Re-Framing Urban Space

Re-Framing Urban Space: Urban Design for Emerging Hybrid and High-Density Conditions rethinks the role and meaning of urban spaces through current trends and challenges in urban development. In emerging dense, hybrid, complex and dynamic urban conditions, public urban space is not only a precious and contested commodity, but also one of the key vehicles for achieving socially, environmentally and economically sustainable urban living. Past research has been predominantly focused on familiar models of urban space, such as squares, plazas, streets, parks and arcades, without consistent and clear rules on what constitutes good urban space, let alone what constitutes good urban space in a "high-density context."

Through an innovative and integrative research framework, *Re-Framing Urban Space* guides the assessment, planning, design and redesign of urban spaces at various stages of the decision-making process, facilitating an understanding of how enduring qualities are expressed and negotiated through design measures in high-density urban environments. This book explores over 50 best practice case studies of recent urban design projects in high-density contexts, including Singapore, Beijing, Tokyo, New York and Rotterdam.

Visually compelling and insightful, *Re-Framing Urban Space* provides a comprehensive and accessible means to understand the critical properties that shape new urban spaces, illustrating key design components and principles. An invaluable guide to the stages of urban design, planning, policy and decision making, this book is essential reading for urban design and planning professionals, academics and students interested in public spaces within high-density urban development.

Im Sik Cho is an assistant professor at the Department of Architecture, School of Design and Environment, National University of Singapore (NUS), where she serves as the leader for urban studies research and teaching and principal investigator for many research projects related to urban space design and participatory planning for sustainable high-density environments.

Chye Kiang Heng is a professor, urban designer and planner. Currently, he is the dean of the School of Design and Environment at the National University of Singapore (NUS). He has published four books and numerous articles and book chapters. He is visiting professor at several leading Asian universities and serves on the editorial board of a number of international journals.

Zdravko Trivic is an assistant professor at the Department of Architecture, School of Design and Environment (SDE), National University of Singapore (NUS). He also worked as a researcher at the Centre for Sustainable Cities (CSAC), SDE, NUS. His research and design work in the areas of urban design and health and space theories has been presented internationally. He has published several book chapters and conference and journal articles.

"For a long time, conscientious professionals have expressed hostility towards dense environments and tall buildings, harboring, instead, the ideals of public spaces in the 'human' scale and the city's rich visual communication in Medieval or nineteenth century urban design. Today, however, anybody can freely eat, profess their love, or read newspapers not only on ground level, but at heights 10 m, 100 m, 1,000 m and 10,000 m above ground. It is now time for classical knowledge to be reconstructed. This book provides stimulating material for architects, urban designers and landscape architects to revisit design philosophies on public spaces and reach brilliant new ideas fit to the realities of today."

—Hidetoshi Ohno, Professor Emeritus, University of Tokyo, Japan

"Focused on the dynamic, high-density cities of East Asia, *Re-Framing Urban Space* argues that we need to move beyond traditional public–private space dualisms, to recognize the increasingly hybrid nature of contemporary cities. Provocative and richly illustrated, yet profoundly pragmatic, this foundational text should sit on every urban practitioner's desk."

—Jennifer Wolch, William W. Wurster Dean, College of Environmental Design, University of California, Berkeley, USA

Re-Framing Urban Space

Urban Design for Emerging Hybrid and High-Density Conditions

Im Sik Cho, Chye Kiang Heng and Zdravko Trivic

Routledge
Taylor & Francis Group

NEW YORK AND LONDON

First published 2016
by Routledge
711 Third Avenue, New York, NY 10017

and by Routledge
2 Park Square, Milton Park, Abingdon, Oxon OX14 4RN

Routledge is an imprint of the Taylor & Francis Group, an informa business

This Work is made possible by the research/work and resultant deliverables from the
project entitled "Urban Space Planning for Sustainable High Density Environments,"
being a critical review on the theories and practices of sustainable high-density
environment, supported by the funding from the Singapore Ministry of National
Development ("MND") and undertaken jointly in collaboration by the Copyright
Owner and Singapore's Urban Redevelopment Authority ("URA"), Housing and
Development Board ("HDB") and National Parks Board ("NParks"). Such research/
work and deliverables form the basis upon which this Work is produced.

Library of Congress Cataloging in Publication Data
Cho, Im Sik, author.
Re-framing urban space : urban design for emerging hybrid and high-density
conditions / Im Sik Cho, Chye-Kiang Heng, and Zdravko Trivic.
pages cm
This Work is made possible by the research/work and resultant deliverables from the
project entitled Urban Space Planning for Sustainable High Density Environments.
1. Public spaces--Social aspects. 2. City planning. 3. Urban density. I. Heng, Chye
Kiang, 1958- author. II. Trivic, Zdravko, author. III. Title.
NA9053.S6C495 2015
307.1'216--dc23
2015008619

ISBN: 978-1-138-84985-3 (hbk)
ISBN: 978-1-138-84986-0 (pbk)
ISBN: 978-1-315-72514-7 (ebk)

Typeset in Avenir LT Pro
by Fakenham Prepress Solutions, Fakenham, Norfolk NR21 8NN
Printed by Bell & Bain Ltd, Glasgow

Contents

CONTENTS

Acknowledgments

This book is a result of the research project "Urban Space Planning for Sustainable High Density Environments," which was conducted at the Centre for Sustainable Asian Cities (CSAC), School of Design and Environment, National University of Singapore (NUS), during 2009 to 2013, in collaboration with URA (Urban Redevelopment Authority, Singapore), HDB (Housing and Development Board, Singapore) and NParks (National Parks Board, Singapore). The project was funded by the Ministry of National Development (MND), Singapore. All copyrights are shared among the National University of Singapore, the collaborating agencies and the publisher.

We also acknowledge valuable contributions to this work made by Dr. Limin Hee as initial principal investigator, Dr. Davisi Boontharm, Dr. Erwin Viray and Dr. Patrick Janssen as collaborators for the research.

We also thank Ivan Kurniawan Nasution for his contribution to the research as research assistant as well as his efforts working on the numerous illustrations presented in this book, a number of part-time student researchers for their timely assistance in various phases of the project, as well as Jinhui Wang for the development of the TUSA (Tool for Urban Space Analysis).

Finally, we acknowledge numerous contributors who agreed to share their material and made this volume a visually enriching read.

Singapore, 2015

Im Sik CHO
Chye Kiang HENG
Zdravko TRIVIC

List of Figure Credits

by-sa/3.0/deed.en; http://creativecommons.org/licenses/by-sa/3.0/legalcode).

2.125   Courtesy of Flickr user "qinrongs" (Qinrong Lim). This image is freely available at https://www.flickr.com/photos/qinrongs/6034378423/sizes/o/. This file is licensed under the Creative Commons Attribution-NoDerivs 2.0 Generic (CC BY-ND 2.0) license (https://creativecommons.org/licenses/by-nd/2.0/; https://creativecommons.org/licenses/by-nd/2.0/legalcode).

2.128b   Courtesy of Flickr user "acnatta" (André Natta). This image is freely available at https://www.flickr.com/photos/acnatta/6286042804/sizes/o/. This file is licensed under the Creative Commons Attribution 2.0 Generic (CC BY 2.0) license (https://creativecommons.org/licenses/by/2.0/; https://creativecommons.org/licenses/by/2.0/legalcode).

2.129a   Courtesy of Wikipedia and Wikimedia user "Another Believer." This Wikipedia and Wikimedia Commons image is from the user Another Believer and is freely available at http://commons.wikimedia.org/wiki/File:Bryant_Park,_New_York_City_(May_2014)_-_08.JPG. This file is licensed under the Creative Commons Attribution-ShareAlike 3.0 Unported license.

2.130a   Courtesy of Flickr user "imgdive" (Banzai Hiroaki). This image is freely available at https://www.flickr.com/photos/imgdive/4591084984/sizes/o/. This file is licensed under the Creative Commons Attribution 2.0 Generic (CC BY 2.0) license (https://creativecommons.org/licenses/by/2.0/; https://creativecommons.org/licenses/by/2.0/legalcode).

2.130b   Courtesy of Flickr user "imgdive" (Banzai Hiroaki). This image is freely available at https://www.flickr.com/photos/imgdive/548444411/sizes/o/. This file is licensed under the Creative Commons Attribution 2.0 Generic (CC BY 2.0) license (https://creativecommons.org/licenses/by/2.0/; https://creativecommons.org/licenses/by/2.0/legalcode).

2.132b   Courtesy of William Cho. This image is from the user williamcho (William Cho) and is freely available at https://www.flickr.com/photos/adforce1/3743214056/sizes/o/. This file is licensed under the Creative Commons Attribution-ShareAlike 2.0 Generic (CC BY-SA 2.0) license (https://creativecommons.org/licenses/by-sa/2.0/).

2.137   Courtesy of Flickr user "準建築人手札網站 Forgemind ArchiMedia." This image is freely available at https://www.flickr.com/photos/eager/8615547244/sizes/o/. This file is licensed under the Creative Commons Attribution 2.0 Generic (CC BY 2.0) license (https://creativecommons.org/licenses/by/2.0/; https://creativecommons.org/licenses/by/2.0/legalcode).

2.138a   Courtesy of Chen Xiuqi.

2.138b   Courtesy of Relan Masato.

2.140a   Courtesy of Chen Xiuqi.

2.141   Courtesy of David Wilkinson.

2.142   Courtesy of Wikipedia and Wikimedia user "Calvin Teo." This Wikipedia and Wikimedia Commons image is from the user "Calvin Teo" and is freely available at http://commons.wikimedia.org/wiki/File:Vivocity_Bayfront_view_at_night.jpg under the Creative Commons Attribution-ShareAlike 3.0 Unported (CC BY-SA 3.0) license (http://creativecommons.org/licenses/by-sa/3.0/deed.en; http://creativecommons.org/licenses/by-sa/3.0/legalcode).

2.143   Courtesy of Flickr user "iedwin.11" (Edwin Lee). This image is freely available at https://www.flickr.com/photos/edwin11/3171189412/sizes/o/. This file is licensed under the Creative Commons Attribution 2.0 Generic (CC BY 2.0) license (https://creativecommons.org/licenses/by/2.0/; https://creativecommons.org/licenses/by/2.0/legalcode).

2.144   Courtesy of Ben Melger.

2.145   Courtesy of Flickr user "Josiah Lau Photography." This image is freely available at https://www.flickr.com/photos/josiahlau/5836835438/sizes/o/. This file is licensed under the Creative Commons Attribution-NoDerivs 2.0 Generic (CC BY-ND 2.0) license (https://creativecommons.org/licenses/by-nd/2.0/; https://creativecommons.org/licenses/by-nd/2.0/legalcode).

2.148   Courtesy of Terence Ong. This Wikipedia and Wikimedia Commons image is from the user Terence Ong and is freely available at http://commons.wikimedia.org/wiki/File:Esplanade_outdoor_performance.JPG. Permission is granted to copy, distribute and/or modify this document under the terms of the GNU Free Documentation License, Version 1.2 or any later version published by the Free Software Foundation; with no Invariant Sections, no Front-Cover Texts, and no Back-Cover Texts. A copy of the license is included in the section entitled GNU Free Documentation License. This file is licensed under the Creative Commons Attribution-ShareAlike 3.0 Unported license and under the Creative Commons Attribution 2.5 Generic license.

2.149a   Courtesy of Chen Xiuqi.

2.150   Courtesy of Wojtek Gurak.

2.156   Courtesy of Relan Masato.

2.157   Courtesy of Relan Masato.

2.171   Courtesy of Relan Masato.

2.172   Courtesy of Relan Masato.

2.173   Courtesy of Chen Xiuqi.

2.181   Courtesy of Larry Yeung.

2.182   Courtesy of Larry Yeung.

2.183   Courtesy of Larry Yeung.

2.185   Courtesy of Larry Yeung.

2.186   Courtesy of Housing and Development Board (HDB), Singapore.

Prologue

Places that evoke long-lasting memories for their visitors are often found in the accessible urban spaces of the city, since these spaces exude their individual charm and endow the city with a collective sense of character. One remembers with fondness the plaza mayors of Spanish cities, the canal streets of many a Dutch city, the sidewalk cafés in Paris and the arcades in Milan, the night markets of Taipei, the *shotengai* or covered shopping streets in Japanese cities, and the *xiang*s and *hutong*s of Chinese cities. More specifically, one recalls place-specific sites like Piazza San Marco in Venice, Times Square in New York, Quiapo in Manila, the Bund in Shanghai, the banks of Kamogawa River in Kyoto, and Insadong in Seoul. Descending deeper into the memory bank, one might recollect particular urban encounters such as a brief afternoon respite reading a guidebook on a bench in a pocket park in Paris or an evening stroll along the quays of Singapore River. Although seemingly generic, these public spaces play a significant role in our experience of the city.

Urban spaces made memorable by the visitor hold even more importance for inhabitants and citizens of the city. These arenas where civic lives intersect not only encapsulate the collective memories of its people but also the stories told by one generation to the next, the hopes and aspirations of the city and its constituents, and the tender moments shared by couples and families. It is in these crucibles that urban identities and social cohesion are forged and the resilience of a city tested. Needless to say, if the urban spaces of a city are successful in achieving these aims, then the city, too, succeeds.

Cities with long histories have a range of such public spaces that, over time, are shaped by and adapted to the different needs of its inhabitants; in this respect, newer urban developments that sprout overnight from speculative real estate play often lack the treasured traits of established public spaces. The beloved spaces of a city take generations to be nurtured into substantial places that are valued by the communities around it, and so the seeds which bear such fruits need to be planted together with the planning and provision of fertile spaces for its growth. In traditional towns and cities, a defined open space, a few benches, a favorite corner café, a water fountain, an old tree, a few raised steps, a thoughtful piece of public art and so on can evolve into the nucleus within or around which meaningful public space forms.

Casual observers familiar with the Western urban paradigm have the misconception that traditional Asian cities—which evolved over millennia under contrastingly different power structures and belief systems—enjoy few, if any, public spaces. (East) Asian cities, founded and transformed through various religious and political ideologies, have formulated their own logic toward the treatment of urban spaces: at bridgeheads, along river banks, around wells, in front of temples, within temple compounds, before administrative buildings and the like.

In the past few decades, the traditional urban tissue of many matured Asian cities has been reworked by rapid urbanization. The hybrid conditions that emerge from these fast-changing cities provide, in some instances, great opportunities for public space creation while, in other circumstances, causing irreversible consequences for the grain and texture of age-old urban districts. In many cases, swaths of existing urban fabric along with their multifarious public spaces have been erased to make way for extensive high-density real estate developments driven by expedience and the maximization of profit. While there are successful examples of new public space created in this dynamic context—a number of which are featured in this volume—the outcome, more often than not, is the proliferation of generic gated communities and the replacement of veritable public domains by exclusive private open spaces. Fortunately, in recent years, forward-looking city managers, developers and architects have collectively produced new typologies of public spaces that are open to the wider community amidst such high-density residential developments. Notable examples are Central Park Beijing apartments (Xincheng gouji) and the Linked Hybrid in Beijing[1] or the private residential developments along Robertson Quay and in One North Residences at Biopolis in Singapore, to name a few.

Commercial retail developments are more concerned than gated residential ones with creating public spaces, if nothing else, to attract the public to frequent their shops. Many such spaces, unfortunately, are privately owned public spaces or pseudo-public spaces operating under a set of motivations that emphasize individualism and consumption over civic interests and collective rewards. This disparity between the private provider and public user of urban open spaces, particularly within the premises of commercial retail developments, can create real barriers in terms of accessibility and inclusiveness. The display of blatant signage warning users of the types of activities that are prohibited and the expression of non-verbal cues, such as indicators of dress code and affordability, impose controls that may make certain public spaces inviting to some but perhaps not to others. In this respect, city governments can contribute (directly and indirectly) to the protection of quality public spaces, since it is at this level of urban planning where complex decisions are made pertaining to land use, by-laws and incentives on development issues. Several examples such as Roppongi Hills[2] and Tokyo Midtown[3] in Tokyo and Ion Orchard[4] in Singapore featured in this volume show the insertion of such facilities and the creation of urban space often near transport nodes.

At the periphery of existing cities, unshackled by historical constraints, new urban forms flourish with mixed results. Particularly in East Asia, these fringe areas are often met with high-density developments. Occasionally, well-conceived master plans give rise to new memorable urban spaces well loved by their users. The lakeside promenade in Suzhou Industrial Park, Treelodge@Punggol[5] in Singapore and Shinonome Codan Court[6] in Tokyo are examples that come to mind.

Equally creditable are the conversions of old industrial buildings and dilapidated production facilities such as 798 Art Zone in Beijing and the old log pond in Yilan. Meanwhile, in other cities, existing infrastructures are improved and provide the city with surprising encounters. New York's High Line Park[7] and Singapore's Kallang River in Bishan Park are noteworthy examples; they are the pride of the city in general, while also serving as an immense resource for local residents who use them on a regular if not daily basis.

The world has undergone rapid changes in the past few decades: the rising middle class and transformed lifestyles in Asia, the emerging complex hybrid urban conditions in dense Asian cities, the processes of globalization and neo-liberalism that are not only dominating much of the developed world but are also eroding the quality of public space, and the list goes on. These changes have both enriched as well as undermined our urban experience. Although there are instances where the urban fabric and spaces of traditional cities have had to give way to modern developments, new typologies have also emerged in the process. Past research has primarily focused on familiar models of urban space, such as squares, plazas, streets, parks and arcades; this volume extends the repertoire to include the expanding typologies of urban spaces emerging today.

These emerging contemporary spaces are shaped by a dynamic process which aims to synergize the various aspects of urban design from spatial configuration and programming to utilization and management. At the same time, however, the hybrid spaces produced are often complicated by tensions and negotiations among diverse users and agencies. The ever-evolving urban conditions of high-density cities call for the re-conceptualization of conventional modes of understanding urban design and public space. *Re-Framing Urban Space* presents an innovative research framework for inciting new knowledge on the complex relationship between density and quality of public space. By re-examining the characteristics and performances of public space, we gain an enriched understanding of how enduring qualities are expressed and negotiated through design and other measures in the increasingly hybrid and high-density urban context. With this broad intention, *Re-Framing Urban Space* aims to achieve three objectives.

First, as the title implies, re-framing urban space is an attempt at rethinking and re-conceptualizing the role and meaning of public spaces within the current global trends and challenges accompanying contemporary urban development. In doing so, the book addresses emerging hybrid urban space typologies in high-density contexts that fall outside conventional notions of public space. Second, this volume aims to demonstrate the application of the Urban Space Framework and Instrument for: (1) the systematic categorization of hybrid conditions and new urban space typologies, and (2) the evaluation and analysis of urban space performance. In this way, the book serves as a guide to assess, plan, design (and redesign) urban spaces at various stages of the decision-making process. Third, with over 50 urban spaces explored through best practice case studies, the book adds practical value to our knowledge of public space in an insightful and visually compelling format.

While the geographic focus of this volume draws attention to (East) Asian cities—in which Asia's rapid pace of urbanization and, hence, potential to exhibit new models of urban space was discussed—the learning points gleaned from such a study also correspond to the experiences of other cities, for example, in Latin America and Africa, with comparatively high-density urban development. Globalization, after all, has enabled the exchange of ideologies and cultures across borders such that urban phenomena once thought to be unique to a particular region are transposed, thus implicating cities on a worldwide scale. Likewise, the scope of the research framework and tools introduced in this book are not city- or region-specific but, rather, holistic and adaptable in their application capabilities to assess and analyze various urban spaces in high-density environments.

With an intention to guide different phases in urban space design, the structure of *Re-Framing Urban Space* reflects the main stages of the design process, namely: *Review, Understanding, Assessment and Analysis, and Application.* Chapter 1, "Review: Urban Space and Current Tendencies in Urban Development," guides the reader through key theoretical and design concepts currently dominating the discourse on public space. The chapter also discusses current trends and challenges in contemporary urban development (such as densification, intensification, hybridization and sustainability), cross-referenced to a number of recent urban design projects in high-density contexts globally. Building on the literature review of relevant urban design theories, concepts, guidelines and practices, Chapter 2, "Understanding: Quality of Urban Space and Design Principles," develops an integrated urban space research framework by which to identify the critical properties and design principles that shape new and emerging quality public spaces in high-density urban environments. Chapter 3, "Assessment and Analysis: Assessing the Quality of Urban Space," offers practical tools to capture, assess and analyze urban space performance based on the systematic framework established in Chapter 2. In closing, Chapter 4, "Application: Guide to Design Actions," suggests practical means of applying the systematic framework and instrument to different design purposes to facilitate optimum design actions to enhance the urban space design quality that is relevant and of interest to urban planners, urban designers, architects and developers.

Re-Framing Urban Space confronts the very real urban conditions of densification and hybridity that are playing out in some cities today, and which are sure to appear in many more cities in the near future. The process of framing the notion of urban space within the context of these emerging conditions, indeed, has created (necessary) conceptual demands for this volume. First, can certain valued qualities of public space be regarded as "timeless"? If so, can these timeless characteristics be achieved under evolving conditions found in hybridized high-density urban environments?

The book is premised on the assertion that public spaces with timeless appeal do and can indeed prosper in hybrid high-density cities; yet, second, how do we move beyond conventional means of studying these emerging typologies of urban space? Third, what innovative approaches in applied research can yield new insights about the timeless qualities of public space? Our initial discussions of framing urban space within today's hybrid and high-density urban contexts consequently led us to the *re-framing* of urban space. In re-framing urban space, we see an opportunity to advance the frontier of knowledge on urban space by opening up possibilities in research and practice for the inclusion of emergent public space typologies where hybrid and high-density urban conditions prevail.

NOTES

1 See Chapter 2, "Urban Space Quality," 15 and 42, and section entitled "Orgware Qualities of Urban Space: An Example" for more details about Dangdai Moma (Linked Hybrid) in Beijing.

2 See Chapter 2, "Urban Space Quality," 12, 20, 27 and 35 for more details about Roppongi Hills in Tokyo.

3 See Chapter 1, section entitled "Mixed-use Developments," and Chapter 2, "Urban Space Quality," 22 and 36 for more details about Tokyo Midtown in Tokyo.

4 See Chapter 2, "Urban Space Quality," 2, 9, 29 and 38 for more details about Ion Orchard in Singapore.

5 See Chapter 2, "Urban Space Quality," 1 and 10, and section entitled "Qualities of Urban Space: An Example of Full Analysis" for more details about Treelodge@Punggol in Singapore.

6 See Chapter 2, "Urban Space Quality," 6, 38, 39 and 40, and section entitled "Hardware Qualities of Urban Space: An Example" for more details about Shinonome Codan Court in Tokyo.

7 See Chapter 1, section entitled "Recreational Green Hybrids," and Chapter 2, "Urban Space Quality," 15, 16, 29, 34, 37, 43 and 45 for more details about the High Line Park in New York.

Urban Space and Current Tendencies in Urban Development

This chapter outlines the contemporary challenges posed for urban design in light of the ongoing debate addressing sustainable urban development, as well as the emergence and criticism of increasingly hybrid urban space typologies in high-density environments. A number of relevant concepts, terms and definitions are critically revisited, such as density, intensity, sustainability, hybrid space and urban space. In reference to emerging hybrid and new urban space configurations in high-density and high-intensity contexts globally, this chapter introduces a number of recent urban design projects, with an aim to outline global contemporary urban development trends, while gradually shifting the focus toward similar trends in Asian cities.

CONTEMPORARY URBAN CONDITIONS

Challenges of Urbanization

The beginning of this century is characterized by the dramatic rise of urban population and urban development globally.[1] For the first time in history, since 2007, more than half of the world's population lives in cities. According to the recently updated United Nations' *World Urbanization Prospects* (2014), currently 54 percent of the world's population resides in urban areas and it is predicted that such a number will increase up to 66 percent by 2050, or more than six billion people living in cities.

While Africa and Asia are currently the least urbanized regions of the world, with urban populations of 40 percent and 48 percent, respectively, it is expected that the fastest and the highest concentration of the world's urban growth would occur in these regions, with 56 percent and 64 percent of their population becoming urban, respectively, by 2050. The majority of the current mega-cities (cities with more than ten million inhabitants)—16 out of 28—are situated in Asia (United Nations, 2014). However, the urbanization process spreads beyond the mega-cities, being even more rapid in smaller cities and towns, bringing dramatic and unprecedented changes. In fact, over the past three decades Asian cities have already experienced the most dramatic urban transformations, characterized by (but not limited to) rapid built and population densification, intensity and diversity of uses and

users, increased mobility and other modes of exchange, and overall complexity of urban living conditions. Such a magnitude of urban development and transformation may be comparable to what the Western world has experienced over the past two centuries.

Such a rapid rise of urban development and urban population globally has inevitably led to higher demands for environmentally, economically and socially sustainable planning. As part of such demands, the provision of "high-quality public spaces" is increasingly seen as one of the key means for fostering environmental and social sustainability, and improving the quality of life in contemporary urban environments (Amin, 2006).

It is now widely accepted that quality public spaces are vital assets for a city's livability and sustainable development, providing social, health, environmental and economic short- and long-term benefits (CABE, 2004; Carmona, 2010a, 2010b; McIndoe et al., 2005). Well designed and managed, public spaces bring communities together, shape the cultural identity of an area, provide meeting places and foster social ties that have been disappearing in many urban areas due to rapid urban transformations. Investment in public space also contributes to environmental sustainability by employing energy-efficient and less polluting design strategies, promoting greenery and biodiversity, delivering developments that are sensitive to their contexts and encouraging walking and cycling, among others. Finally, the presence of good urban design potentially attracts other investments, strengthens the local economy, and is thus a vital business and marketing tool. Such a recent shift in understanding the role of urban design in sustainable urban development goes beyond the beautification of the built environment and marks the beginning of the "new urban revolution," as pointed out by Ali Madanipour (2006).

The main challenge of urban design today is thus to create (and re-create) good urban spaces with the ability to accommodate and respond to diverse, intense, hybrid, dynamic, contested and often unprecedented urban conditions. Consequently, the ways we understand, analyze, design, redesign and utilize urban spaces require both quantitative and qualitative re-conceptualizations. This includes challenging and reassessing the existing notions of density, space, typology and "publicness," among others, in the context of high-density, high-intensity urban environments.

The role of quality public space in sustainable urban development becomes particularly critical in high-density contexts, and especially in those cities for which due to scarcity of land (such as Tokyo or Singapore, among others) densification may not be a matter of conscious or desirable choice, but rather an inevitable challenge. The specific governmental, spatial, economic and socio-cultural conditions of many East Asian cities have over time formed a unique platform for the high-density urban form explorations with the primary aim of optimizing the available space by maximizing capacity, while challenging the possibilities of retaining or enhancing the quality and livability in such environments. Various challenges and limitations led these cities to accept and embrace new hybrid modes of living and management, spatial and functional organization that differ considerably from the conventional urban development typologies.

Accordingly, this book aims to challenge the limits of high-density, high-intensity hybrid and dynamic development up to which the performance and vitality of urban space would remain satisfactory or even improved. Consequently, the broader aim is to explore ways of how to assure a holistic approach to environmental, social and economic sustainability, while not losing one to the other in the process of urban space development.

What is Density?

Common approaches to understanding, measuring and investigating the density of urban environments are mainly focused on built structures and capacities, with a set of objective indexes that express the concentration of built structures and/or people within a given area. This is physical or built density. Some of the most common measurements of physical density are the ratio of the building footprint to a given site, i.e. site coverage or building coverage ratio (BCR) and the ratio of building area to a given site area, such as gross plot ratio (GPR) or floor area ratio (FAR). In addition, human density refers to the concentration of people in a particular space and is typically expressed by the number of people living in the area and the number of dwelling units in the area, often in reference to age, gender, ethnicity, education and other demographic differentiators.

While such quantitative measures establish common and useful language for planners, urban designers and architects, they seem to neglect the qualitative aspects of density and intensity coming from users' perception and multi-sensory facets of urban experience. Density indexes per se are not sufficient to fully define and understand urban density. They are relevant and meaningful only when seen in relation to a specific context. High density is often defined differently in different cultures. A specific number of dwelling units per hectare might be considered high density in one context, but low or medium in another. Finally, the same values of built and population density indexes can result in a different form and scale of the built environment. The high-rise neighborhoods in Singapore and low-rise urban blocks in Amsterdam, for instance, may have similar FAR values, while being very different in their spatial configuration.

In fact, "soft" information that originates from users' subjective spatial experience and perception of an urban setting is often more evident and more powerful than the underlying density numbers. The human perception of density differs from the scientific one, expressed through space and population density indexes. It refers to a set of bodily and mental mechanisms and processes, which serve to organize, identify and interpret all sensory information available in space. It is thus crucial for understanding, responding to and interacting with the built environment. Accordingly, in addition to the "objective" measures of urban density, the perceived density is expressed in more subjective terms. It refers to an evaluation of spatial conditions, including estimations of the amount of people within a space, space availability and spatial arrangement (Cheng, 2010; Rapoport, 1975), a process molded by users' cognitive abilities, socio-cultural backgrounds, learned experiences and memories (Alexander, 1993; Malnar & Vodvarka, 2004).

Perceived density is related to but also confused with crowding, being described as the negative assessment of density that causes psychological stress in space users (Churchman, 1999). Certain spatial conditions, such as limited space, channeled movement or level of enclosure, could intensify the experience of crowding (Mackintosh et al., 1975; Saegert, 1979). Even though it may be a prerequisite for causing a sense of crowdedness, density by itself is not sufficient to create a crowding experience (Stokols, 1972).

In order to fully understand and enhance the performance and livability of urban spaces in high-density conditions, a more holistic and intuitive approach that would incorporate both "hard" (physical environment) and "soft" (user's perception) information on density and intensity of urban spaces is needed.

Is the Denser the Better?

Increase in density of urban form and urban population is a worldwide trend and it is thus unsurprising that it has received a considerable amount of attention in contemporary research and academic discussions, especially in reference to its high impact on environmentally and socially sustainable urban development. Yet, in light of the ongoing debate, there is no clear consensus as to whether high density is a good or a bad condition for the city and its dwellers.

The majority of continuously growing recent literature advocates for high-density, high-intensity, compact, mixed-use and pedestrian-oriented urban development as the desired strategies for sustainable urban growth, as opposed to unsustainable sprawl development (see, e.g., Chan & Lee, 2007, 2009; Ewing et al., 2008; Jenks et al., 1996; Newman & Kenworthy, 2006; Sabaté Bel, 2011). In line with such an understanding, it is often argued that the cities of today should be compact and densely populated with people, activities and movement, while maintaining the right balance to ensure non-oppressive conditions for their inhabitants (see, e.g., Jenks & Dempsey, 2005; Mehaffy & Salingaros, 2011; Uytenhaak, 2008). However, the attempts to define such a "right balance" in more specific terms, such as the "optimum" levels of density or mixes of uses that a more sustainable urban form necessitates, are rare (Talen, 2011).

One of the key arguments in favor of the high-density compact urban development refers to its positive environmental and economic impacts in comparison to low-density sprawl development. It is claimed that high-density compact urban models tend to lower the consumption of energy and other resources (Speir & Stephenson, 2002), decrease ecological footprint and air pollution (Stone Jr., 2008), as well as reduce transportation and infrastructure costs, construction and management expenses, and are thus considered economically more viable (Bramley & Morgan, 2003; Bunker, 1985; Burton, 2000a; Collie, 1990; Glynn, 1981; Newman & Kenworthy, 2006). Among other positive social impacts, studies argue that higher density eases the access to services and facilities and, in such a way, enables higher walkability and active living (see, e.g., Forsyth et al., 2008; Greenwald & Boarnet, 2001; Heath et al., 2006; Moudon & Lee, 2003; Norman et al., 2006; Talen, 1999, 2011). Higher density increases proximity and enhances mix, diversity, social interaction, community well-being and overall quality of life (Dittmar & Ohland, 2003; Duany & Plater-Zyberk, 2001; Ewing et al., 2008; Gehl, 2010; Hillier & Hanson, 1984; Jacobs, 1961; Newman & Kenworthy, 2006; Popkin et al., 2009; Salingaros, 1998; Song & Knaap, 2004; Turner & Berube, 2009). However, there is no axiomatic relationship between social mix and use mix (Bramley & Power, 2009).

Such a favorable understanding of high-density conditions is, however, relatively recent. Negative experiences in the nineteenth century's industrial cities, when high concentrations of people were associated with poor hygiene, disease, fire hazards and deaths, led to favoring low-density urban development. Some sociological and psychological research suggests that increasing urban density causes greater physiological and psychological stress, social disorder (increasing violence, crime, suicide rates and drug addiction), ill-health conditions and violation of personal space (Evans et al., 2002; Gómez-Jacinto & Hombrados-Mendieta, 2002; Newman & Hogan, 1981; Regoeczi, 2003). Other studies claim that the modern, highly dense residential areas considerably reduce the level of spontaneous interaction among residents, as they create a condition that is stressful and that violates their personal space. As a result, the increased need for privacy encourages people to maintain their distance and withdraw from social contact (Bridge, 2002; Freeman, 2001; Madanipour, 2003; Nasar & Julian, 1995; Simmel, 1995; Tonkiss, 2005).

Finally, recent studies continue to report that, given the choice, people generally prefer low-density suburban living (Chatterjee, 2009; Gordon & Richardson, 1997). Living in high-density public housing is still often associated with the socio-cultural stigma of poverty (Harper, 2014; Seo & Chiu, 2014). However, in their recent research conducted in Singapore, Hong Kong and Australia, Yuen and colleagues (2006) argue that high-rise, high-density living is not only a dominant and inevitable model in many Asian cities that cope with land scarcity, rapid urban growth, population growth and housing shortage, such as Hong Kong, Singapore or Tokyo, among others, but is also an accepted and sometimes even favored lifestyle. According to them, many of the problems that have long been associated with the early types of high-rise housing are now increasingly being seen as a result of the lack of neighborhood facilities, poor maintenance and management (e.g., lift breakdowns, fire risks or crime in the lifts) and non-strategic selection of residents.

Intensity—Complexity—Urbanity

The density of an urban environment is clearly not the only and sufficient measure of good performance, sustainability and quality of urban living. Density per se is a neutral condition that has neither positive nor negative value, yet considerably affects physical, functional and operational complexities of urban spaces, both positively and negatively.

In *Cities Full of Space*, Uytenhaak (2008) states that an overall sense of density results from the number, diversity, proximity and intensity of people, structures and infrastructures, movements and urban activities. Urban density is thus understood as a relational and dynamic phenomenon. It is the proximity that is one of the main attractors of the city; the closeness to others stimulates higher opportunities for communication, cooperation and influence. Accordingly, denser city environments tend to generate higher levels of interaction among people, establishments and institutions than sparser city environments (Salmon, 2012). But density alone is insufficient to warrant desirable interactions for living, working and recreation. It is often the subtle differences in the quality, not the quantity, of interactions, which make one city or neighborhood more attractive than another.

While urban density is a quantitative category, urban intensity is a more qualitative expression of density, characterized by the volume of spatial interactions that occur to accommodate various activities, both currently and in the future. As Issarathumnoon (2013) describes in her study of Bangkok, "vivid and fluid public/ private interfaces—the ambiguous territories between public spaces and private spaces … the soft boundaries contributed by cloud-liked informal features … to temporarily occupy space, and multi-layered spatial usages" suggest how the urban space and its perimeters can "provide good opportunities for constructing urban intensity" (pp. 22–23) that leads to the multi-functional use (i.e., the plurality) of urban space.

According to the renowned and one of the most influential urban geographers, Jane Jacobs (1961), one of the essential qualities of livable cities is a high degree of consciously organized complexity. Cities are composed by spatial segments, which are interrelated and form an organic whole. According to Hillier (2007), cities are "stocks of buildings which are linked by space and infrastructure"; yet this physical structure hosts complex economic, social, cultural and environmental processes. In the context of higher density these processes are further challenged, while intensifying the level of urban complexities and potentially leading to new spatial, programmatic and organizational manifestations of urban space relationships.

The concept of urban space as a complex system has been well established within academia over the past few decades, drawing its foundation mostly from mathematics, fractal and informational theories, such as the extensive work on urban complexity by Michael Batty (2005) or Nikos A. Salingaros (1999, 2000, 2011), among many others. For Salingaros, urban space is not merely an empty open space, but rather a raft of information that arises from the available physical structures, surfaces and activities (building façades, the pavement and local nodes, such as trees and urban furniture) and interacts with human consciousness. While the spatial plan arrangement is important, the way users build conscious connections with the surroundings is a more critical aspect.

However, complexity should not be mistaken for "compli-catedness." Complexity cannot be generated solely by erecting complex structures or adding disintegrated fragments, as has been attempted in many contemporary urban space projects. According to Salingaros and Mehaffy (2012), the "complicatedness" is the mere result of an irrelevant and unconnected complexity. In contrast, like nature, complexity evolves in time through the process of organizing different and often conflicting elements and cycles into an integrated system.

Density, intensity, complexity, as well as diversity and flexibility, are terms that are often associated with urbanity. Pont and Haupt (2009: 165) point out various studies which have recognized urbanity as a concept that is frequently used to describe a human condition of plurality, difference, interaction and communication (Hajer, 1989; Heeling et al., 2002: 101; Jacobs, 1961; Meyer et al., 2006; Urhahn Urban Design, 2000; Van der Wouden, 1999; Zijderveld, 1983). Radović (2013) states that "many manifestations of intensity are closely related to urbanity" and "its various definitions can be qualified by degrees of intensity, as expressed in diverse spatial and/or temporal urban situations." According to Lozano (1990), urbanity, as the potential for inhabitants and institutions in a town or city to interact, is partly created by density and, in turn, encourages higher density. A dense concentration of people is, according to both Jacobs and Lozano, one of the prerequisites for a flourishing and diverse city: "The other factors that influence how much diversity is generated, and where, will have nothing much to influence if enough people are not there" (Jacobs, 1961: 205, cited in Pont & Haupt, 2009).

REDEFINING URBAN SPACE

Public Space—Urban Space—Hybrid Space

In high-density conditions, space becomes not only a precious commodity but also a place of complex and dynamic spatial and programmatic transformations, confrontations and dialogues. In this light, the common definitions of public and private space and their physical, functional and operational properties need to be reassessed.

Public Space: Definitions

Public space is a multi-dimensional concept and has multiple and sometimes contradictory definitions (Kohn, 2004). Yet, the ease with which the term "public space" is commonly used contrasts sharply with its growing complexity, including typology, use, ownership and management aspects. Influenced by the idea of the "entrepreneurial city" and neo-liberal theories (Brenner & Theodore, 2002; Harvey, 1989; MacLeod, 2002), city authorities and developers, even planners and designers, commonly use the term "public space" in an intuitive and taken-for-granted fashion, while barely being concerned with the nuances of the level of the "publicness" of public spaces.

Public space is typically defined as an accessible physical space for all citizens, regardless of age, gender, race, ethnicity or socio-economic status with free circulations of people and goods at all times (Carmona et al., 2003; Shaftoe, 2008). It is also described as a symbol of democracy and sociability, of resistance against the aggressive processes of commercialization and globalization (Mitrasinovic, 2006), a space of debate and negotiation, of protest and expression of the interests of minorities (Watson, 2006), with diversity and difference as its major elements (Young, 1990). In its broadest sense, the public space concept does not necessarily imply physical space, but rather includes physical, symbolic and procedural facets (Iveson, 2007). According to some authors (see, e.g., Ellin, 1996; Watson, 2006), it even refers to all communal and non-private arenas of social life, including all media and, more recently, the internet.

Recent academic debates on contemporary public spaces range from the negative and pessimistic to the more positive and optimistic. The pessimistic view, however, prevails, emphasizing the erosion of the essential characteristics of public space due to various social, political and economic factors, especially commercialization, commodification, the intrusion of the private market into the realm of public culture, and over-control (see, e.g., Carmona, 2010a, 2010b; Crawford, 1992; Dovey, 1999, 2010; Kohn, 2004; Low & Smith, 2006; Pimlott, 2008/2009; Zukin, 1995, 2000). As a result, these factors have led to the "end of public culture" (Sennett, 1977), the play of neo-liberal forces over the public realm (Brenner & Theodore, 2002; MacLeod, 2002), the erosion of community (Kohn, 2004; Low and Smith, 2006; Putnam, 2000; Watson, 2006), a public lulled by the "cappuccino" culture (Atkinson, 2003; Jackson, 1998; Smith, 1996; Zukin, 1995, 2000); and over-emphasis on safety issues, maintenance and control (Davis, 1998; Loukaitou-Sideris & Banerjee, 1998; Mitchell, 1995; Sorkin, 1992).

Such a critique, however, tends to idealize the notion of public space, emphasizing traditional and somewhat nostalgic dialectics which oppose the private and the public, true and false publicness, space and place, aesthetics and ethics.[2] In this view, the emerging hybrid forms of urban spaces are often ignored or rejected. They are categorized as the "PROPASt" (privately owned publicly accessible spaces) category (Mitrasinovic, 2006) and thus are often regarded as "quasi-public" (Dovey, 1999, 2010; Pimlott, 2008/2009) or even "non-places" since they have no roots in tradition, history and culture (Augé, 1995). For Kohn (2004), for instance, public spaces are only those that are owned by the government, have no restricted access and foster interaction. Such a traditional attitude toward the public realm seems to be somewhat problematic and insufficient for understanding the contemporary contexts of emerging new hybrid urbanities and modes of publicness.

The unstable definition of both public and private spheres creates a weak edge on both territories, as their complexities are intertwined and affect each other. The borders between the public and the private have recently been increasingly blurred, and both spheres have gradually acquired some characteristics of the other. Madanipour (2003, 2006) also notes that as much

as the private realm influences the public, society is also the realm of the private, pointing out that there is no clear-cut separation between public and private. Publicness depends on how people characterize the private, and thus there are many shades of publicness and privacy creating a fluctuating, often tense, semi-public–private or "neo-public" continuum (Dimmer et al., 2005; Nielsen, 2004; ZUS, 2006). Due to the hybridization of the public and the private, it is necessary to re-conceptualize the notion and definition of public space in a more flexible and inclusive manner.

Urban Space

More optimistic interpretations of the current state of contemporary public spaces argue that the perception of the decline of the public realm is largely based on a construction of the ideal of public spaces, which is falsely equated with absolute democracy, classlessness and diversity (see, e.g., Banerjee, 2001; Brill, 1989a, 1989b; Carr et al., 1992; Goss, 1996; Jackson, 1998; Loukaitou-Sideris & Banerjee, 1998; Worpole & Knox, 2007). A mono-dimensional view of publicness is also largely influenced by the emphasis on ownership over space (Carmona & De Magalhães, 2008; De Magalhães, 2010; Hajer & Reijndorp, 2001), which is one of the reasons why we still know too little about the expanding and increasingly hybrid urban space typologies in highly dense contexts emerging today.

According to Habermas (1989), the notion of public space is a historical product, which originated from the differentiation between the state, civil society and the market, as well as the consolidation of modern notions of private property. The relationship between public space and public life has always been dynamic and reciprocal, leading to new forms of publicness that often require new types of spaces. In this more optimistic view, publicly accessible spaces are often defended, as they represent essential components of economic growth and development, affecting the surrounding property values and attracting local retail development (Feehan & Heit, 2006; Nielsen, 2004). Moreover, publicly accessible spaces have also been described as having the ability to serve social ends (Miller, 2007), connect neighborhoods and even promote democracy and civic virtue (Benhabib, 1996; Habermas, 1984). A number of research studies have shown that the contemporary trend toward urban space design with elements of retail, leisure and tourism contribute to the intensification of both individual hedonism and friendship or public respect (Binnie et al., 2006; Gregson et al., 2002; Miller, 2001).

In this view, it may be equally valid to argue that public space is not necessarily declining but rather expanding, offering new modes of "publicness" due to increased opportunities for various forms of exchange (see, e.g., Carr et al., 1992; Coleman, 2006;

Hertzberger, 2005; Nielsen, 2004; Solà-Morales, 1992; Worpole & Knox, 2007).

Political and economic shifts, globalization and technological changes (most importantly in transport and communication) in the second half of the twentieth century, have accelerated changes in the ways public spaces are provided and managed (Schmidt & Németh, 2010). New public space provision and management mechanisms increasingly involve a bigger role of other (non-public) social agents, especially in the private and voluntary sectors (De Magalhães, 2010), and such a trend is likely to continue in the future. Regardless of the position in debates on contemporary public spaces, be it "erosion of the public character" of public space and public sphere, or a "new mode of publicness," conceptual and empirical explorations of the emerging types of public spaces, regarding both the risks and the potentials, are relevant and needed. As people seek both shared space and privacy, finding a "right balance" between the two in planning public spaces in a high-density context is critical. Moreover, rather than holding firmly to past and existing public spheres as a reference to ideal publicness, one needs to consider the ongoing production of "counter-public spheres" which have capacities to develop new public scenes (Iveson, 2007).

Accordingly, instead of adopting classical definitions of public space, the term "urban space" takes into account emerging types of spaces that may not be publicly owned or managed yet increasingly act as public spaces. Urban space is closer to the notion of "collective space," suggested by Spanish architect Manuel de Solà-Morales (1992), where different groups coexist and interact on a competitive basis. Van Alen Institute's exhibition "OPEN: New Designs for Public Space" held in New York in 2003 showcased this recent trend of hybrid urban space development across the world, exploring their typological, morphological, infrastructural, programmatic and operational complexities (Gastil & Ryan, 2004). According to Ellin (1996) and Worpole and Knox (2007), among others, public spaces should in fact include all physical spaces that are not strictly private, but in which social and civic functions of a public character are performed. This even includes spaces of cafés, bars or bookstores (Banerjee, 2001; Oldenburg, 1999). In fact, many of today's public spaces emerged from private squares, such as Georgian and Victorian squares in London (De Magalhães, 2010).

In his research, Francis (2003) introduced the term "urban open space" as publicly accessible open spaces which are designed and built for activity and enjoyment. The word "open" is used in Lynch's (1981) interpretation of it, which relates primarily to the accessibility of space. He mentions that public access is a critical factor for the quality of open space. Accessibility opens up all sorts of interactions with and within the space, including conflicts;

it fosters the diversity of user groups in terms of age, sex, social status or cultural background. The lack of access enhanced by strict management or over-design may considerably reduce the quality of public space. Privately owned open space, however, can increase the level of "publicness" by allowing people to freely dwell, express and act in space, as well as to utilize, appropriate and modify it (Francis, 2003; Lynch, 1981).

Finally, one may need to notice that the boundaries between the public and the private have always been blurry in the context of Asian cities, forming a fluctuating continuum of negotiated semi-public and semi-private spaces. With increased density and rise of the economy (as well as specific climate, as in the case of tropical cities like Singapore), such a condition has created a logical ground for new hybrid urban developments to emerge and be accepted as the extension of the public sphere.

Hybrid Urban Space

Familiar models of urban space include those predicated on the relationship between the form of urban space and the use and socio-cultural meaning of these spaces in the development of typologies. Commonly addressed types of public space, such as squares, plazas, streets or parks, had not only made the city readable, but also held the meanings and uses that were understood by everyone. Past research has been predominantly focused on such models of urban space, without consistent and clear rules on what constitutes good urban space, let alone what constitutes good urban space in a "high-density context." Consequently, we still know too little about the expanding typologies of urban spaces emerging today, such as mixed transit and commerce-led spaces (e.g., subway stations and airports), multi-leveled and elevated spaces (e.g., roof parks and pedestrian bridges and underpasses), and intensified mixed-use residential developments, among others. Some of these spaces may be found in the existing buildings and infrastructures, whose uses are increasingly being transformed today in such a way that they are acquiring the role of civic places. Childs (2004) calls such spaces the "unsung civic places."

While the conventional types of public spaces and their timeless values remain immensely important, exploring new ways of attaining and sustaining such values, as well as investigating possible new values and modes of publicness, in high-density conditions, is of high relevance and much needed. New urban conditions shaped by rapid urbanization, rise in urban population, densification of urban form, migration and the increasing cultural diversity of cities, among other factors, are leading to a multiplicity of hybrid space typologies. The ways in which public spaces are conventionally understood, designed, utilized and managed necessitate continuous re-conceptualizing.

Rather than reviewing a history and taxonomy of conventional types of public spaces, it is more relevant, and in fact necessary, to acknowledge and examine the shifting meanings and use of places over time, the deformations of typologies of spaces, as well as the importation of new typologies and their reconstitution in high-density contexts.

In an attempt to define the hybridization process in an architectural context, Joseph Fenton (1985) provides the most cited reference. Fenton clearly acknowledges that the fully hybrid architecture in the American context resulted as a response to the increased pressures created by the escalating land values and the constraints of the urban grid in the late nineteenth century.

His concept of architectural hybridization and "hybrid vigor" has originated from genetics, referring to the cross-breeding of different species in order to strengthen particular characteristics of the new hybrid species. Such a process, however, involves both the possibilities and the risks, and mixing for the sake of mixing may engender sterility and fake coexistence, rather than spaces with superior or advanced characteristics.

While focusing primarily on buildings in the context of the American metropolis, Fenton (1985) distinguishes three basic types of hybrids and their combinations, namely: the fabric hybrid, the graft hybrid and the monolith hybrid. The fabric hybrid is derived directly from the structure and measurements of the surrounding urban context; it is a volumetric infill of the grid. The graft hybrid represents a combination of different building forms within an urban block that articulate the different functions they house. The monolith hybrid is often a high-rise structure that merges different programs under a unifying skin. In his *Delirious New York*, Rem Koolhaas (1978) also investigates the hybrid and generic qualities of the skyscrapers of Manhattan, highlighting the countless possibilities for different programs to coexist on different floors and behind a singular envelope. Yet, an architectural hybridization is a process that is manifested beyond the physical complexity and the mere mixing of multiple programs within a single structure. True hybridization requires greater interaction between structural and programmatic pieces, and the mutual intensification and activation of the surrounding context.

Finally, the process of hybridization deeply affects the nature of contemporary urban spaces. While redefining the site, the contemporary hybrid developments redefine the form, the scale, the enclosure and the location of public spaces, the ways they interact with their surroundings and the ways they are used, experienced and managed. In such a way, the urban space becomes fully hybridized with other functions of the development.

Accordingly, we distinguish three mutually overlapping modes of hybridization expressed by the emerging urban space developments in high-density contexts, namely: spatial, programmatic and/or operational (ownership) hybridization.

Spatial Hybrids
Spatial hybridization of urban space is reflected through structural complexity and technological innovations and their relationship to the surrounding context, forming new spatial conditions for access, connectivity, physical flexibility and innovative public uses. Complex forms, layouts, hybrid indoor–outdoor interfaces and thresholds, underground, multi-level or elevated public spaces are some of the design manifestations of new hybrid urban space developments. In the context of the design of new spatial hybrids, the plan loses its primacy, and the section and three-dimensional modeling become crucial. In the context of Asian cities, *The Making of Hong Kong* by Shelton et al. (2011) and *Learning from the Japanese City* by Shelton (2012) convincingly explore new models of the compact, high-rise, volumetric, dense and intense urbanism that is emerging, particularly in China and Japan. In these contexts, hybrid development results from the reassessment and redefinition of the site (the ground), as well as of the movements and functions that form the large and highly complex volumetric network of urban spaces.

Programmatic Hybrids
Programmatic or functional hybrids combine various activities that are mutually synergetic and compatible while suggesting unconventional ways of space usage. Typical contemporary mixed-use developments tend to place "everything under one roof" in order to induce the condition of heterogeneity, diversity and density of "city-like" experiences. However, they often result in creating conditions of co-presence, segregation and conflicts, rather than coexistence, cohabitation, integration and mutual synergy. Flexible and multi-functional design and programming are some of the mechanisms encouraged by the new large-scale developments in order to maximize the use of space and cater to all user groups. Railway stations and other transportation infrastructures are some examples of functional hybridization.

Operational Hybrids
Urban public space is a human-constructed common that in high-density and high-intensity conditions turns into a congestible good that often generates rivalry and conflicts (Dietz et al., 2002; Neuts, 2011; Poklembovái et al., 2012). Operational hybridization refers to new conditions for spatial negotiation, in terms of redefining the conventional notions of boundaries, territoriality and accessibility through negotiated ownership, temporary appropriation, safety optimization, use, time and capacity regulations, and the management of (and over) space.

In contemporary hybrid urban developments the contractual relationships, such as public–private partnerships, play an increasingly important role (De Magalhães, 2010). Although, at present, the predominant ways of public space governance, provision and management may still appear quite traditional, the gradual transfer of responsibilities for public space governance from public to private sectors through various types of contracts is inevitable, changing the very notion of public spaces.

Emerging Hybrid Urban Space Typologies

Emerging hybrid urban spaces are dynamic and often conflicting systems of synergies between spatial configurations, programs, ways of utilization and management, charged by the intense tensions and negotiations between the diverse users and agencies. In order to understand such complexities we look at over 50 dense, intense, hybrid, complex and dynamic contemporary urban spaces, the majority of which are located in Asia, including cases from Singapore, Tokyo, Osaka, Beijing, Hong Kong and Seoul, but also New York, Melbourne, Berlin, Rotterdam and Copenhagen, among others.

In selecting the case studies, the main focus was on spaces that fulfill at least one of the following criteria:

- space is dense in terms of built density of the site and/or of the immediate surrounding context;
- space is dense in terms of population density or number of users (capacity);
- space is intense in terms of high concentration and diversity of activities and users;
- space is hybrid and complex in form, program and/or governance (ownership and management);
- space represents an emerging typology of public space;
- space offers new programs and/or considerably new ways of utilization in existing typologies of public spaces.

These criteria do not necessarily refer to best practices in terms of quality, performance or success, but rather to good examples of the investigated conditions (built and population density, intensity of use, hybridity and spatial innovation). For example, observed high density of users (crowdedness) does not necessarily relate to high urban performance, although it may be an indicator of its popularity or intensity. Similarly, urban spaces that are less crowded, such as Henderson Waves in Singapore or Dangdai Moma in Beijing, should not be a priori discarded from the selection as potential good practices.

Any attempt to classify contemporary hybrid urban space developments into rigid and static spatial typologies would be an immensely difficult and, perhaps, even unnecessary challenge.

Our initial hybrid typologies are formed in reference to the primary use of urban space. These include *intensified residential developments, mixed-use developments, infrastructural transit-led spaces, recreational green hybrids and hybrid urban voids*. The types proposed are, however, not exhaustive, as most of the spaces investigated are in fact fully eligible for more than one category. Moreover, while some of these descriptive themes used to categorize emerging urban space developments may not be read as hybrid per se, our interest lies in highlighting the most apparent hybrid properties of investigated spaces in reference to high-density and high-intensity conditions. In other words, our attempt is to capture the unique, unconventional, dynamic and often unstable qualities of these typologies that resulted from varied levels of spatial, functional and operational hybridization.

Intensified Residential Developments

Undoubtedly the most apparent impact of densely built and populated areas on quality of life are found in housing environments. In response, new residential developments and community centers often **oppose conventional housing schemes**. Apart from the "typical" formal play areas (such as playgrounds and sport grounds), open green spaces and other amenities, urban spaces in new residential developments are increasingly adopting various forms and mixed activities (with emphasis on sociability) catering to both residents and general public (visitors), while creating **new conditions for social exchange and negotiation**. Although such a design strategy may not be entirely new, some recent housing developments in high-density contexts showcase considerable levels of innovation and experimentation resulting from spatial, functional and operational hybridization. **Vertical open spaces, elevated and multi-level podiums, roof gardens and sky bridges** are some of the recent re-invented typologies that offer alternative ways of space usage and intensification of usage vertically, while at the same time ensuring the comfort of urban dwellers through alternative amenities and recreational spaces for social interaction (Pomeroy, 2011; Yeh, 2011). Apart from providing multi-level networks of pedestrian spaces, such amenities also offer attractive new ways to perceive and experience the city (from above) and to redefine privacy—qualities that are becoming increasingly valued among high-rise residents (Osmundson, 1999; Yuen et al., 2006).

Pinnacle@Duxton (Figure 1.1) is a pioneering high-density public housing model as the result of a response to population growth in Singapore. With the increase of plot ratio—three times that of typical public housing blocks in Singapore, with an average gross plot ratio (GPR) of about 3.00—the Pinnacle@Duxton integrates **elevated public amenities (a public podium and two sky bridges)** as a form of compensation to detachment from the street level. Located at the 26th and the 50th levels, the

1.1 Elevated public space (sky bridge)—Pinnacle@Duxton, Singapore.

bridges act not only as connections between seven residential blocks, but also as public spaces for residents and the general public. While the bridge at the 26th level may be accessed only by the residents, the roof-top sky bridge is accessible by the general public on payment of a small fee. Crowd control measures are also implemented, with the capacity of visitors limited to 200 per day. **Different levels of publicness** were imposed due to various factors, such as the privacy of residents, the maintenance and vertical circulation control, among others. The amenities on the 26th level sky bridge include social services and recreational facilities, such as a Residents' Committee center (RC), a community plaza, a jogging track, an elderly fitness corner, an outdoor gym, a children's playground and two view decks. The main nodes of activities at the roof-top, such as playgrounds and seating areas, are located between the blocks with pathways meandering around the periphery providing great panoramic views of the city center. Although somewhat fragmented, the overall experience within the different segments of the Pinnacle@Duxton is pleasant.

Another example that aims to activate a three-dimensional pedestrian network is *Jianwai SOHO* (Figure 1.2) in the central area of Beijing's CBD. This mega-complex, which includes 20 high-rise towers, four villas with 20 **roof-top gardens** and 16 pedestrian lanes, houses luxury residential, commercial and office functions.

Inspired by the **maze** of alleys in North African Islamic cities, the project attempts to reconstruct, more or less successfully, their rich, diverse and vivid everyday-life settings and ambience, through a **multi-level network** of public spaces, narrow streets, covered passageways, pocket spaces and accessible green roofs. The basement level of the development is reserved for cars, while the landscaped ground level is completely liberated for pedestrians. The apartment towers and low-rise commercial buildings form a loose checkerboard plan at the ground level. Instead of organizing the project around a large park or other focal point, the ground plane is riddled with sunken gardens that knit the two levels together and allow daylight to reach even the lowest levels. This multi-level space between the buildings is the most unique and striking element of the design. The roof of the commercial buildings features green pedestrian walkways that connect all the buildings and allow free movement through the complex.

Multi-level publicly accessible networks, **micro-urbanism** and **porosity** are some of the major characteristics of the recent intensified housing projects by Steven Holl Architects, including the **Dangdai Moma**[3] (also known as **Linked Hybrid**) in Beijing and **Sliced Porosity Block** (also known as **Raffles City**) in Chengdu, that aim to push the boundaries of the typical residential complexes in China. **Sliced Porosity Block** (Figure 1.3)

1.2 Multi-level network of public spaces—Jianwai SOHO, Beijing, China.

1.3 Open gated community—Sliced Porosity Block, Chengdu, China.

1.4 Mixed-use large-scale development—Tokyo Midtown, Tokyo, Japan.

is a housing complex with five high-rise towers that envelop an **elevated public podium** situated on top of a shopping mall. This mixed-use housing development, with direct access to a subway line, provides a variety of programs, including offices, serviced apartments, a hotel, cafés and a restaurant. With the provision of diverse activities and ease of accessibility, it is fast becoming one of the most established retail, dining and entertainment centers in Chengdu, with a high frequency of visitors. The large public space of more than 300,000 square meters consists of three valleys with water ponds that also serve as skylights to the six-storey shopping area below. These water gardens reflect three temporal dimensions of the design concept: a Fountain of the Chinese Calendar Year, a Fountain of the Twelve Months and a Fountain of Thirty Days. The voids of the towers at the podium level accommodate three pavilions: a pavilion of history, a light pavilion and a local art pavilion, creating attractive light effects in the evenings.

Mixed-Use Developments

Characterized by **high diversity and intensity of users and activities** in one place (predominantly commercial), emerging mixed-use mega-complexes often mark the city areas, becoming their new focal points and creating new identities of urban districts. Although heavily criticized for diminishing the public realm, mixed-use developments are seen as one of the dominant models of contemporary urban development and their contribution to the new public realm should not be ignored. Also under pressure of sustainability paradigms, new trends in designing retail-focused spaces show a considerable shift from "conventional shopping mall" developments. With fewer financial constraints, mixed-use complexes are often seen as arenas for **unconventional experimentations** with urban space typologies and innovative uses.

Tokyo Midtown (Figure 1.4) is a 569,000-square-meter **mixed-use** development in Tokyo, comprising office, residential, commercial, hotel, museum and leisure spaces. The main landmark is the Midtown Tower which is the second-tallest building in Tokyo (53 floors and 248m high) and the fifth tallest in Japan. The project was designed by a number of world-renowned architects. Midtown Tower, Midtown East and Midtown West were designed by the architectural firm Skidmore, Owings & Merrill (SOM) and Nikken Sekkei; landscape design of the Hinokicho park (40,000 square meters) was by EDAW; the Suntory Museum of Art was designed by Kengo Kuma; Sakakura Associates designed the Residential Wing and underground spaces; and Communication Arts was in charge of the design of the retail Galleria. At the edge of Hinokicho Park is Design Sight 21_21, a 1,700-square-meter design gallery created by fashion designer Issey Miyake and architect Tadao Ando. **Environmental preservation**, environmentally conscious design, and **community participation** are valuable aspects of this mega-complex. With various art and culture programs and contemporary outdoor artwork, Tokyo Midtown is a good example of exploring the **interactive** relationships between site and context, indoor and outdoor environment, users and space, as well as enhancing urban space identity through artistic means.

Taikoo Li Sanlitun (Figure 1.5) is another mixed-use mega-complex located in the most mature retail area in Beijing. It comprises five shopping malls, and five office and four residential towers of varying heights, linked by a dynamic **three-dimensional pedestrian network** of sky bridges, alleys, piazzas and a sunken garden, reinterpreting the idea of a compact city and creating a dynamic interplay between various indoor and outdoor spaces and activities.

Relatively simple in form, the *Sony Centre* (Figure 1.6) in Potsdamer Platz area, Berlin is a complex **mixed-use private development**, parts of which are open and accessible to the public. During the 1990s it attracted bitter criticism for drawing its inspiration from the shopping mall and for being heavily **branded**. The central space of the development is the Forum, a circular atrium space covered by a large canopy, which acts as a kind of event and exhibition space, displaying an array of Sony products. Apart from visual technology and entertainment-related facilities, such as an IMAX theater, art and film museums and a Sony-style store, the development also contains a mix of shops and restaurants, apartments and offices, a hotel and a conference center. Free Wi-Fi connections are available for all visitors.

A recently opened building (October 2014), the **Market Hall (Markthal)** (Figure 1.7) in Rotterdam, is one of the latest examples of **intense hybrid urban space** developments. It combines a food market, retail, housing, parking and public space functions (228 apartments, 100 fresh market produce stalls, food-related retail units, preparation and cooling space, a supermarket and 1,200 parking spaces). During the day (from 9 a.m. to 8 p.m.),

the covered square serves as a central market hall, while after business hours the hall becomes an enormous sheltered public space. The result is a covered square which acts as a central market hall during the day, while after business hours it remains lively due to people frequenting the restaurants on its first floor.

Metropol Parasol (Figure 1.8) is an **iconic multi-level mixed-use** development located in La Encarnación square, in the old quarter of Seville, Spain. Its major feature is a wooden structure consisting of six parasols in the form of giant mushrooms, one of the largest such constructions in the world. The complex is organized on four levels. The underground level houses the Antiquarium, a museum that displays Roman and Moorish remains discovered on site. The ground street level houses the Central Market, on top of which is an open-air public plaza shaded by the wooden parasols. The roof levels of the structure contain **panoramic ramps and terraces** and a restaurant, offering one of the best views of the city center.

Insadong Ssamziegil (Figure 1.9) is a colorful shopping and culture complex in Insadong, Seoul, that features cafés, galleries, and workshops that mix modern and traditional Korean styles. The complex opened in 2004 and is now a destination in itself and an important centerpiece of Insadong. Ssamziegil may be modern, but its construction blends well into the surrounding traditional neighborhood. The whole area takes up 3,967 square meters (42,700 square feet). The 500-meter (1,640-foot) ramp footpath that wraps around the courtyard as it ascends to the roof is the main feature of this complex, which resembles a small Insadong alleyway and **brings the horizontal character of the street to a vertical dimension**. Like a spiral, the ramp envelops the public area and people can see various events on the ramp. There are 70 small shops about 10 square meters (107 square feet) in size along this footpath and 12 of the workshops on the first floor, which were in situ before Ssamziegil was constructed, have since been modernized. The fourth floor features a sky garden, a gallery, a crafts exhibition hall, a book café, and other urban spaces to rest.

Infrastructural Transit-Led Spaces

New transportation hubs (such as subway and train stations) and bridges, as well as reused dated infrastructural systems, increasingly adopt planning and design strategies that emphasize community, accessibility, pedestrian-friendliness and culture as new, important values. Transportation spaces thus function not only as transit nodes, but as rich, **complex** and **dynamic** spaces with **multiple functions** on **multiple spatial levels**, enhancing the economic viability of the station and its surrounding area. Among the case studies are Shinjuku subway stations in Tokyo; Kyoto Station in Osaka; the Central Mid-levels Escalator in Hong Kong; and A8ernA in Koog aan de Zaan, the Netherlands.

1.5 Mixed-use large-scale development—Taikoo Li Sanlitun, Beijing, China.

1.6 Branded private mixed-use development—Sony Centre, Berlin, Germany.

1.7 Market covered by residential arch—Market Hall (Markthal), Rotterdam, the Netherlands.

1.8 Iconic public space—Metropol Parasol, Seville, Spain.

1.9 Elevated spiral shopping street—Insadong Ssamziegil, Seoul, South Korea.

According to Grossman (2000, p. 2, par. 5),

having [train] stations [in Japan] adopt local community themes requires that the plaza once again be viewed as the focal point of a meaningful urban design (or "machi zukuri"). It is unlikely the station plaza could ever serve demand for open space, due to size restrictions. However, there are strong movements to support the station plaza as the impetus from which integrated plans for pedestrian-oriented designs may originate.

Kyoto Station (Figure 1.10) in Osaka designed by Hiroshi Hara marks a new era of high-rise developments in the city, being among the first train stations that have introduced a variety of programs to transit-led facilities under one 15-storey roof.

It contains a shopping mall, cafés and restaurants, museums and exhibition venues, a movie theater, a hotel, a game center, government offices and multi-storey parking garages. With its valley-like hollow space, the station building creates an artificial interior landscape and a composite spatial layout that reflects the complexity of major Japanese cityscapes: vertical dimensions, interlocking networks, fluidity of space and discontinuities of scale. In somewhat theme-park manner, Kyoto Station **juxtaposes familiar and traditional with novel and high-tech**: the atrium of American malls, the traditional public space of Western cities and the transportation hub of Japan. It is possible to move around within this space without seeing or coming into actual contact with the railway.

With 10 platforms serving 20 tracks and 12 train links, and over 200 exits, including the underground arcades, *Shinjuku Station*

1.10 Multi-functional transit hub—Kyoto Station, Osaka, Japan.

(Figure 1.11) is the world's busiest transport hub with an average of 3.64 million people using the station each day. It offers a **vast and complex network** of commercial spaces at various levels, as well as performance spaces for various cultural and social events, making it one of the most common **meeting points** in the city. New modes of publicness are not static, but rather transient and always evolving, seeking flexibility and experimentation. While the cost of building underground structures is very high, due to limited land availability and increasing population, exploring such alternative possibilities for expanding the **underground network** of public spaces while linking it with the existing street level networks is much needed.

The Central Mid-levels Escalator (Figure 1.12) in Hong Kong is the longest outdoor covered escalator system in the world, covering over 800 meters in distance and elevating at over 135 meters. It was constructed in 1993 to provide a better commute by linking areas within the Central and Western District in Hong Kong Island. The project was criticized as being a "white elephant," since it failed to achieve the primary objective of reducing traffic between the Mid-levels and Central areas, as well as overrunning its original budget. However, in spite of such critique, the Central Mid-levels Escalator made a substantial impact on how public facilities and spaces around are used. Since the escalator system opened, most pedestrians started gathering at the elevated level, rather than at the street level (as in the past). This has opened up large tracts of intermediate levels above ("SoHo") and below ("NoHo") Hollywood Road to both pedestrians and commerce. Many restaurants have opened around all the elevated levels, on the first or second floors of the buildings already present. Previously private and exclusive spaces on the upper levels became accessible to the public, creating a **dynamic 3D network of public and semi-public spaces**. The

1.11 Multi-level public network—Shinjuku Station, Tokyo, Japan.

Central Mid-levels Escalator is a good example of an innovative and **integrated type of elevated public space**, which is very relevant in highly dense urban conditions.

A8ernA (Figure 1.13) is an exceptional example of infrastructural space **reuse** and reactivation. Namely, the new public space development in Koog aan de Zaan makes use of the dead space under the A8 motorway bridge that passes through the heart of this small town near Amsterdam, while reconnecting the two parts of the town and providing a better connection to the river. Its program of amenities and activities has been established in a highly **participatory** fashion, based primarily on citizens' demands. The entire arcade space is divided into three well-differentiated zones. The central square accommodates a supermarket, flower and pet shops, and a light fountain. The eastern end offers a small harbor with panoramic platform, while the western side comprises various spaces for teenagers, such as a graffiti zone (the so-called "graffiti gallery"), a skating rink, a break-dance stage, table-tennis desks, a small football pitch, a basketball court, lovers' corners, as well as a car park for 120 vehicles.

1.12 Elevated public infrastructure—The Central Mid-levels Escalator, Hong Kong.

1.13 Reactivation of dead infrastructural space—A8ernA, Koog aan de Zaan, the Netherlands.

1.14 Elevated parkway that reuses an old railway—the High Line Park, New York, USA.

Recreational Green Hybrids

Recreational urban spaces primarily include green spaces and, based on urban footprint, may be further classified as parks, green promenades (linear parkways) and park bridges (elevated parks). Green spaces that appear as part of other developments of different primary uses (such as small green areas or community gardens in housing precincts, or commercial and mixed-use developments) are classified only as secondarily recreational.

The *High Line Park* (Figure 1.14) is an **elevated** 1.6-kilometer-long **privately managed parkway system** (the world's longest green roof) in New York. Following the community-led efforts, this development transforms an existing unused infrastructure—an old railway for freight transport on the western side of Manhattan Island—into a public park. With its numerous points of access from street level, and its connections to adjacent buildings, it enriches the public space network of the city, while providing visual relief and new vantage points to the waterfront, the neighborhood and even the Statue of Liberty in the distance. Various tours, lectures, performances and events for the whole family are offered with or without charge, focusing on the High Line Park's design, gardens, history and public art projects.

Namba Parks (or *Nankai Namba*) (Figure 1.15) is a **mixed-use large-scale** complex located adjacent to Namba Station, one of the most important transportation hubs in the Osaka region in Japan. The main conceptual premise of Namba Parks is of a canyon coursing through an elevated urban park, while offering a combination of retail, entertainment, cultural, office and residential space. The roof park slopes upward, approximately eight levels from the main entrance, offering a number of green outdoor common areas. Although somewhat island-like and self-centered, Namba Parks represents one of the most successful **privately managed** public spaces adjacent to transportation infrastructure, a **green transit-oriented development**, where economic performance and quality green design emerge as a single objective.

Henderson Waves (Figure 1.16) is a segment of the 9-kilometer southern ridge trail, a **green connector** in Singapore. The bridge resides directly above Henderson Road, acting as the main connector between Telok Blangah Hill Park and Mount Faber Park. Spanning 284 meters and reaching a height of 36 meters, it is the highest pedestrian-only bridge in Singapore. An elaborated wave-like form establishes the bridge as a key feature and visual

1.15 Large-scale terraced roof-top park—Namba Parks, Osaka, Japan.

1.16 Green connector, pedestrian bridge as public space—Henderson Waves, Singapore.

landmark within the large recreational infrastructure. While by and large located in a nature park and a relatively low-density setting, as well as being mostly a weekend destination, overseas examples (such as the High Line Park in New York) have shown that the same technique could work equally well in a high-density urban setting, while encouraging more intense everyday usage.

Hybrid Urban Voids

Although attributed as "conventional" urban space typologies, urban voids retain special attention in high-density contexts. Pedestrian-friendly city zones, emerging from initiatives for the **reclamation of urban streets** and other space often taken over by cars or underused, are essential for making highly dense contemporary cities **more walkable, building better communities**

and improving the overall quality of life. Some such cases include Times Square and Bryant Park in New York; Superkilen in Copenhagen; Clarke Quay in Singapore; and Skatepark @ Westblaak Avenue and Schouwburgplein in Rotterdam.

Times Square (Figure 1.17) is a recently **pedestrianized street** in the New York downtown area, with the goal to ease traffic congestion and improve the livability of the area. The reclaiming of the street for pedestrians turned Times Square into an enjoyable and eventful public space, while stitching up the urban fabric and giving the entire downtown a new identity. Pedestrian-friendly features include cycle lanes, clearly marked out pedestrian zones (painted and blocked with potted plants), and sturdy movable tables, chairs and umbrellas that make the space **highly interactive and flexible**. The red steps of the TKTS

1.17 Flexible pedestrian space—Times Square, New York, USA.

booth represent the main landmark in Times Square, an important point for social interaction, resting and people-watching. In fact, a massive ongoing reconstruction project involves re-paving the pedestrianized streets and replacing aged and cluttered infrastructure with a more modern one, including electrical outlets to eliminate the need for generators at large events and concerts. Reconstruction work is estimated to be completed by 2015. Times Square is one of the most successful redevelopments attracting both local visitors and tourists.

Superkilen (Figure 1.18) is a new pedestrian park street in Copenhagen, Denmark that celebrates the **diversity** of more than 60 nationalities living in that city. This colorful and dynamic linear public space is 750 meters long, offering bike lanes, playgrounds, spaces for basketball, football, cultural activities, picnics, socializing and relaxing. It comprises three main areas: a red square, a black market and a green park. The red square, painted in bright red, orange and pink, serves as an extension to the activities in the nearby sports hall, providing recreational and cultural activities. The black market at the center is a meeting place with dynamic walking surfaces, offering a variety of seating, a Moroccan fountain, barbecue grills, tables for playing backgammon and chess, and a Japanese octopus playground. The green park caters primarily to children, young people and families, providing pitches for hockey and basketball, as well as attracting people for picnics or sunbathing.

Cheonggyecheon stream (Figure 1.19), a 5.8-kilometer-long recreational urban space in downtown Seoul, is the result of a massive **urban renewal** project that included demolishing an elevated freeway and reviving a historic Cheonggyecheon stream

1.18 New pedestrian park street—Superkilen, Copenhagen, Denmark.

which once passed beneath it. Such an intervention created a **vibrant sunken ecological corridor** for pedestrians, cyclists and wildlife, offering pockets for play, relaxation, picnics and cultural performances, a number of sculptures and historic artifacts along the way, and, in such a way, reconnecting the once divided northern and southern parts of the city. The design of the stream progressively transforms from the predominant hardscape of Cheonggye Plaza into more landscaped and softer wetland zones before joining the Jungraechon stream which further leads out into the Han River. The result is an interactive yet calm green urban oasis amid the tall cityscape and bustling street traffic that also provides flood protection, increases biodiversity, reduces urban heat, reinforces surrounding businesses and in such a way contributes to **sustainable** urban development.

Skatepark @ Westblaak Avenue (Figure 1.20) in Rotterdam is the biggest open-air skating space in the Netherlands resulting from the revitalization of an underused wide traffic island in the middle of the city. Although dominated by the **specific use** and catering to the **specific user groups**, this public space has proved to be vibrant and well integrated, with almost continuous occupation. One of the essential elements of such integration was the involvement of local skaters throughout the design process, upon whose feedback the entire project has been designed. The central zone offers 11 distinct areas of facilities and equipment for skating, pirouettes and aerial acrobatics, all differentiated by color codes. Next to the skating area stands a café restaurant, also providing various services for skaters and other visitors, including maintenance and event management.

Clarke Quay (Figure 1.21) is an attractive tourist and **night-time pedestrian area** characterized by a **mix of modern and traditional values**, as well as **unique design features**. Set against the backdrop of rows of shop fronts, it offers an array of cafés, bars and restaurants, night clubs, entertainment spots and retail shops. Within the internal pedestrianized streets, the threshold between inside and outside is blurred as commercial activities extend onto the streets. A unique spatial feature is a giant canopy made out of connected transparent umbrella-like elements that brings strong

1.19 Sunken parkway—Cheonggyecheon stream, Seoul, South Korea.

1.20 Space for specific use—Skatepark @ Westblaak Avenue, Rotterdam, the Netherlands.

1.21 Night-time pedestrian area—Clarke Quay, Singapore.

1.22 Exploration of topographic relationship—Ewha Campus Complex, Seoul, South Korea.

1.23 Flexible multi-functional green space—Bryant Park, New York, USA.

1.24 "Fractal" public space—Federation Square, Melbourne, Australia.

visual identity and serves as a micro-climate system, improving users' comfort in the adverse tropical weather conditions.

Located in one of the most popular shopping districts in Seoul, **Ewha Campus Complex (ECC)** at Ewha Womans University (Figure 1.22) offers a new type of public space by exploring the **topographic relationship** between the architecture and the landscape. The new complex, with a library, a bookstore, a gym, a movie theater, cafés and other cultural facilities that are accessible by the general public, resembles a green "hill" split by a 25-meter-wide and 250-meter-long "valley." This monumental **canyon-like space** slopes down in the opposite direction to the topography of the roof and is surrounded by glass walls with entrances to the building at different levels. At the northern end, the ramp turns into stairs forming an outdoor amphitheater. This spatially **dynamic** space provides a new gateway to the university campus and is open to the public, expressing an attempt to reconnect private institutional space with the city.

Bryant Park (Figure 1.23) is a 39,000-square-meter privately managed public park in midtown Manhattan. It is known worldwide as one of the most successful restoration projects that involved **public–private partnership** and solving social issues through good design. It is a destination for a large number and a wide range of users. During lunch-hours in the warm weather months, the park typically hosts over 5,000 businesspeople while totaling about 20,000 visitors by the end of the day. Among the amenities available are a French-style Carousel, Citi Pond, the Reading Room (an open-air library), a boule board, chess tables, extensive gardens and seasonal planting displays, table tennis, the Bryant Park Grill, free wireless access, ice-skating rink during the winter, 8-foot-wide umbrellas, as well as 2,000 **movable chairs** to take in the sights. Being the only large-scale public park in midtown Manhattan, Bryant Park is an attractive location for **various public and private events**, such as concerts, performances, exhibitions, fashion shows, literary events and product launches.

Federation Square (Figure 1.24) is one of the **new landmarks** of Melbourne famous for its bold fractal architecture and vibrant year-round event calendar. Built above the railway, this complex development provides a **creative mix of activities** and attractions to engage visitors, including art galleries, cinemas, tourist services, retail and dining. With its **diverse network of public spaces**, including the central open square and adjacent covered arcades, Federation Square rapidly became an important meeting place in the heart of the city.

NOTES
1 In 2010, the world's population reached 6.9 billion people, and it is expected to attain 9.3 billion in 2050 and 10.1 billion by 2100 (United Nations, 2014).

2 In her book *The Human Condition* (1958), German-American political theorist Hannah Arendt traces the public versus private space dichotomy back to Greek Polis by juxtaposing its *Oikia* and *Agora*. The *Oikia* was the ideal form of private space—space of production and reproduction, space of necessity, while the *Agora* was the opposite—the ideal form of the public space, space of the freedom of speech and action. While being opposites, the two spaces shared at least one common element: a clear boundary that defined them.
3 Detailed information about Dangdai Moma (Linked Hybrid) in Beijing, China may be found in Chapter 2, "Orgware Qualities of Urban Space: An Example."

REFERENCES
Alexander, E. R. (1993). Density Measures: A Review and Analysis. *Journal of Architectural and Planning Research*, 10(3), 181–202. doi:10.1177/08854129922092478.
Amin, A. (2006). Collective Culture and Urban Public Space. *City*, 12(1), 5–24. doi:10.1080/13604810801933495.
Arendt, H. (1958). *The Human Condition*. Chicago, IL: University of Chicago Press.
Atkinson, R. (2003). Domestication by Cappuccino or a Revenge on Urban Space? Control and Empowerment in the Management of Public Spaces. *Urban Studies*, 40(9), 1829–1843. doi:10.1080/0042098032000106627.
Augé, M. (1995). *Non-places: Introduction to an Anthropology of Supermodernity*. London: Verso.
Banerjee, T. (2001). The Future of Public Space: Beyond Invented Streets and Reinvented Places. *APA Journal*, 67(1), 9–24. doi:10.1080/01944360108976352.
Batty, M. (2005). *Cities and Complexity: Understanding Cities with Cellular Automata, Agent-based Models, and Fractals*. Cambridge, MA: MIT Press.
Benhabib, S. (1996). *Democracy and Difference: Contesting the Boundaries of the Political*. Princeton, NJ: Princeton University Press.
Binnie, J., Holloway, J., Millington, S., & Young, C. (eds) (2006). *Cosmopolitan Urbanism*. New York: Routledge.
Bramley, G., & Morgan, J. (2003). Building Competitiveness and Cohesion: The Role of New House Building in Central Scotland's Cities. *Housing Studies*, 18, 447–471. doi:10.1080/02673030304245.
Bramley, G., & Power, S. (2009). Urban Form and Social Sustainability: The Role of Density and Housing Type. *Environment and Planning B: Planning and Design*, 36(1), 30–48. doi:10.1068/b33129.
Brenner, N., & Theodore, N. (eds) (2002). *Spaces of Neoliberalism: Urban Restructuring in North America and Western Europe*. Oxford, and Boston, MA: Blackwell.
Bridge, G. (2002). The Neighbourhood and Social Networks. *CNR Paper 4*, School of Policy Studies, Centre for Neighbourhood Research, Bristol University.
Brill, M. (1989a). An Ontology for Exploring Urban Public Life Today. *Places*, 6(1), 24–31.
Brill, M. (1989b). Transformation, Nostalgia and Illusion in Public Life and Public Place. In I. Altman & E. Zube (eds). *Public Places and Spaces*, Vol. 10 (Human Behavior and Environment series) (pp. 7–30). New York: Plenum.
Bunker, R. (1985). Urban Consolidation and Australian Cities. *Built Environment*, 11, 83–96. doi:10.1080/00420980050162184.
Burton, E. (2000a). The Compact City: Just or Just Compact? A Preliminary Analysis. *Urban Studies*, 37, 1969–2001. doi:10.1080/00420980050162184.
CABE. (2004). *The Value of Public Space—How High Quality Parks and Public Spaces Create Economic, Social and Environmental Value.*

Retrieved from https://www.designcouncil.org.uk/sites/default/files/asset/document/the-value-of-public-space.pdf.

Carmona, M. (2010a). Contemporary Public Space: Critique and Classification, Part One: Critique. *Journal of Urban Design, 15*(1), 125–150. doi:10.1080/13574800903435651.

Carmona, M. (2010b). Contemporary Public Space, Part Two: Classification. *Journal of Urban Design, 15*(2), 265–281. doi: 10.1080/13574801003638111.

Carmona, M., & De Magalhães, C. (2008). *Public Space: The Management Dimension*. London: Routledge.

Carmona, M., Heath, T., Oc, T., & Tiesdell, S. (2003). *Public Places Urban Spaces: The Dimensions of Urban Design*. London: Architectural Press.

Carr, S., Francis, M., Rivlin, L. G., & Stone, A. M. (1992). *Public Space*. Cambridge and New York: Cambridge University Press.

Chan, E. H. W., & Lee, G. K. L. (2007). Critical Factors for Improving Social Sustainability of Urban Renewal Projects. *Social Indicators Research: An International and Interdisciplinary Journal for Quality-of-Life Measurement*. doi:10.1007/s11205-007-9089-3.

Chan, E. H. W., & Lee, G. K. L. (2009). Design Considerations for Environmental Sustainability in High Density Development: A Case Study of Hong Kong. *Environment, Development and Sustainability, 11*, 359–374. doi:10.1007/s10668-007-9117-0.

Chatterjee, M. (2009). Perception of Housing Environment among High Rise Dwellers. *Journal of the Indian Academy of Applied Psychology, 35*(Special Issue), 85–92. Retrieved from http://medind.nic.in/jak/t09/s1/jakt09s1p85.pdf.

Cheng, V. (2010). Understanding Density and High Density. In L. Ng (ed.), *Designing High-density Cities for Social and Environmental Sustainability* (pp. 3–16). London: Earthscan.

Childs, M. C. (2004). *Squares: A Public Place Design Guide for Urbanists*. Albuquerque: University of New Mexico Press.

Churchman, A. (1999). Disentangling the Concept of Density. *Journal of Planning Literature, 13*(4), 389–411. doi:10.1177/08854129922092478.

Coleman, P. (2006). *Shopping Environments: Evolution, Planning and Design*. Amsterdam: Elsevier.

Collie, M. (1990). The Case for Urban Consolidation. *Australian Planner, 28*, 26–33. doi:10.1080/07293682.1990.9657455.

Crawford, M. (1992). The World in a Shopping Mall. In M. Sorkin (ed.), *Variations on a Theme Park: The New American City and the End of Public Space* (pp. 3–33). New York: Hill and Wang.

Davis, M. (1998). *City of Quartz: Excavating the Future in Los Angeles*. London: Pimlico.

De Magalhães, C. (2010). Public Space and the Contracting-out of Publicness: A Framework for Analysis. *Journal of Urban Design, 15*(4), 559–574. doi:10.1080/13574809.2010.502347.

De Sola-Morales, M. (1992). Public and Collective Space: The Urbanisation of the Private Domain as a New Challenge. In *A Matter of Things*. 2008. Reprint. Rotterdam: NAi Publishers.

Dietz, T., Dolšak, N., Ostrom, E., & Stern, P. C. (2002). The Drama of the Commons. In E. Ostrom, T. Dietz, N. Dolšak, P. C. Stern, S. Stronich, & E. U. Weber (eds), *The Drama of the Commons* (pp. 3–35). Washington, DC: National Academy Press.

Dimmer, C., Golani Solomon, E., & Klinkers, K. (2005). *Shinonome: New Concepts of Public Space*. Retrieved from https://www.academia.edu/712234/Shinonome_New_Concepts_of_Public_Space.

Dittmar, H., & Ohland, G. (2003). *The New Transit Town: Best Practices in Transit-oriented Development*. Washington, DC: Island Press.

Dovey, K. (1999). *Framing Places: Mediating Power in Built Form*. New York: Routledge.

Dovey, K. (2010). *Becoming Places: Urbanism/Architecture/Identity/Power*. New York: Routledge.

Duany, A., & Plater-Zyberk, E. (2001). *Suburban Nation: The Rise of Sprawl and the Decline of the American Dream*. San Francisco, CA: North Point Press.

Ellin, N. (1996). *Postmodern Urbanism*. Oxford: Blackwell.

Evans, G. W., Lercher, P., & Kofler, W. W. (2002). Crowding and Children's Mental Health: The Role of House Type. *Journal of Environmental Psychology, 22*, 221–231.

Ewing, R., Bartholomew, K., Winkelman, S., Walters, J., & Anderson, G. (2008). Urban Development and Climate Change. *Journal of Urbanism, 1*, 201–216. doi:10.1080/17549170802529316.

Feehan, D., & Heit, M. D. (2006). *Making Business Districts Work: Leadership and Management of Downtown, Main Street, Business District and Community Development Organizations*. New York: Haworth Press.

Fenton, J. (1985). *Hybrid Buildings*. New York: Pamphlet Architecture; Princeton, NJ: Distributed by Princeton Architectural Books.

Forsyth, A., Hearst, M., Oakes, J. M., & Schmitz, M. K. (2008). Design and Destinations: Factors Influencing Walking and Total Physical Activity. *Urban Studies, 45*, 1973–1996. doi:10.1177/0042098008093386.

Francis, M. (2003). *Urban Open Space: Designing for User Needs*. Washington, DC: Island Press.

Freeman, L. (2001). The Effects of Sprawl on Neighbourhood Social Ties: An Explanatory Analysis. *Journal of the American Planning Association, 67*(1), 69–77. doi:10.1080/01944360108976356.

Gastil, R., & Ryan, Z. (2004). *Open: New Designs for Public Spaces*. New York: Van Allen Institute.

Gehl, J. (2010). *Cities for People*. Washington, DC: Island Press.

Glynn, T. (1981). Psychological Sense of Community: Measurement and Application. *Human Relations, 34*, 789–818. doi:10.1177/001872678103400904.

Gómez-Jacinto, L., & Hombrados-Mendieta, I. (2002). Multiple Effects of Community and Household Crowding. *Journal of Environmental Psychology, 22*(3), 233–246. Retrieved from: http://dx.doi.org/10.1006/jevp.2002.0236.

Gordon, P., & Richardson, H. (1997). Are Compact Cities a Desirable Planning Goal? *Journal of the American Planning Association, 63*(1), 95–106. doi:10.1080/01944369708975727.

Goss, J. (1996). Disquiet on the Waterfront: Reflections on Nostalgia and Utopia in the Urban Archetypes of Festival Marketplaces, *Urban Geography, 17*(3), 221–247.

Greenwald, M. J., & Boarnet M. G. (2001). Built Environment as a Determinant of Walking Behaviour: Analyzing Non-work Pedestrian Travel in Portland, Oregon. *Transportation Research Record, 1780*, 33–42. doi:10.3141/1780-05.

Gregson, N., Crewe, L., & Brooks, K. (2002). Shopping, Space, and Practice. *Environment and Planning D: Society and Space, 20*(5), 597–617. doi:10.1068/d270t.

Grossman, M. L. (2000). Tokyo Railway Station Spaces—Modern Day Sakariba. In *Moving Landscape, IO Internet Magazine*. Helsinki. Retrieved from: http://www.helsinki.fi/iiaa/io/io2000.pdf.

Habermas, J. (1984). *The Theory of Communicative Action*. Cambridge: Polity Press.

Habermas, J. (1989). *The Structural Transformation of the Public Sphere*. Cambridge, MA: MIT Press.

Hajer, M. (1989). *De stad als publiek domein*. Amsterdam: Wiardi Beckman Stichting.

Hajer, M., & Reijndorp, A. (2001). *In Search of New Public Domain*. Rotterdam: NAi Publishers.

Harper, C. (2014). Density, Productivity and Propinquity: Strategies and Tactics for Housing Design at Higher Urban Densities. In R. Cavallo, S. Kamossa, N. Marzot, P. M. Birghouder, & J. Kuijper (eds), *New Urban Configurations* (pp. 370–375). Delft: Delft University Press.

Harvey, D. (1989). From Managerialism to Entrepreneurialism: The Transformation of Urban Governance in Late Capitalism, *Geografiska Annaler, 71*B, 3–17.

Heath, G. W., Brownson, R. C., Kruger, J., Miles, R., Powell, K. E., & Ramsey, L. T. (2006). The Effectiveness of Urban Design and Land Use and Transport Policies and Practices to Increase Physical Activity: A Systematic Review. *Journal of Physical Activity and Health, 3*(Supplement 1), S55–S76.

Heeling, J., Meyer, H., & Westrik, J. (2002). *Het ontwerp van de stadsplattegrond*. Amsterdam: Uitgeverij SUN.

Hertzberger, H. (2005). *Lessons for Students in Architecture*. Rotterdam: 010 Publishers.

Hillier, B. (2007). *Space is the Machine*. Retrieved from: http://eprints.ucl.ac.uk/3848/1/SpaceIsTheMachine_Part1.pdf.

Hillier B., & Hanson J. (1984). *The Social Logic of Space*. Cambridge: Cambridge University Press.

Issarathumnoon, W. (2013). Bangkok Urban Intensities: A Contribution of Vivid and Fluid Public/Private Interfaces. In D. Radović (ed.), *Mn'M Workbook 1: Intensities in Ten Cities* (pp. 18–23). Tokyo: IKI (International Keio Institute) + flick studio co., ltd.

Iveson, K. (2007). *Publics and the City*. Oxford: Blackwell.

Jackson, P. (1998). Domesticating the Street: The Contested Spaces of the High Street and the Mall. In N. R. Fyfe (ed.), *Images of the Street: Planning, Identity, and Control in Public Spaces* (pp. 176–191). London: Routledge.

Jacobs, J. (1961). *The Death and Life of Great American Cities*. New York: Random House.

Jenks, M., & Dempsey, N. (eds) (2005). *Future Forms and Design for Sustainable Cities*. London: Architectural Press.

Jenks, M., Burton, E., & Williams. K. (eds) (1996). *The Compact City: A Sustainable Urban Form*. London: Spon.

Kohn, M. (2004). *Brave New Neighbourhoods: The Privatisation of Public Space*. London: Routledge.

Koolhaas, R. (1978). *Delirious New York: A Retroactive Manifesto for Manhattan*. New York: Monacelli Press.

Loukaitou-Sideris, A., & Banerjee, T. (1998). *Urban Design Downtown: Poetics and Politics of Form*. Berkeley, CA: University of California Press.

Low, S., & Smith, N. (eds) (2006). *The Politics of Public Space*. London: Routledge.

Lozano, E. E. (1990). *Community Design and the Culture of Cities: The Crossroad and the Wall*. New York: Cambridge University Press.

Lynch, K. (1981). *A Theory of Good City Form*. Cambridge, MA: MIT Press.

Mackintosh, E., West, S., & Saegert, S. (1975). Two Studies of Crowding in Urban Public Spaces. *Environment and Behavior, 7*(2), 159–184. doi:10.1177/001391657500700203.

MacLeod, G. (2002). From Urban Entrepreneurialism to a "Revanchist City"? On the Spatial Injustices of Glasgow's Renaissance. In N. Brenner & N. Theodore (eds), *Spaces of Neoliberalism: Urban Restructuring in North America and Western Europe* (pp. 254–276). Oxford: Blackwell.

Madanipour, A. (2003). *Public and Private Spaces of the City*. London: Routledge.

Madanipour, A. (2006). Roles and Challenges of Urban Design. *Journal of Urban Design, 11*(2), 173–193. doi:10.1080/13574800600644035.

Malnar, J. M., & Vodvarka, F. (2004). *Sensory Design*. Minneapolis: University of Minnesota Press.

McIndoe, G., Chapman, R., McDonald, C., Holden, G., Howden-Chapman, P., & Sharpin, A. B. (2005). The Value of Urban Design: The Economic, Environmental and Social Benefits of Urban Design. Ministry for the Environment, Manatū Mō Te Taiao, Wellington. Retrieved from: http://www.mfe.govt.nz/sites/default/files/value-of-urban-design-full-report-jun05_0.pdf.

Mehaffy, M., & Salingaros, N. A. (2011). Frontiers of Design Science: The Network City. Metropolis, December 2011. Retrieved from: http://www.metropolismag.com/Point-of-View/December-2011/Frontiers-of-Design-Science-The-Network-City/.

Meyer, H., de Josselin de Jong, F., & Hoekstra, M. J. (eds) (2006). *Het ontwerp van de openbare ruimte*. Amsterdam: Uitgeverij SUN.

Miller, D. (2001). *The Dialectics of Shopping*. Chicago, IL: Chicago University Press.

Miller, K. F. (2007). *Designs on the Public: The Private Lives of New York's Public Spaces*. Minneapolis: University of Minnesota Press.

Mitchell, D. (1995). The End of Public Space? People's Park, Definitions of the Public, and Democracy. *Annals of the Association of American Geographers, 85*(1), 108–133. doi:10.1111/j.1467-8306.1995.tb01797.x.

Mitrasinovic, M. (2006). *Total Landscape, Theme Parks, Public Space*. Aldershot: Ashgate.

Moudon A. V., & Lee, C. (2003). Walking and Bicycling: An Evaluation of Environmental Audit Instruments. *American Journal of Health Promotion, 18*, 21–37. Retrieved from: http://dx.doi.org/10.4278/0890-1171-18.1.21

Nasar, J., & Julian, D. (1995). The Psychological Sense of Community in the Neighbourhood. *Journal of the American Planning Association, 61*(2), 178–184. doi:10.1080/01944369508975631.

Neuts, B. (2011). Determining the External Social Costs of Public Space Crowding: Life in a Tourist Ghetto. Retrieved from: http://dlc.dlib.indiana.edu/dlc/handle/10535/7324.

Newman, P., & Hogan, T. (1981). A Review of Urban Density Models: Toward a Resolution of the Conflict Between Populace and Planner. *Human Ecology, 9*(3), 270–302. doi:10.1007/BF00890739.

Newman, P. W. G., & Kenworthy, J. R. (2006). Urban Design to Reduce Automobile Dependence. *Opolis: An International Journal of Suburban and Metropolitan Studies, 2*(1), 35–52.

Nielsen, T. (2004). Ethics, Aesthetics and Contemporary Urbanism. *Nordisk Arkitekturforskning: Nordic Journal of Architectural Research, 2004*, 23–46.

Norman, G. J., Nutter, S. K., Ryan, S., Sallis, J. F., Calfas, K. J., & Patrick, K. (2006). Community Design and Access to Recreational Facilities as Correlates of Adolescent Physical Activity and Body-mass Index. *Journal of Physical Activity and Health, 3*(Supplement 1), S118–S128.

Oldenburg, R. (1999). *The Great Good Place: Cafés, Coffee Shops, Bookstores, Bars, Hair Salons and the Other Hangouts at the Heart of a Community*. New York: Marlowe.

Osmundson, T. (1999). *Roof Gardens: History, Design and Construction*. New York; London: W. W. Norton.

Pimlott, M. (2008/2009). The Continuous Interior: Infrastructure for Publicity and Control. *Harvard Deign Magazine, 29*, 75–86.

Poklembovái, V., Kluvánková-Oravskáii, T., & Finkaiii, M. (2012). Challenge of New Commons—Urban Public Spaces. Paper presented at the First Global Thematic IASC Conference on the Knowledge Commons, Louvain-la-Neuve, Belgium, September. Retrieved from: http://biogov.uclouvain.be/iasc/doc/full%20papers/Poklembova.pdf.

Pomeroy, J. (2011). High-density Living in the Asian Context. *Journal of Urban Regeneration and Renewal, 4*, 337–349. Retrieved from: http://www.pomeroystudio.sg/uploads/wysiwyg/high%20density%20living.pdf.

Pont, M. B., & Haupt, P. (2009). *Space, Density and Urban Form*. Rotterdam: NAi Publishers.

Popkin, S. J., Levy, D. K., & Buron, L. (2009). Has HOPE VI Transformed Residents' Lives? New Evidence from the HOPE VI Panel Study. *Housing Studies, 24*, 477–502. doi:10.1080/02673030902938371.

Putnam, R. (2000). *Bowling Alone: The Collapse and Revival of the American Community*. New York: Simon & Schuster.

Radović, D. (2013). Intensities in Ten Cities. In D. Radović (ed.), *Mn'M Workbook 1: Intensities in Ten Cities* (pp. 6–8). Tokyo: IKI (International Keio Institute) + flick studio co., ltd.

Rapoport, A. (1975). Toward a Redefinition of Density. *Environment and Behavior, 7*(2), 133–158. doi:10.1177/001391657500700202.

Regoeczi, W. C. (2003). When Context Matters: A Multilevel Analysis of Household and Neighborhood Crowding on Aggression and Withdrawal. *Journal of Environmental Psychology, 23*(4), 451–464. Retrieved from: http://dx.doi.org/10.1016/S0272-4944(02)00106-8.

Sabaté Bel, J. (2011). In Search of the Best City Measures: Ten Propositions. In W. Ng, J. K. Chan, K. M. Cheah, & I. S. Cho (eds), *Vertical Cities Asia: International Design Competition, Vol. 1* (pp. 14–25). Singapore: National University of Singapore.

Saegert, S. (1979). A Systematic Approach to High Density Settings: Psychological, Social, and Physical Environmental Factors. In M. R. Gurkaynak & W. A. LeCompte (eds), *Human Consequences of Crowding* (pp. 232–245). New York: Plenum Press.

Salingaros, N. A. (1998). Theory of the Urban Web. *Journal of Urban Design, 3*, 53–71. doi:10.1080/13574809808724416.

Salingaros, N. A. (1999). Urban Space and Its Information Field. *Journal of Urban Design, 4*(1), 29–49. doi:10.1080/13574809908724437.

Salingaros, N. A. (2000). Complexity and Urban Coherence. *Journal of Urban Design, 5*(3), 291–316. doi:10.1080/713683969.

Salingaros, N. A. (2011). Urbanism as Computation. In J. Portugali, H. Meyer, E. Stolk, & E. Tan (eds), *Complexity Theories of Cities Have Come of Age: An Overview with Implications to Urban Planning and Design* (pp. 245–268). Heidelberg: Springer.

Salingaros, N. A., & Mehaffy, M. (2012). Science for Designers: The Meaning of Complexity. Retrieved from: http://www.metropolismag.com/pov/20120330/science-for-designers-the-meaning-of-complexity.

Salmon, F. (2012), Why Jobs Require Cities. *Reuters, Analysis & Opinion*, February 2. Retrieved from: http://blogs.reuters.com/felix-salmon/2012/02/02/why-jobs-require-cities/.

Schmidt, S., & Németh, J. (2010). Space, Place and the City: Emerging Research on Public Space Design and Planning. *Journal of Urban Design, 15*(4), 453–457. doi:10.1080/13574809.2010.502331.

Sennett, R. (1977). *The Fall of Public Man*. Cambridge: Cambridge University Press.

Seo, B., & Chiu, L. H. R. (2014). Social Cohesiveness of Disadvantaged Communities in Urban South Korea: The Impact of the Physical Environment. *Housing Studies, 29*(3), 407–437. doi: 10.1080/02673037.2013.803519.

Shaftoe, H. (2008). *Convivial Urban Spaces: Creating Effective Public Spaces*. London: Earthscan.

Shelton, B. (2012) (2nd edn). *Learning from the Japanese City: Looking East in Urban Design*. Abingdon, Oxon: Routledge.

Shelton, B., Karakiewicz, J., & Kvan, T. (2011). *The Making of Hong Kong: From Vertical to Volumetric*. New York: Routledge.

Simmel, G. (1995). The Metropolis and Mental Life. In P. Kasnitz (ed.), *Metropolis: Center and Symbol of our Times* (pp. 30–45). New York: New York University Press.

Smith, N. (1996). *The New Urban Frontier: Gentrification and the Revanchist City*. London: Routledge.

Song, Y., & Knaap, G-J. (2004). Measuring Urban Form: Is Portland Winning the War on Sprawl? *Journal of the American Planning Association, 70*, 210–225. doi:10.1080/01944360408976371.

Sorkin, M. (ed.) (1992). *Variations on a Theme Park: The New American City and the End of Public Space*. New York: Hill & Wang.

Speir, C., & Stephenson, K. (2002). Does Sprawl Cost Us All? Isolating the Effects of Housing Patterns on Public Water and Sewer Costs, *Journal of the American Planning Association, 68*(1), 56–70. doi:10.1080/01944360208977191.

Stokols, D. (1972). On the Distinction Between Density and Crowding: Some Implications for Future Research. *Psychological Review, 79*(3), 275–277. doi:10.1037/h0032706.

Stone Jr., B. (2008). Urban Sprawl and Air Quality in Large US Cities. *Journal of Environmental Management, 86*(4), 688–698. doi:10.1016/j.jenvman.2006.12.034.

Talen, E. (1999). Sense of Community and Neighbourhood Form: An Assessment of the Social Doctrine of New Urbanism. *Urban Studies, 36*, 1361–1379. doi:10.1080/0042098993033.

Talen, E. (2011). Sprawl Retrofit: Sustainable Urban Form in Unsustainable Places. *Environment and Planning B: Planning and Design, 38*, 952–978. doi:10.1068/b37048.

Tonkiss, F. (2005). *Space, the City and Social Theory*. Cambridge: Polity Press.

Turner, M. A., & Berube, A. (2009). *Vibrant Neighborhoods, Successful Schools: What the Federal Government Can Do to Foster Both*. Washington, DC: The Urban Institute.

United Nations. (2014). *World Urbanization Prospects*. United Nations. Retrieved from: http://esa.un.org/unpd/wup/Highlights/WUP2014-Highlights.pdf.

Urhahn Urban Design (2000). *De woonwijk van de toekomst*. Ideeënboek t.b.v. Bouwfonds prijsvraag. Georganiseerd door NIROV.

Uytenhaak, R. (2008). *Cities Full of Space: Qualities of Density*. Rotterdam: 010 Publishers.

Van der Wouden, R. (ed.) (1999). *De stad op straat. De openbare ruimte in perspectief*. Den Haag: Sociaal en Cultureel Planbureau.

Watson, S. (2006). *City Publics: The (Dis)Enchantments of Urban Encounters*. London: Routledge.

Worpole, K., & Knox, K. (2007). *The Social Value of Public Space*. York: Joseph Rowntree Foundation.

Yeh, A. G. O. (2011). High-density Living in Hong Kong. *LSECities: Cities, Health and Well-being*. Retrieved from: http://files.lsecities.net/files/2011/11/2011_chw_3050_Yeh.pdf.

Young, I. M. (1990). *Justice and the Politics of Difference*. Princeton, NJ: University Press.

Yuen, B., Yeh, A. G. O., Appold, S. J., Earl, G., Ting, J., & Kwee, K. L. (2006). High-rise Living in Singapore Public Housing. *Urban Studies, 43*(3), 583–600. doi:10.1080/00420980500533133.

Zijderveld, A. C. (1983). *Steden zonder stedelijkheid. Cultuurhistorische verkenning van een beleidsprobleem*. Deventer: van Loghum Slaterus.

Zukin, S. (1995). *The Cultures of Cities*. Oxford: Blackwell.

Zukin, S. (2000, 2nd edn). Whose Culture? Whose City? In R. LeGates & F. Stout (eds), *The City Reader* (pp. 131–142). London: Routledge.

Zones Urbaines Sensibles (ZUS). (2006). Laboratorium Rotterdam: DECODE SPACE! In Search of New Perspectives on/for Public Space. Case Study, Erasmus Medical Centre. *OASE, 71*, 104–139.

2

Quality of Urban Space and Design Principles

Building upon the literature reviews of relevant urban design theories, research concepts, guidelines and practices, this chapter outlines the original framework developed to holistically and systematically understand the desired qualities of contemporary urban spaces in high-density environments, while elaborating on specific design principles, design measures and best practices.

What is the value of urban design?
What constitute good public spaces?
Is the quality of public space measurable?
Can good public space be deliberately created?

VALUE AND BENEFITS OF QUALITY URBAN DESIGN

It is now widely accepted that well-designed and well-managed public spaces are the vital assets for a city's livability and sustainable development, and have social, health, environmental and economic short- and long-term benefits (CABE 2004; CABE & DETR, 2001; McIndoe et al., 2005; PPS, 2008). Poor urban design may lower the quality of life, limit employment opportunities and generate a wide range of unsustainable costs for the community and the city as a whole.

Social and Health Benefits

Public spaces are open to all, regardless of ethnic origin, age or gender, and as such represent a democratic forum for citizens and the society. When properly designed and managed, they bring communities together, provide meeting places and foster social ties of a kind that have been disappearing in many urban areas. These spaces shape the cultural identity of an area, are part of its unique character and provide a sense of place for local communities. Provision of good public spaces:

- enhances social interaction and user participation;
- caters to all, and especially the aging population;
- encourages a more outdoor lifestyle;
- fosters a sense of belonging and pride in an area;
- increases perceptions of safety and security within and beyond developments;

- provides opportunities for physical activity and play;
- enhances the attractiveness of routes for walking and cycling, encouraging healthier lifestyles;
- reduces road accidents through appropriately managing different transport modes and prioritizing the pedestrian, etc.

Economic Benefits

A high-quality public environment can have a significant impact on the economic life of urban centers and is thus an essential part of any successful regeneration strategy. The presence of good urban design attracts investments and is a vital business and marketing tool. As suggested by CABE & DETR (2001), good public spaces can strengthen the local economy by:

- attracting local visitors and tourists;
- responding to occupiers' demands;
- attracting investment through high-quality improvements;
- producing high returns on investments (enhancing rental and capital value through good urban design);
- reducing management, maintenance, energy and security costs;
- differentiating places and raising their prestige, etc.

Environmental Benefits

Investment in public space contributes to environmental sustainability by:

- reducing the impact of climate change;
- creating more energy-efficient and less polluting development;
- minimizing carbon emissions through the choice of materials and construction technologies, as well as through the encouragement of walking and cycling;
- delivering development sensitive to its context;
- returning inaccessible or run-down areas and amenities to beneficial public use;
- revitalizing urban heritage, etc.

Everyone benefits from high-quality urban spaces: investors through favorable returns on their investments and through satisfying occupiers' demand; developers by attracting investors; designers (good urban design is crucially dependent on their input); occupiers (owners) from the better performance, loyalty, health and satisfaction of their employees and clients; everyday users and society as a whole from the economic advantages and through access to a better-quality environment and an enhanced range of amenities and facilities; and public authorities by meeting their obligation to deliver a well-designed, economically and socially viable environment.

QUALITY OF URBAN SPACE

Due to the increased global attention that has been given to urban design and its role in sustainable development in the past decades, attempts to describe, assess and improve the design and quality of public spaces have been numerous. However, a consensus on what constitutes good public space, let alone what constitutes high-quality urban space in a high-density context, has not yet been reached. The perceived divide between the aesthetics and ethics of public space is difficult to bridge, and current approaches to the design of public space tend to emphasize aesthetics over more amorphous needs since they are not easily translated into design vocabulary. The ways in which public spaces are perceived, designed, used, experienced and maintained inevitably change over time, directly reflecting their particular historical, social, economic and cultural contexts.

In the nineteenth century, the rise of new building materials and technologies allowed for new types of public spaces to emerge, such as exhibition halls, covered markets, shopping arcades and railway stations. Camillo Sitte witnessed this intense change in European cities, where it was triggered by new economic factors and the increased demand for sanitation and transport. In his book *City Planning According to Artistic Principles* (1965), Sitte criticized the late nineteenth century urbanism for its obsession with order and regularity, arguing for the creative qualities of "traditional" urban spaces, with their accent on irregularity.

New political and economic shifts, globalization, and technological advancement in the second half of the twentieth century have further accelerated changes in the provision, design and management of public spaces (Schmidt & Németh, 2010). Yet, in spite of the recent global attention given to urban design, the results are often described as disappointing, and good examples as scarce, suggesting that the quality of public spaces today is progressively diminishing (Chapman, 2011; Sandercock & Dovey, 2002). However, such a situation does not result from the absence of shared perceptions of what good and desirable qualities of public spaces are, but rather from the difficulties of collaborative decision-making, of integrated creation and maintenance of these

spaces in practice (Mayer & Seijdel, 2005; Sandercock & Dovey, 2002).

The "Classics" and the "Followers"

While the intention of this section is not to provide a historical overview of urban design and planning, it is important to mention some of the most influential urban design theories and concepts, such as those proposed by the so-called "urban design classics," including Kevin Lynch, William Whyte and Jane Jacobs, among others, upon which the more recent frameworks to describe and assess the desirable qualities for successful public spaces are built.

In his *A Theory of Good City Form*, for example, Kevin Lynch (1981) identifies five dimensions of good urban space performance. These are namely vitality, which refers to the degree to which the spatial form supports uses and users; sense, which mainly relates to the degree of spatial legibility; fit, which informs on the ability of spatial form to encourage users' interaction and support their behavioral patterns; access, including also the availability of diverse uses; and control, referring to rules and regulations shared by all users of public space. In their paper "Towards an Urban Design Manifesto," Jacobs and Appleyard (1987) proposed seven qualities of good urban environments, namely livability; identity and control; access to opportunities, imagination and joy; authenticity and meaning; community; self-reliance; and social equity (environment for all).

In Canter's (1977) diagram or "visual metaphor" of a place, the place results from the interaction between its main constituents, namely actions and activities; physical attributes (the physical shape and parameters of the setting); and conceptions (multi-sensory experience and perception, including mental maps, mental images and classifications of desirability and undesirability). Expanding on Canter's model, Punter's (1991) model of "sense of place" provides more details on the components of the physical setting (townscape, built form, permeability, landscape, furniture), activity (land use, pedestrian flow, behavior, patterns, noise and smell, vehicle flow) and meaning or imageability (legibility, cultural associations, perceived functions, attractions and qualitative assessments). Finally, building upon the work of Relph (1976), Canter (1977) and Punter (1991), Montgomery (1998) recognizes three main elements that constitute good public space, namely activity, mainly a product of vitality and diversity; image, which relates to people's perception of space and involves symbolism, imageability, association; and form, which describes the physical condition of the place, including scale, shape, permeability, etc. Based on these three elements, Montgomery further identifies 25 principles for achieving good urbanity, yet emphasizing that these principles should not be treated as axioms but rather as "an illustrated discussion of the qualities of successful urban places" (1998, p. 113).

In their book *People Places*, Marcus and Francis (1997) developed 15 general criteria for quality public places, some of which are accessibility, comfort, safety and security. They proposed a "design review checklist" specific to particular types of public space, as an attempt to propose guidelines and inform clients, designers and planners on how to create "pleasing, comfortable, accessible, supportive, meaningful, and beautiful people places" (1997, pp. 80–84). The criteria are derived from the review of seven types of open space, namely urban plazas, neighborhood parks, mini-parks, campus outdoor spaces, elderly housing outdoor spaces, childcare open spaces and hospital outdoor spaces. While the selected spaces represent a considerable variety of uses and user groups, including those that are less conventional and rarely addressed in public space research, the researchers consider only outdoor spaces and seem to encourage very specific typologies of public spaces, neglecting the importance of emerging hybrid environments.

While we may agree that good public spaces may have as many as possible of these characteristics, the quality of public spaces should be seen as relative, dynamic and pluralistic, as many of these attributes would only be present in degrees. On the other hand, instead of looking at positive or desirable qualities of public spaces, some research frameworks focus on key factors that undermine the quality of public spaces. According to Williams and Green (2001), such undermining factors include traffic, business activity, antisocial behavior and crime, poor design, conflicting roles and privatization of the public realm, arguing that they can be eliminated through good design.

Placemaking

In the "placemaking" approach, the focus shifts from the physical space toward activities, the local community and social aspects. The concepts of placemaking originated in the 1960s, based on the pioneering works of Jane Jacobs (1961) and William Whyte (1980, 1988), and followed by others, such as Gehl and colleagues (1996, 2001, 2010), for instance. Since 1975, the PPS, Project for Public Spaces (2008), has been developing an extensive placemaking approach, as well as one of the most comprehensive of the available frameworks for public space. The four key attributes of successful places, presented in their "Place Diagram," are:

- access and linkages, including the ways in which a place should be visually and physically connected to its surroundings;
- comfort and image, addressing more tangible design aspects;

- uses and activities, including the main attractors for people to come to a place, and to come back;
- sociability, addressing the most difficult quality of place, which is creating a comfortable environment for social interaction between local users and strangers.

Within each of these four attributes, the PPS further differentiates two groups of criteria, namely the intangibles, which describe the more intuitive and qualitative aspects of space, and measurements or tangibles, which give weight to the quantitative aspects. Finally, the "Place Diagram" serves as a tool to help people evaluate any public space, either good or bad, and is very easy to use by the design professionals, various clients and laymen, providing a platform for integrated placemaking involving all actors.

Another well-known, practical and frequently referred placemaking framework, created based on the extensive research on urban life on the streets of Zürich, Copenhagen, Melbourne and Sydney, among others, is that developed by Gehl (1996, 2010). In his work, Gehl continuously explores and re-explores the more sensitive views to understanding and creating better "lives between buildings." In *Life between Buildings* (1996) and *Cities for People*, Gehl (2010) develops a series of arguments and suggestions for making lively, safe, sustainable and healthy cities with an emphasis on the "human dimension." The result is "the toolbox of principles" and design recommendations, ranging from the largest scale of city planning to the smallest dimension of qualities at "eye level." The criteria to evaluate the pedestrian-friendly spaces are categorized into three groups: protection, comfort and delight. With the recommendations for planners and designers, which are framed in a "dos and don'ts" manner, Gehl's framework has a highly practical and somewhat instrumental value.

Convivial Space

Apart from the physical, psychological, sensual and geographical facets, the concept of "convivial space" emphasizes the "managerial" and negotiating aspects of public spaces (Childs, 2004; Harries, 1997; Illich, 1985; Shaftoe, 2008). Illich's (1985) proposition of a convivial society suggests that people should not be mere consumers of urban spaces. Instead, conviviality is achieved through individual freedom and personal interdependence, while also shaping and enriching public spaces according to people's own tastes and needs. Similarly, Harries (1997) criticizes the dominant formalist and aesthetic approach in urban design, instead emphasizing its responsibility to serve the community by playing both an ethical and a political role. Shaftoe (2008) further describes convivial urban spaces as rich, vibrant and enjoyable open spaces where people can socialize, encounter differences,

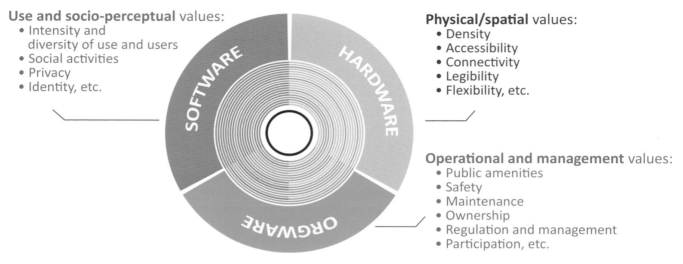

Use and socio-perceptual values:
- Intensity and diversity of use and users
- Social activities
- Privacy
- Identity, etc.

SOFTWARE

HARDWARE

ORGWARE

Physical/spatial values:
- Density
- Accessibility
- Connectivity
- Legibility
- Flexibility, etc.

Operational and management values:
- Public amenities
- Safety
- Maintenance
- Ownership
- Regulation and management
- Participation, etc.

2.1 The Urban Space Framework: HARDware, SOFTware and ORGware components.

negotiate and resolve conflicts, and practice tolerance and solidarity. For Childs (2004), convivial spaces are made through a deep understanding of *civitas* (the ways in which people gather), *genius loci* (the spirit of the place and interaction with landscape) and *urbanitas* (traditions of built form).

"Publicness" of Public Space

Rather than exploring the quality of public spaces, some studies have attempted to develop frameworks and tools to measure the level of their "publicness," such as the recent research by Van Melik et al. (2007), Németh and Schmidt (2007), Varna and Tiesdell (2010) and Marcuse (2005). Although they overlap on many levels, and the quality of space depends considerably on its level of publicness, these two groups of studies should not be misinterpreted. In their study, Varna and Tiesdell (2010) conceptualized a "star model," derived from a triangular model recognizing three key dimensions of publicness: the legal, managerial and design-oriented. These three dimensions are further broken down into five sub-dimensions: control, civility (managerial), ownership (legal), physical configuration and animation. While proposing a scale for measuring each sub-dimension, the authors admit that the act of "weighting" is debatable, since it involves the inconsistency of subjectivity and judgment. The study by Németh and Schmidt (2007) focused on identifying the hybrid conditions of public space, based on the combination of ownership and operation, including: publicly owned and operated, privately owned and publicly operated, publicly owned and privately operated, and privately owned and operated. Similarly, Marcuse (2005) differentiates six levels of ownership, ranging from fully

public to completely private, considering the hybrid relationships between function and use.

The most influential work for this research, however, is that of Carmona (2010a, 2010b) and colleagues (Carmona & De Magalhães, 2008; Carmona et al., 2010), who strongly criticize the stagnant condition of the ongoing debate on the decline of public space. Carmona argues that there is a considerable degree of privatization of public space, and vice versa, which is not necessarily an undesired or "bad" phenomenon. Many of these hybrid spaces perform well and are successful in supporting the exchange of goods, experiences, information and ideas. In *Public Places Urban Spaces*, Carmona and colleagues (2010) offer a comprehensive literature review of urban design theories and practices, while proposing a framework of six key dimensions for looking at urban design and public space today: morphological, perceptual, social, visual, functional and temporal. Understanding the implementation and management processes is seen as crucial for the performance of public space. In his recent papers, Carmona (2010a, 2010b) highlighted three critical perspectives for approaching the complexity of contemporary public spaces, namely the design, socio-cultural and political economy perspectives. These three perspectives are used to arrive at the three major aspects—function, perception and ownership—which help categorize the emerging, increasingly hybrid typologies of public spaces. However, Carmona's attempt to identify and classify the hybrid conditions of contemporary public spaces mainly contributes to measuring the gradients of publicness, from the most "public" to the most "private," rather than the "quality" of urban spaces.

URBAN SPACE FRAMEWORK:

HARDWARE—SOFTWARE—ORGWARE

Building on the extensive literature review, as well as perceived spatial, functional and operational complexities and hybrid properties of emerging types of urban spaces, an original and holistic conceptual urban space framework is proposed.

The Urban Space Framework, as illustrated in Figure 2.1, recognizes three equally important and interdependent components that influence and shape urban space typology and performance, namely HARDware, SOFTware and ORGware. HARDware refers to physical and geometrical properties, i.e., design values of space. SOFTware involves uses, social and perceptual values of urban space. Finally, ORGware relates to operational and management aspects of public space. The three components are interdependent and inevitably overlap on various levels, providing a holistic and comprehensive platform for understanding how new hybrid urban spaces in high-density contexts operate and perform. In such a way, the Urban Space Framework suggests that good urban space performance results from the synergy of high-quality design, thoughtful mix of activities and good provision of amenities and management.

In this chapter, each component—HARDware, SOFTware and ORGware—is introduced and elaborated through "urban space attributes," "urban space qualities" and "design principles."[1] In total, the Urban Space Framework consists of 13 urban space attributes, 47 urban space qualities and 94 design principles. Each urban space quality is defined by two design principles. Design principles are explained using three sections that respond to three key questions, namely:

- What—stating the content of the design principles.
- Why—providing an overview of the potential benefits once the principles are implemented, drawing from the relevant literature review and research findings.
- How—providing reference to good design practices, selected from the urban spaces investigated in this research, while highlighting some specific design measures and considerations.

The principles should not be read in isolation, but rather as intertwined ingredients that together form the quality of urban space. The majority of urban space qualities and design principles are phrased in such a way that they are of particular relevance to design practitioners, while a very small number of principles may not be under the direct influence of urban designers. Although most of the qualities and principles do not necessarily derive from or are specifically tailored for high-density conditions, many new urban spaces interpret and express these "timeless" qualities in ways that differ considerably from the conventional types of public spaces. Accordingly, greater attention is intentionally given to principles that are more directly design-oriented as well as appearing to be more critical in high-density hybrid urban environments.

As a synthesis of urban space qualities and principles, each urban space component—HARDware, SOFTware and ORGware—is summarized by detailed analysis of an exemplary case study, namely Shinonome Codan Court, Tokyo, Japan for HARDware; Skypark@VivoCity, Singapore for SOFTware; Dangdai Moma (Linked Hybrid), Beijing, China and Sliced Porosity Block (Raffles City), Chengdu, China for ORGware. Finally, Chapter 2 concludes with a summary of the Urban Space Framework fully applied to analyze one good practice: Treelodge@Punggol, Singapore.

HARDWARE:

PHYSICAL AND GEOMETRICAL PROPERTIES OF URBAN SPACES

A number of analytical concepts and research methods focusing on spatial and morphological qualities of historical and contemporary cities have been proposed (see, e.g., Alexander et al., 1987; Carr et al., 1992; Cullen, 1961, 1968; Gehl & Gemzoe, 2001; Jacobs, 1961; Lynch, 1960; Salingaros, 1998, 1999, 2000), revealing their potential to be used as planning and design tools.

For Carmona and colleagues (2010), the design perspective is framed by the discussion between the physical configuration and function, space and use. Physical configuration is mostly discussed in terms of territoriality, borders, accessibility, visual permeability, as well as time and use control, regulation or restriction (Németh & Schmidt, 2007, 2011; Oc & Tiesdell, 1999). According to Talen (2011), the five most important dimensions of good urban form (i.e., sustainable urban spaces) are: accessibility, connectivity, density, diversity and nodality. For Varna and Tiesdell (2010), key qualities of physical configuration are: connectivity; visual access; and thresholds and gateways. For them, the physical configuration refers to micro-design (i.e., the design of public space itself), while macro-design involves the surrounding context and refers to animation. Animation relates to the degree to which spatial design supports and meets human needs, as well as to the degree to which the space is actively used and shared among different groups and individuals. As such, the Urban Space Framework recognizes it as having both software and orgware properties.

Based on extensive review of these frameworks, the Urban Space Framework recognizes seven HARDware attributes, crucial for nodal, spatial and environmental performance of urban spaces. These urban space attributes are: accessibility, connectivity, mobility means, legibility and edges (porosity), spatial variety, environmentally friendly design strategies and users' comfort (Figure 2.2).

Nodal Value

The nodal value refers to an ability of space to provide an adequate number of physical and activity nodes and their connections, as well as to establish good and safe access for all users, including formal and informal, main and alternative entrances by different mobility means. It has been empirically proven that the number of nodes and their connections directly correlate to higher livability of a built environment (Alexander, 1965; Gehl, 1996).

Spatial Value

The spatial value deals with the morphological value of the urban space, evaluative qualities such as legibility, permeability, spatial variety and adaptability. Legibility may be understood as

a function of balancing between the content and accessibility to various stimuli available in space, which is crucial for navigating and understanding the space. Good understanding of urban space involves understanding from both within and outside its spatial boundaries, which implies rich and clear interactions between the space and the surrounding context.

Environmental Value

The environmental value assesses the environmental benefits as well as human comfort achieved and experienced within the urban space. The main parameters are greenery and water features, ecology, and the implementation of environmentally friendly design strategies, shade and comfort. Greenery is measured as the efforts that the space employs in terms of publicly accessible landscaping to heighten perception, user–space interaction and restorative effects, as well as to contribute to the alleviation of the urban heat phenomenon (Marcus & Francis, 1997).

URBAN SPACE FRAMEWORK

HARDWARE		Values: Attributes:	Urban Space Quality:
	NODAL VALUE	A: ACCESSIBILITY	1: Pedestrian Access Points 2: Universal Access 3: Types and Distribution of Universal Access 4: Prioritizing the Pedestrians
		B: CONNECTIVITY	5: Movement Patterns 6: Node Connectivity 7: Sightlines and Way-Finding
		C: MOBILITY MEANS	8: Bicycle-friendly Design 9: Public Transport 10: Vehicular Access 11: Drop-Off and Taxi Stands
	SPATIAL VALUE	D: LEGIBILITY & EDGES	12: Spatial Layout 13: Focal Points of Activity 14: Visual Landmarks 15: Permeability
		E: SPATIAL VARIETY	16: Spatial Variety 17: Spatial Adaptability
	ENVIRONMENTAL VALUE	F: ENVIRONMENTALLY FRIENDLY DESIGN	18: Greenery and Water – Availability and Access 19: Greenery – Form, Pattern and Diversity 20: Biodiversity 21: Environmentally Friendly Strategies 22: Environmental Integration
		G: USER COMFORT	23: Protection from Weather Conditions 24: Shade and Sunlight 25: Air Control and Optimization 26: Noise Control and Optimization

2.2 Hardware urban space component.

URBAN SPACE ATTRIBUTE

A ACCESSIBILITY

Accessibility is typically described as a measure of interaction between the users and the cadastral patterns of the city (Carmona et al., 2010). It refers to an ability of the user to access the space with regard to any control or exclusion strategies that may or may not be present. Good accessibility is considered to be one of the most important components of good urban form and, together with connectivity, a prerequisite for a space to function well, as it frames the interaction not only between space and its surroundings, but also between users and space (e.g., Carr et al., 1992; Jacobs, 1961; Jacobs & Appleyard, 1987; Lynch, 1981; Salingaros, 1999). According to Carr and colleagues (1992), three modes of access exist, namely **visual**, **physical** and **symbolic** access. Visual access allows people to observe the space before entering, while the physical access may not be provided. Physical access, whether accompanied or not by visual access, defines the level of inclusion and exclusion of a public space. Symbolic access refers to spatial and perceptual clues that signal whether the space feels threatening or inviting.

Although essentially being a physical attribute of space, certain measures of accessibility may considerably influence socio-perceptual and operational performances of urban space. Accessibility has been associated with increased interaction (Dittmar & Ohland, 2003), smart growth (Song & Knaap, 2004), active living (Heath et al., 2006; Norman et al., 2006), safety, and health (Greenwald & Boarnet, 2001; Handy et al., 2002; Moudon & Lee, 2003). It affects the degree of permeability, connectivity, security and safety of the urban space. Accessibility also relates to choices of access, including universal access and access by means of public transportation. According to Salingaros (1999), good urban space prioritizes pedestrians by providing a variety of easily accessible pedestrian paths that are protected from non-pedestrian traffic and designed according to universal standards in order to cater to all user groups, especially the disabled, children and the elderly, and in such a way increase the degree of social equity in space. Finally, accessibility also relates to operational aspects of urban space that may involve time regulation and management, as well as the existence of entrance fees.

Accessible space is designed for inclusion rather than exclusion, ensuring proactive and integrated consideration rather than reactive tacked-on provision.

URBAN SPACE QUALITY

1 Pedestrian Access Points

What?
Design Principles
- Provide sufficient number of pedestrian access points.
- Distinguish formal access points (main entrances) from informal.

Urban space should be physically accessible by foot from the main road or any adjacent road or pedestrian bridge/underpass. From the urban spaces investigated, it is advisable to provide no fewer than two access points from the main ground level to urban space. This should also apply to vertical access to elevated and/ or multi-level spaces.

Access to urban space can be formal and informal. Formal access refers to the main and direct entrances to urban space. Informal access further increases users' choice, convenience and comfort of movement. It relates to secondary entrances and exits, such as those from the back lanes, through surrounding buildings, by a bridge or through an underground passage. These alternative access points may not offer the most direct or shortest paths to main space, but they are sometimes also identified as short cuts. Access may also be measured by the length of physically accessible urban space boundary.

Why?
- Good pedestrian access is one of the crucial factors for an urban space to function well (Whyte, 1980), as it encourages logical movement and desired behaviors, while enhancing the level of inclusiveness (Carmona et al., 2010).
- Good accessibility allows both transient and stationary activities to occur (Gehl, 1996; Lynch, 1960).

How?
Design Measures and Considerations
- Consider using distinct architectural elements and design measures to distinguish main entrances from alternative informal access points, including size and additional visual information, such as gates, porches, colors and signage.

Reference to Good Practices

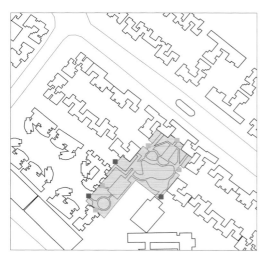

HORIZONTAL ACCESS: A clear hierarchy of the spatial layout and signage is used to define main entrances. In residential precinct *Meridian at Punggol*, Singapore (Figures 2.3a, top, and 2.3b, bottom), three horizontal formal access points (in red) and five informal access points (in orange) are well distributed, clearly visible and easily accessible from the road. Formal access to central green space is accentuated by implementing covered walkways, while one of the informal access points passes through the food court.

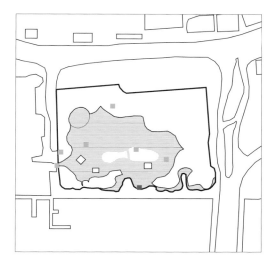

VERTICAL ACCESS: A park at the roof-top of a shopping mall, the **Skypark at VivoCity** in Singapore (Figures 2.4a, top left, and 2.4b, top right), is accessible by one outdoor access point from the ground pedestrian level—a staircase (in red)—and six informal access points—through the mall (in orange). A number of vertical access points lead to elevated urban space of the **Treelodge@Punggol**, a renowned public housing complex in Singapore (Figures 2.4c, bottom left, and 2.4d, bottom right). A grand staircase serves as the direct and most prominent pedestrian access. Alternative vertical access points (lifts and stairs) are "hidden" under the elevated space, where the car-parking area is located.

URBAN SPACE QUALITY

2 Universal Access

What?
Design Principles
- Provide means of universal access when level changes occur.
- Provide sufficient number of universal access points.

A fair amount of universal access ensures safety and equity of an urban space, especially considering the vulnerable user groups, such as the elderly, children, pregnant women and people with disabilities (Carmona et al., 2010; Levine, 2003).

Why?
- Universal access promotes inclusivity, improves usability and safety (Jacobs, 1961; Salmen, 1996), and contributes to "conviviality" of public space (Shaftoe, 2008).

Reference to Good Practices

How?
Design Measures and Considerations
- Ensure smooth accessibility for wheelchair users, the elderly, pregnant women and children, by avoiding rough textures and uneven surfaces. Ensure clear pathways with no obstruction (Levine, 2003).
- Ramps' gradient should not exceed 1:12 ratio and should apply resistant surfaces. Whenever an accessible route crosses a curb, install a ramp with a gradient no greater than 1:12 (Levine, 2003).
- Inclined moving walkways should cater to users with strollers or wheelchairs.
- Hallways and corridors should be wide enough to accommodate two people passing in the opposite direction. All hallways and corridors should be evenly lit (Levine, 2003).

UNIVERSAL ACCESS: A fair amount of **universal access points** as alternatives to staircases should be provided whenever level changes occur. Ramps are effective to accommodate slight level changes (***Ion Orchard***, Singapore; Figure 2.5).

URBAN SPACE QUALITY

3 Types and Distribution of Universal Access

What?
Design Principles
- Provide different types of universal access.
- Distribute universal access points fairly and logically.

The provision of different types of universal access such as ramps, elevators, escalators and travelators is encouraged. Moreover, dispersing the location of universal access is advisable, as it increases choice and affects the intensity of people and activity within urban space.

Why?
- Different types of universal access increase the choice of pedestrian movement (Levine, 2003).
- Good distribution of access points increases choice and avoids crowding (Salingaros, 1999).

Reference to Good Practices

How?
Design Measures and Considerations
- Universal access points are often difficult to find and entail longer or more complicated routes. All universal access means should be located along accessible routes, with the shortest distance to main entrances (Levine, 2003). They should run in the same direction of main pedestrian movement.
- Use different materials, floor textures or colors to differentiate main pathways and universal access (Levine, 2003).
- When both are provided, elevators should be in proximity to escalators.
- Additionally, due consideration should be given to designing street furniture, crossings, tactile paving, information boards, way-finding facilities and parking adequate for people with disabilities (Hong Kong Planning Department, 2006).

TYPES OF UNIVERSAL ACCESS: Covered travelators are a highly effective response to uphill conditions, **continuous** and **gradual level changes**, as in the *Central Mid-levels Escalator*, Hong Kong (Figure 2.6a, left). Escalators and elevators are more convenient for **connecting different levels in elevated or multi-level developments**, such as *Namba Parks* in Osaka, Japan (Figure 2.6b, right).

URBAN SPACE QUALITY

4 Prioritizing the Pedestrians

What?
Design Principles
- Provide safe and direct pedestrian access that clearly prioritizes pedestrians over vehicular traffic.
- Make the core of urban space completely pedestrianized.

Pedestrian space is the core of public space (Salingaros, 1999), and pedestrian movement in and around urban space should be clearly prioritized over vehicular traffic, with an accent on safety. This involves adequate and logically placed pedestrian crossings, bridges and underground passages, good pedestrian signalization, and protection of pedestrian space from vehicular and other modes of mobility, such as cycling.

Why?
- The provision of safe and direct pedestrian access allows a sufficient number of people to dwell in urban space, which is a prerequisite for generating quality public life (Carmona et al., 2010; Gehl, 1996, 2010; Marcus & Francis, 1997).
- Good pedestrian access promotes inclusivity and equality in urban space (Carmona et al., 2010).

How?
Design Measures and Considerations
- Wherever possible, provide the most direct access to core urban space and avoid pedestrian bridges and underpasses.
- If the grade separation between vehicles and pedestrians is necessary, pedestrian bridges should be as short as possible, while free-standing footbridges should be avoided. Instead, where possible, the design should allow direct connection between the origin and the destination point at the elevated levels. The design should also consider the aesthetics of the footbridge structures, including introducing soft landscape elements to make the pedestrian journey more pleasant. Similarly, for pedestrian underpasses, the design should employ quality and well-designed walling and flooring materials, good lighting, signage and other elements to enhance the visual comfort, legibility and safety of pedestrians (Hong Kong Planning Department, 2006).
- Set a clear boundary between pedestrian and vehicular traffic.
- Make the core of the urban space completely pedestrianized.
- Avoid staggered pedestrian crossings with islands that may restrict pedestrian flow and cause inconvenience (Hong Kong Planning Department, 2006).
- Consider employing traffic-calming design measures, such as narrowing roads, pinch points, speed bumps and raised crossings, as well as differentiation in colors and materials, to slow down or reduce vehicular traffic and improve safety for the pedestrians and cyclists on streets surrounding urban space (Hong Kong Planning Department, 2006).

Reference to Good Practices

SAFE AND DIRECT PEDESTRIAN ACCESS: The provision of adequate pedestrian crossings is crucial for **safe connectivity and accessibility**. *Hachiko Square* in Shibuya, Tokyo (Figure 2.7) is the busiest simultaneous pedestrian crosswalk in the world.

SHARED SPACE: Appropriate signage, safety fences and different **pavement surfaces** are some of the efficient ways to **clearly demarcate** areas for vehicular and pedestrian traffic. *Onden Road* in Tokyo (Figure 2.8a, top) is a narrow pedestrian street that is shared between cyclists and pedestrians. *Qianmen Street* in Beijing (Figure 2.8b, bottom) is a good example of a pedestrian street shared with slow-speed streetcars.

PEDESTRIANIZED STREETS: Fully pedestrianized areas safeguard pedestrian movement and **foster** an array of different types of **activity**, while enhancing **safety**. Ever since it was pedestrianized, *Times Square* in New York (Figure 2.9) is now an enjoyable and eventful public space and the world's most visited place, with more than 350,000 pedestrian visitors a day. At the "mock-up" stage, pedestrian-friendly features were introduced. The existing asphalt was painted in vivid colors to demarcate pedestrian zones and clearly distinguish them from vehicular and cycling traffic. Sturdy, movable tables, chairs and parasols made this experimental urban space **highly dynamic, interactive and flexible**. Today, the revamped space has granite pavement instead of asphalt, while additional, more permanent structures are still being built.

URBAN SPACE ATTRIBUTE

B CONNECTIVITY

Connectivity refers to the degree to which environments offer points of connection and contact at a range of scales and purposes (Talen, 2011). A well-connected space is integrated within local movement patterns and systems.

"Semi lattice structure" (Alexander, 1965), "urban web" (Salingaros, 1999), "capital web" (Buchanan, 1988) and "space syntax" (Hillier, 1996a, 1996b) are some of the concepts developed based on complexity of physical and functional interconnections in built environments. Maximizing connectivity in urban space, by providing a larger number of main and alternative routes, such as streets, sidewalks and pathways, increases the opportunities for social interaction and exchange (Alexander, 1965; Hillier & Hanson, 1984; Salingaros, 1998). It is generally agreed that the large-scale urban blocks, cul-de-sacs and tree-like street networks rarely provide good connectivity (Alexander, 1965). Accordingly, Jacobs (1961) argues that flexible arrangements of smaller urban blocks, with multiple connections, permit more flexible paths, while attracting users and encouraging the growth of diversity of use.

URBAN SPACE QUALITY

5 Movement Patterns

What?
Design Principles
- Establish direct and safe connection to dominant external movement route.
- Provide well-interconnected internal pathways.

Urban space is not a singular entity, but is rather part of a larger network established by cohesive connections between urban nodes. Places that are well connected to external pedestrian networks are more likely to encourage pedestrian movement and to support a vital and viable range of uses. Carefully planned sightlines and views also considerably contribute to better movement and connectivity.

It is thus important to establish direct connections to the most dominant external movement route(s) and to avoid detours and complicated access paths. Within the boundaries of urban space good internal connection should be established, with pathways that are interconnected and do not create dead-end situations.

Why?
- Connecting to external movement enhances the urban network, which in turn generates life and activity in urban space (Carmona et al., 2010; Jacobs, 1961; Salingaros, 1999).
- Interconnected pathways increase the possibility of incidental contact and social interaction (Carmona et al., 2010; Jacobs, 1961).
- Interconnectivity reduces congestion (Salingaros, 1998), while also reducing the opportunities for crime (Southworth & Ben-Joseph, 1997).

How?
Design Measures and Considerations
- New urban space should be well integrated into the existing urban surroundings. Existing points of access and connection points for both people and vehicle circulation should be analyzed and clear connections to existing routes and surrounding amenities should be established during the initial stage of urban space design (Urban Design Compendium, 2007).

Reference to Good Practices

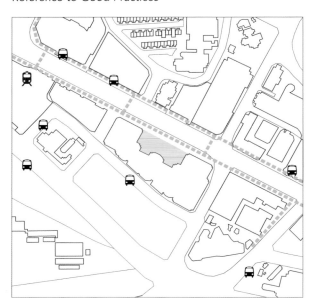

CONNECTION TO EXTERNAL PATHS: Locate urban space next to **existing local movement pattern**, such as a main street, a shopping center or a subway station, to enhance the **connectivity** of space and bring positive **density and intensity** of uses and users into urban space. *Civic Plaza* in Singapore (Figures 2.10a, left, and 2.10b, right), used for both formal and informal events, benefits from being located within the main pedestrian network threading through Orchard Road, while offering convenient and seamless access from and to the pedestrian walkway and neighboring malls, Wisma Atria, Lucky Plaza and Paragon.

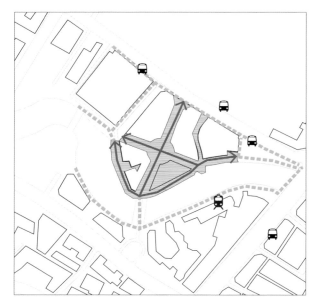

INNER CONNECTIVITY: Well-interconnected pathways increase **choices** of movement through and within urban space. In *Clarke Quay* in Singapore (Figures 2.11a, left, and 2.11b, right), good inner connectivity **activates** different parts of urban space, such as the river quay, the café and dining areas, and the central event plaza.

URBAN SPACE QUALITY

6 Node Connectivity

What?
Design Principles
- Support transient activities; connect important activity nodes in immediate surroundings.
- Provide facilities for long-term activities within urban space.

Movement is at the heart of the urban experience and is an important factor in generating life and activity (Carmona et al., 2010). The movement is itself an activity that often generates other activities (Carmona et al., 2010; Gehl, 1996; Hillier, 1996b; Jacobs, 1961; Salingaros, 1998). The availability and interrelationship of different types of physical and activity nodes available in and around public space are crucial to facilitate and direct urban movement (Hillier, 1996b).

It has been empirically proven that the number of nodes and their connections directly correlate to a higher livability of a built environment (Alexander, 1965; Gehl, 1996). As suggested by Salingaros (1998), good connectivity can be achieved by linking three distinct types of nodes, namely natural elements, human activity nodes and architectural elements.

A well-connected urban space does not only support transient activities. Too much emphasis on movement reduces the opportunities for contact. Good urban space also functions as a destination and a people's magnet, promoting long-term activities and functioning as a social space, engaging people in economic, social and cultural transaction. Accordingly, adding more break points with the provision of amenities designated for active uses,

interaction, resting and informal activities would increase the opportunity for social exchange.

Why?
- Good connectivity encourages movement, which contributes to intensification of social contact and interaction, while generating diversity of use and users (Carmona et al., 2010; Jacobs, 1961).
- Good connectivity encourages people to walk and cycle, and thus has potential health benefits (Frank & Engelke, 2001).
- Well-connected spaces contribute to a greater sense of safety and security by bringing more "eyes on the street" and encouraging natural surveillance (Jacobs, 1961; Shaftoe, 2008).
- Space that is well equipped with a variety of amenities supports the creation of activity nodes. Amenities increase animation of space and attract people (Shaftoe, 2008), while enabling necessary transient activities (daily activities such as walking to the bus stop, for instance) to transform into longer-term optional and social activities (Gehl, 1996).

How?
Design Measures and Considerations
- Activity nodes within urban space should be exposed to surrounding pedestrian links to attract users; consider breaking through or perforating any unnecessary hard and opaque boundaries to create viewpoints and clear vistas (Urban Design Compendium, 2007).
- Avoid dead-end situations; if unavoidable, treat dead-end areas as pocket spaces with specific functions, such as small and more private gatherings.

Reference to Good Practices

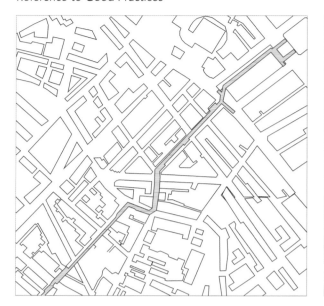

TRANSIENT/ADJACENT ACTIVITIES: *The Central Mid-levels Escalator* in Hong Kong (Figures 2.12a, left, and 2.12b, right) is about a 800-meter-long infrastructure that supports pedestrian movement, while connecting important nodes of activities within the Central and Western districts of Hong Kong. After its opening in 1993, it soon became a memorable and attractive feature in the dense and intense city center that made a substantial positive impact on its surroundings. While the escalator itself does not offer much, except for its primary function—passing through—since it opened, it has increased the number of pedestrians in the area and triggered various activities on and around it. The first and second floors of the surrounding buildings started opening up to pedestrians offering various commercial activities. The result is a dynamic three-dimensional network of public and semi-public pedestrian spaces that enhances and integrates the transitory, informal and everyday experiences of the highly dense city center.

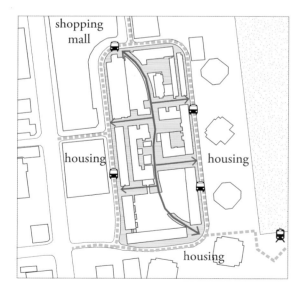

INTERCONNECTED ACTIVITY NODES: Good urban space connects several nodes of activities and is well integrated into local movement patterns. The residential complex *Shinonome Codan Court* in Tokyo (Figures 2.13a, left, and 2.13b, right) provides a three-dimensional pedestrian network to support both transient and stationary long-term activities. Even though its urban space caters primarily to local residents, it also serves as a connector from a shopping mall on one side to the train station and bus stops on the other side of the development. At the same time, this residential urban space also functions as a destination and encourages long-term activities, by providing various amenities, such as pocket spaces with formal and informal seating with shade, green areas, playgrounds, commercial and community activities along the main spine. Moreover, the edge of the development is visually porous, which makes it inviting and improves the sense of safety.

URBAN SPACE QUALITY

7 Sightlines and Way-Finding

What?
Design Principles
- To provide good visibility of horizontal and vertical directions.
- To provide good visibility to main entrance and exit points.

As described by Kevin Lynch (1960), legible environments are those that people can easily structure into accurate images, which are used to react to the environment more effectively. According to the "convex isovist" principle and space syntax (Hillier, 1996a, 1996b), a connective space is one where all points within the space may be seen from all points within that space. The larger the area that may be seen from all points in the space, the better the connectivity and the greater the opportunity for pedestrians to move around.

Why?
- Good visibility of different directions increases vitality and users' choices (Jacobs, 1961) and helps users to easily orientate within the space and find exits in case of emergency.
- Good visibility attracts users and enhances the feeling of safety in space (Jacobs, 1961).

How?
Design Measures and Considerations
- Ensure that the main points of the entrance and exit are visible from both inside-out and outside-in.
- Incorporate visual signals and way-finding facilities where needed.

Reference to Good Practices

INNER VISIBILITY: Good **spatial layout** and clear **visibility** of horizontal and vertical directions from both outside-in and inside-out encourage **movements** and increase users' **choice, way-finding and safety**, as in *Insadong Ssamziegil* in Seoul (Figure 2.14).

URBAN SPACE ATTRIBUTE
C MOBILITY MEANS

While highlighting the importance of good pedestrian access, a successful urban space is ideally accessible by all types of mobility means. This includes all modes of transportation, especially public transport and cycling, as well as taxis and private cars. However, spaces should not be dominated by their presence (Shaftoe, 2008; Urry, 2007). Provision of vehicular access has long been a basic requirement for various types of urban developments, which ended up in creating spaces for vehicles rather than for people, as well as a series of traffic and environmental problems globally. In response, current trends in urban planning and urban design tend to emphasize the importance of good public transportation, walkability and cycling rather than on traditional overuse of cars. Thus, access to and by public transportation and cycling should be addressed with higher priority.

URBAN SPACE QUALITY

8 Bicycle-Friendly Design

What?
Design Principles
- Provide sufficient bicycle stand facilities.
- Provide designated cycling areas/lanes.

While traveling by car in general provides increased mobility and convenience for longer distances, it also causes various mobility conflicts, parking, cost- and pollution-related problems in contemporary cities. It is now accepted globally that well-designed walking and cycling environments are more sustainable alternatives to typical car-centric development and automobile dependency, while allowing for more pleasant and efficient land use, and in such a way improves the overall quality of life, promotes social equity and addresses environmental concerns.

A successful urban space should be easily accessible by bicycle. Where possible, designed cycling-related facilities should be provided to allow cycling within or through urban space. Informal cycling may be permitted only if safety conditions allow. Additionally, to further promote cycling, urban spaces may also consider introducing skate parks and other recreational areas specifically designed for "extreme" rolling sports, such as skateboarding, BMX free-style biking, riding scooters and rollerblade skating.

Why?
- Good provision of cycling facilities, such as bike lanes, bike stands and bike shelters, increases mobility choices and promotes cycling, which in turn has health and environmental benefits, while bringing positive density and extending the vitality and life of the urban space (Frank & Engelke, 2001; New York City Department of Transportation, 2009).
- Cycling has health benefits, especially in regard to obesity and physical activity (Frank & Engelke, 2001; Lopez & Hynes, 2006). Studies have shown that cycling to work can decrease mortality by as much as 40 percent (Andersen et al., 2000)
- Well-designed cycling lanes enhance safety, comfort and mobility in and around urban space, as well as calming vehicular traffic (New York City Department of Transportation, 2009).

How?
Design Measures and Considerations
When designing bicycle-friendly urban spaces, it is critical to ensure safety. Wherever possible, provide dedicated safe areas for all, ensure that potential conflicts with other users are removed, demarcate cycling lanes visually, ensure safe crossings for cyclers, and provide shade and adequate public bike parking, among other considerations.

- Consider providing bicycle racks near to pedestrian crossings, bus stops and subway entrances to promote cycling as a commuting alternative (City of New York, 2010). Safe bike stand facilities should be available within the urban space or in its immediate vicinity (up to two minutes' walking distance/ up to 200m).
- Cycling lanes should be well separated from pedestrian walkways. If the lane is shared between pedestrians and cyclists, the advisable lane width should not be less than 3 meters.
- Separate bike lanes and vehicular traffic. It is advised to use physical demarcation, such as grade separation, median or locating bike lanes in between pedestrian and parking lanes to avoid conflict between cyclists and cars (City of New York, 2010).
- In busy commercial areas, separate bike paths should be 2.5 to 3 meters wide, and 1.5 to 2.5 meters wide in residential areas (New York City Department of Transportation, 2009).

Reference to Good Practices

DEDICATED BICYCLE PARKING: Provision of adequate **bicycle parking stands** within **walking distance** from the *Taikoo Li Sanlitun* in Beijing (Figure 2.15) invites a wider range of different **user groups**.

DEDICATED BICYCLE LANES: Provision of adequate bike lanes, separated from pedestrian lanes and seating areas, enhances mobility and access to space, as proven in *Superkilen*, Copenhagen (Figure 2.16), often described as the most bicycle-friendly city in the world.

URBAN SPACE QUALITY

9 Public Transport

What?

Design Principles

- Locate space close to public transportation.
- Provide choice of public transportation.

Proximity to good public transport and facilities (including buses, trams, trains, ferryboats, etc.) is essential in reducing the number of car journeys (CABE, 2008) and making a place more accessible to a variety of user groups, especially the vulnerable. While public transport may not be within the scope and influence of urban designers, the design of urban space should take advantage of the nearest public transport facility as one of the major daily attractors.

The effective use of public transport has been linked to access to and the choice of different modes of transport, but also to other factors such as perceptions of convenience, practicality, safety, comfort and cost (QUT & ISR, 2009).

New transportation hubs themselves not only function as transit nodes, but are increasingly becoming attractive destinations, meeting places with a wide choice of additional long-term activities.

Why?

- Good public transportation promotes equity and increases conviviality of the urban space (CABE, 2008; Shaftoe, 2008; Urry, 2007; WHO, 2007).
- Provision of various mobility services means increased choice of access and caters to vulnerable user groups, including children, women, the elderly and the disabled, as well as low-income users (CABE, 2008; Urry, 2007).
- Interconnection of different modes of transport strengthens the urban web network (Salingaros, 1999).

How?

Design Measures and Considerations

- If possible, locate bus stops at the shortest distance to urban space (preferably up to 400 meters or five minutes' walking distance), without obstructing the main pedestrian traffic flow (Levine, 2003).
- Integrate bus stops along well-connected streets; provide clear signage and information facilities at buildings, bus stops and major intersections to ensure good way-finding. Design bus stops for the convenience of pedestrians, including shelters, seating amenities and/or places for relaxing (City of New York, 2010).

Reference to Good Practices

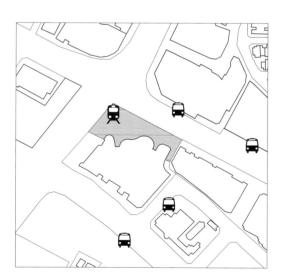

ACCESS TO PUBLIC TRANSPORTATION: *Ion Orchard Plaza* (Figures 2.17a, left, and 2.17b, right) in Singapore is a good example of benefiting from **direct access** to public transportation facilities. The plaza is located on the top of underground train stations. Access to the plaza is provided directly from the subway station or through the adjacent shopping mall. Bus stations are also available within 400-meter **walking distance** from the plaza. The success of Ion Orchard Plaza considerably depends on this facility.

INTEGRATION WITH PUBLIC TRANSPORTATION: *Shibuya Station* in Tokyo is one of the busiest train stations in the world, catering to 2.4 million passengers on an average weekday. As the result of a redevelopment project which started in 2005, the station's existing functions and facilities have been enhanced and new ones created, with an emphasis on expansion and enrichment of public spaces around the station to form a new pedestrian network consisting of underground public squares, walkways and decks. The most well-known node around Shibuya Station is *Hachiko Square* (Figure 2.18). This rectangular space is the busiest simultaneous pedestrian cross-walk in the world, used by approximately one million people each day, with as many as 10,000 people crossing during a single cycle of the traffic lights. In spite of being hectic and providing only limited seating amenities, this dynamic square is an extremely popular tourist destination, people-watching site and a common local meeting place before a night out that challenges the space capacity and pedestrian mobility issues, density and intensity, in an extraordinary and unique manner.

INTEGRATION WITH PUBLIC TRANSPORT INFRASTRUCTURE: In *Sengkang Sculpture Park* in Singapore (Figure 2.19), situated **in-between the public train stations** and the **residential** area, elevated train infrastructure is used as a sheltered space for both **necessary** and **optional activities**.

URBAN SPACE QUALITY

10 Vehicular Access

What?
Design Principles
- Provide parking facilities.
- Provide parking facilities integrated within space without conflicting with pedestrian movement.

Cities today are still dominated by cars as the preferred mode of mobility by the majority. Historically, a car has often been described as a "source of freedom" that enables fast, reliable, flexible and convenient movement to almost any destination in the city (Urry, 2007). However, cars also create a number of problems, including environmental issues, traffic congestion and conflicts with pedestrians, among others. Current trends in urban planning and urban design emphasize the importance of good public transportation and cycling facilities as viable and more sustainable alternatives to automobiles, and thus advocate that these should be given higher priority.

However, ideally, good public spaces are accessible by all means of transportation, including cars. Thus, wherever possible, good vehicular access and parking facilities that are well separated from pedestrian areas should not be ignored. It is preferred that such parking facilities should be integrated within urban space or located within reasonable walking distance from the urban space (up to 400m).

Reference to Good Practices

Why?
- Provision of parking facilities increases mobility and movement of people and goods through the city (Urry, 2007).

How?
Design Measures and Considerations
- Consider parking facilities with care and only when there is space available. Focus on public transportation, cycling and walkability first.
- Where possible, avoid parking at the street level.
- Locate parking at a distance that encourages people to use more active modes of travel such as walking, cycling and public transport (City of New York, 2010).
- Provide options for parking in different lots, and provide signage or maps for way-finding (Levine, 2003).
- Consider parking space measurements (Development and Building Control Division, 2011, ch. 2), as well as standards of parking capacity (Development and Building Control Division, 2011, Appendix A).
- At least 20 percent of the parking capacity should cater to people with disabilities, marked with appropriate symbols (Levine, 2003).

INTEGRATED PARKING FACILITIES: In *Treelodge@Punggol*, Singapore (Figure 2.20a, left), parking facility is **integrated** right **under** the main urban space, which increases **convenience**, while successfully **separating vehicular traffic from pedestrian activity**. In another Singapore housing precinct, the *Meridian at Punggol* (Figure 2.20b, right), the roof-top of a multi-storey car park is **utilized** as a green recreational space. Although such a design solution is highly **efficient** in terms of space economy and **land utilization in high-density contexts**, **good pedestrian accessibility** to such spaces is required in order to ensure its vitality.

URBAN SPACE QUALITY

11 Drop-Off and Taxi Stands

What?
Design Principles
- Provide safe drop-off points.
- Provide taxi stands.

In addition to good vehicular access, it is important to equip the urban space with safe pick-up and drop-off points, with access for the disabled. Moreover, although not necessarily in the power of an urban designer, large and vibrant urban spaces should preferably incorporate designated taxi stands or these should be found in their proximity.

Reference to Good Practices

Why?
- Provision of drop-off points and taxi stands caters to vulnerable user groups, children, women, the elderly and the disabled (CABE, 2008; Urry, 2007). It increases efficiency, safety, convenience and comfort.

How?
Design Measures and Considerations
- Locate drop-off points within the shortest distance to the main entrance without obstructing the pedestrian flow. Provide at least one accessible route from public transport stops, parking spaces and drop-off points to the main entrances (Levine, 2003).

DROP-OFF POINTS AND TAXI STANDS: Drop-off, pick-up points and taxi stands **located at the entrance** of *Raffles Place Park*, Singapore (Figure 2.21) facilitate the **movement of both people and goods**.

URBAN SPACE ATTRIBUTE
D LEGIBILITY AND EDGES

Experience of urban environment is, above all, a kinesthetic experience, a dynamic activity involving movement and time. To support such an activity, information available in and around the space should be readable and legible. Legibility is a function of balancing between the content and accessibility to various stimuli available in space, which is crucial for navigating and understanding the space.

As Lynch (1960) claimed, a legible environment is an axiom for helping people structure their mental image accurately, which as a result helps them react to their environment more effectively. He suggested five physical attributes of legible environment: paths, edges, landmarks, nodes and districts. Lynch's legibility aspects are embedded in urban morphology, and manifested as cadastral patterns. In channeling the movement of people, goods and information within the city, the structure of urban patterns plays an important role. An essential aspect of movement and legibility in urban space is the permeability of its edges, which is defined as the extent to which an environment allows a choice of routes both through and within it (Carmona et al., 2010).

URBAN SPACE QUALITY

12 Spatial Layout

What?
Design Principles
- Make pedestrian networks visible and differentiated from other activities.
- Create a hierarchy of pedestrian networks.

In high-density compact conditions, maintaining a simple and clear spatial layout is sometimes an obvious challenge. In highly complex environments the numbers and complexities of various stimuli in urban space increase. In such a context the need for structuring the mental image about the space accurately becomes essential for easier navigation through space and an efficient reaction to environmental clues. Pedestrian walkways need to be clearly established and differentiated from spatial nodes catering to more stationary and space-defined activities (such as sport grounds) in order to avoid any possible conflicts between the two modes of activities. Moreover, a clear hierarchy of the pedestrian network is needed, including differentiating major from minor pedestrian routes by size/width, shape, material/texture/color, weather protection elements, etc.

Why?
- Clear identification and differentiation of pedestrian walkways from other grounds ensures safety, smooth movement and connectivity, while avoiding potential conflicts with the main activity nodes.
- Good differentiation between major and minor pedestrian routes within the overall pedestrian network gives hierarchy and structure to pedestrian connections, which also improves legibility and way-finding.
- Differentiation of pedestrian networks enriches the visual, tactile and kinesthetic quality of an urban space.

How?
Design Measures and Considerations
- Make the overall pedestrian system obvious using spatial layout, visibility and informational facilities, such as maps, signage and directions.
- Create the hierarchy of the pedestrian network using width, scale, elevation, greenery, shelters, seating, colors and textures (Levine, 2003).
- In order to create a high-quality pedestrian environment, design the pavement with adequate width to accommodate pedestrian movement, street furniture and landscaping. Visually attractive, interesting and high-quality pavement surfaces guide the flow, and make the urban space more inviting and legible (Hong Kong Planning Department, 2006).
- Orientate pedestrian walkways toward interesting vistas. Include trees and objects, as well as exterior lighting along the street to direct vision and enrich the walking experience (City of New York, 2010).

Reference to Good Practices

HIERARCHY OF PEDESTRIAN NETWORK: In **large-scale** developments with **dynamic topography, multiple levels** and **complex interaction between indoor and outdoor spaces**, such as *Roppongi Hills* in Tokyo (Figures 2.22a, top left, 2.22b, top right, and 2.22c, bottom), the hierarchy of the pedestrian network is particularly important. The hierarchy is established through **scale**, differentiation in floor **materials** and **colors**, and **landscape and architectural elements**, such as **canopies or urban furniture**.

URBAN SPACE QUALITY

13 Focal Points of Activity

What?
Design Principles
- Provide diversity of activity nodes.
- Make activity nodes visible.

A legible space allows major activity nodes to be easily identified. In order to function well, an urban space needs to provide a fair distribution of different nodes and focal points of activities. According to Alexander and colleagues (1987), a maximum distance between nodes of activities for a pedestrian path, for instance, to be interesting and lively is 300 meters. It is important to establish a hierarchy of nodes so that users can read the activities in space intuitively.

Reference to Good Practices

Why?
- Nodes of activity enhance natural self-surveillance and safety, as the presence of people acts as a deterrent to crime.
- Different types of activities increase users' choice and create an inviting environment for different user groups.
- Activity nodes stimulate spontaneous activities and interaction.
- Visibility of activity nodes invites users to both participate and withdraw from the activities.

How?
Design Measures and Considerations
- Locate recognizable structures around the centers of activity to motivate intuitive understanding of activities occurring in urban space.

DIVERSITY OF ACTIVITY NODES: *SCAPE Event Space in Singapore (Figures 2.23a, top, and 2.23b, bottom) establishes two major activity nodes concentrated around the multi-functional sports ground and a weekend market space.

DIVERSITY OF ACTIVITY NODES: An LED screen at the center of ***The Place*** in Beijing (Figure 2.24) operates as a constantly active "theatrical space" offering interaction and people-watching from the adjacent amphitheater seating. In winter, this covered space turns into an ice-skating rink.

URBAN SPACE QUALITY

14 Visual Landmarks

What?
Design Principles
- Provide landmarks.
- Provide diversity of landmarks.

Visual landmarks can be any physical node, object or structure that is clearly different from the rest of the space, has unique visual characteristics, and helps the user to navigate and understand the space. They can be objects of particular visual characteristics—unique façades, shapes, materials, colors, outstanding scale, etc.—or prominent solitary objects—monuments, sculptures, fountains, solitary trees, explicit signs, visual displays, etc. On a larger scale, a whole development may itself also be identified as a landmark in reference to its larger surroundings.

Why?
- Landmarks serve as point of reference to orientate in space, and thus enhance legibility (Hirtle, 2008; Lynch, 1960).
- Landmarks contribute to the aesthetic quality and identity of an urban space (Lynch, 1960).

How?
Design Measures and Considerations
- Locate landmarks strategically, such as near the centers of activity or at the junctions of main pathways. Provide vistas to landmarks, and offset street angles to enhance surprise and theatricality (Urban Design Compendium, 2007).
- Consider the illumination of buildings as different points of reference during night-time.

Reference to Good Practices

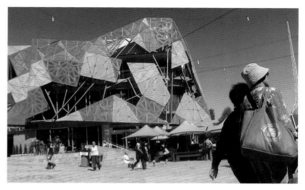

VISUAL LANDMARKS: Unique and **iconic architectural features**, such as the fractal façade of **Federation Square** in Melbourne (Figure 2.25), serve as clear and memorable visual landmarks.

VISUAL LANDMARKS: On a more micro-scale, unique **artworks and furniture** bring identity to a place and serve as important reference points, such as the open amphitheater in **Dhoby Ghaut Green** in Singapore (Figure 2.26).

URBAN SPACE QUALITY

15 Permeability

What?
Design Principles
- Provide good visual connection with surroundings.
- Activate impermeable edges.

Establishing a good visual and physical relationship with the immediate surrounding context is a necessity. The majority of surrounding surfaces at the main pedestrian level should be visually porous or see-through to ensure safety and enhance the contact between the inner and the outer, the public and the private domains. The number of doors and entrances that are directly visible from public space is claimed to be a good indicator of the potential for street life (Carmona et al., 2010; Gehl, 1996). While views into the building provide interest for passers-by, views from the building put "eyes on the street" and contribute to safety. If visual permeability is reduced, the boundary should be visually active and rich, rather than passive and blank (Gehl, 1996; Hong Kong Planning Department, 2006; Yeang, 2000).

Why?
- Good visibility invites more "eyes on the street," which encourages natural surveillance (Jacobs, 1961; Shaftoe, 2008).

- Good visual connection makes urban space approachable or inviting.
- Active qualities of the edge of urban space enrich the visual quality of the space and make walking experiences and street life more enjoyable (Carmona et al., 2010; Gehl, 1996; Hong Kong Planning Department, 2006).

How?
Design Measures and Considerations
- Consider transparent materials and voids to enhance the connection between outdoor and indoor spaces and to make spatial edges visually active.
- Building façades and podium edges should be rich in architectural detailing and in the choice of building materials to evoke interest, particularly at the lower levels (Hong Kong Planning Department, 2006).
- Locate nodes of activity with large numbers of people sitting and lingering (such as cafés) at the edges of urban space to attract other people (City of New York, 2010).
- Retail frontage is highly encouraged in areas with high pedestrian flows (Hong Kong Planning Department, 2006).
- Incorporate temporary and permanent public art installations that are visible from the outside (City of New York, 2010).

Reference to Good Practices

VISUALLY POROUS BOUNDARY: The views of bustling city life and activities of the surrounding context add visual quality and complexity to elevated spaces, such as the ***High Line Park*** in New York (Figure 2.27).

VISUALLY POROUS BOUNDARY: Visual permeability is one of the main qualities of *Dangdai Moma* in Beijing (Figure 2.28), whose design aims to promote interaction through its porous and generous publicly accessible urban spaces.

URBAN SPACE ATTRIBUTE

E SPATIAL VARIETY

Spatial variety is an attribute of an environment that relates to visual and experiential as well as functional diversity provided within the setting. It also relates to the capacity of urban space to adjust to and accommodate a number of different activities, which may include flexible structures employed to increase users' comfort and choice.

URBAN SPACE QUALITY

16 Spatial Variety

What?
Design Principles
• Divide space into sub-spaces.
• Differentiate visual and experiential qualities of sub-spaces to enhance spatial variety.

Urban spaces that provide a variety of forms, scales, spatial arrangements, height–width relationships, colors, materials, patterns, architectural styles, details and uses are often perceived as less monotonous and more engaging, evoking a feeling of richness and dynamism, and attracting diverse user groups and activities. Increasing complexity, however, inherits the danger of creating urban spaces that are "too varied" and perceptually broken into disjointed entities. It is thus important to maintain a balance between the visual and experiential identity of the entire space as a whole and the distinctive qualities of its sub-spaces. In high-density environments, such qualities may be critical for users' subjective perception of density and crowd and, subsequently, for the successful performance of public urban space.

Why?
• It is often argued that contemporary urban spaces appear monotonous, oversized, empty, static, unpleasant and even intimidating. Subdivision into smaller spatial segments increases the diversity and variety of experiential settings for users while stimulating different activities (Marcus & Francis, 1997). Moreover, breaking a large-scale setting into sub-spaces may reduce its intimidating effects while offering a balance between exposure and intimacy, visibility and partial visibility, and maintaining a visual and physical connection to the entire setting as a whole.

How?
Design Measures and Considerations
Possible ways to achieve clear spatial subdivision are:

• by **articulating the edges** of urban space and employing **tall structural elements**, such as walls, columns, eaves and canopies, as well as tall trees, to create arcades, niches and shaded sub-spaces;
• by employing **low barriers**, such as fences, low walls, plants or furniture;
• through articulation of **pavements** to indicate soft boundaries by using different materials, textures, colors and patterns, as well as elevation.

Similarly, possible ways to differentiate sub-spaces are by:

• different **shapes/forms**;
• spatial hierarchy, i.e., different **sizes and proportions**;
• different levels of **sunlight exposure and enclosure**;
• different **pavements and surrounding surfaces**—material, texture, color, pattern, greenery;
• different **arrangement of seating amenities**.

Reference to Good Practices
The ***High Line Park*** in New York is one of the good examples of a rich variety of spatial experiences along its route, while maintaining the strong identity as a whole. This elevated parkway offers a series of distinct, easily identifiable and dynamic yet well-connected spatial segments.

Spatial variety and rich walking experiences partially result from the full utilization of the existing qualities available in the immediate **context**, represented through a series of successful interactions with the surrounding **buildings** and different **views** of the city. Special features, such as the street amphitheater and historical remnants of the rail tracks integrated with its planting, as well as segments where it passes under or joins adjacent buildings, help define different sub-spaces of the parkway (Figures 2.29a, 2.29b and 2.29c).

The dynamic **geometry** of the park, including variations in **shape and width** of the main path, slight **level changes** and additional spaces separated from the main circulation, further contributes to spatial subdivision and variety. Finally, lucid use of **materials** and **landscaping**, **water features** and **seating amenities** of different types and arrangements creates an array of sensory rich settings for distinct nodes of passive and active engagements, as well as exposed and intimate activities, and in such a way promotes social activities (Figures 2.30a and 2.30b).

SPATIAL VARIETY: Physical interaction with surroundings, vantage points and historical traces—the **High Line Park**, New York, USA (Figures 2.29a, 2.29b and 2.29c, top to bottom).

SPATIAL VARIETY: Landscaping, seating and water amenities increase the choice and variety of urban settings—the *High Line Park*, New York, USA (Figures 2.30a, top, and 2.30b, bottom).

SUBDIVISION BY GREENERY: Different patterns and forms of greenery not only contribute to perceptual experience, but also mark the spatial division and encourage different kinds of activities, as in the case of **Bryant Park** in New York (Figure 2.31). Tall trees at the periphery provide shade, which enhances the comfort level and invites more intimate activities, while the central pen green lawn caters to more exposed activities and larger events.

SUBDIVISION BY PAVEMENT COLORS AND TEXTURES: The use of materials of different textures and colors to enhance spatial differentiation and demarcate different activities is particularly obvious in **Superkilen**, Denmark (Figure 2.32).

URBAN SPACE QUALITY

17 Spatial Adaptability

What?
Design Principles
- Accommodate temporary programs.
- Implement flexible layouts and structural elements.

Urban space should possess an ability to adjust to and accommodate a number of different activities, and to be flexible and dynamic in terms of both structure and functional program in order to increase users' comfort and choice. Temporary programs invite large numbers of people and promote the economic life of the site and its surroundings. In highly dense environments such qualities may be crucial, due to lower availability of physical space yet greater intensity of use. Spaces that allow the user to change their uses based on different needs and to provide means for organizing and facilitating occasional events invite positive density to intensify urban life, and increase livability and conviviality of the city (Shaftoe, 2008). Urban spaces equipped with surfaces, furnishings, structures, amenities and services that may be appropriated and modified by the public enable a diverse and flexible range of uses. It is both economical and socially enriching, as it ensures "long and affectionate occupation of the public space" (Wall, 1999, p. 245).

Why?
- The capacity of urban space to allow temporary programs and provide different arrangements and conditions increases the diversity and length of uses, while also motivating the use of space at different times of the day, week and season (Jacobs, 1961).
- Benefits of achieving structural and programmatic flexibility are multiple, ranging from the enhancement of social interaction, a sense of belonging and privacy, to increased comfort level regardless of the weather conditions, which all relate to strong links between hardware and software components (McIndoe et al., 2005; Shehayeb, 1995).

How?
Design Measures and Considerations
To ensure the capacity for temporary programs and increase the structural flexibility of space:

- Check that the **size** of the space is appropriate—large spaces have greater potential to accommodate multiple functions.
- Provide **covered or enclosed spaces** to facilitate uses regardless of the weather conditions.
- Equip the space with necessary **infrastructure** and amenities.
- Consider providing **flexible/movable walls, plateaux, roofs and furniture**.

Reference to Good Practices
Schouwburgplein (Figure 2.33) is an open square situated in the center of Rotterdam, surrounded by the municipal theater, a music hall and a movie theater complex. It is an **interactive and flexible urban stage** elevated 35 centimeters above street level, an open theater that is adaptable to a number of small- and large-scale, short- and long-term **events**. The most prominent features of the square are four 35-meter-tall crane-like light structures. These red **hydraulic elements** are **interactive,** and their position and configuration can be changed by a **publicly accessible control panel**. The space also offers custom furniture, a long wooden bench facing the central stage in the sunniest part of the square.

The floor, which is in fact the roof of an underground parking area, is equipped with **built-in elements** to house **tents and fencing for temporary events**, electricity and water, including an interactive fountain (Figure 2.34). The perforated metal panels are lit from below with white, green and black fluorescent tubes that also contribute to interactivity. Although criticized by the Project for Public Spaces for its inability to provoke uses that are not programmed, this contemporary square is an example of the successful transformation of a previously dead urban space into a vibrant and playful outdoor venue, whose design emphasizes the importance of **void** and flexibility in a high-density context.

2.33 Flexible urban stage—***Schouwburgplein***, Rotterdam, the Netherlands.

2.34 Interactive temporary structures—***Schouwburgplein***, Rotterdam, the Netherlands.

MOVABLE/ADJUSTABLE FURNITURE: Provision of movable chairs, tables and adjustable umbrellas encourages social interaction and allows different activities at different times of the day. Very successful examples are found in **Times Square**, New York (Figure 2.35a, top) and **Raffles Place Park**, Singapore (Figure 2.35b, bottom).

URBAN SPACE ATTRIBUTE

F ENVIRONMENTALLY FRIENDLY DESIGN

Urban form has a considerable impact on environmental benefits, as well as on human comfort, which is achieved and experienced within the urban space. The main parameters include greenery and water features, ecological considerations, the implementation of environmentally friendly design strategies, and sensorial comfort. Spaces and natural features that are well integrated into the physical environment incite interactions both with and within space, while also contributing to the alleviation of the urban heat phenomenon; their benefits include a better micro-climate, a restorative environment and community bonding (as in the case of community gardening).

In addition, introducing environmentally friendly features into new urban developments and communities often requires people to adapt to new lifestyles, such as walking instead of using cars for traveling short distances (Young Foundation, 2009).

URBAN SPACE QUALITY

18 Greenery and Water: Availability and Access

What?

Design Principles

- Provide sufficient greenery and water features.
- Create an inviting setting that allows interaction with greenery and/or water.

Natural features, including all types of greenery and water elements, improve the overall aesthetic quality of urban space. Besides visual perception, they also stimulate auditory, olfactory and tactile sensations, and create the most powerful of sensory experiences, calming, restorative and stress-relieving effects that attract people (Shaftoe, 2008; Ulrich et al., 1991). The provision of landscaping elements, trees, grass patches and lawns, shrubs and bushes, lakes, ponds and fountains, among others, significantly improves the overall comfort and micro-climate of urban spaces, enhancing passive and active recreational uses, and thus positively affecting human well-being (e.g., CABE, 2010; Carmona et al., 2010; Kellert & Wilson, 1993; Marcus & Francis, 1997).

However, the provision of landscape is insufficient per se. Access to nature, interactivity and diversity is one of the critical factors that the design of an urban space needs to address in order to foster bodily engagement and social interaction.

Accessible and attractive natural features invite users to interact with greenery and water as well as with other users, and thus stimulate formal and informal social activities in urban space. Placing interactive water features next to a seating area, for example, or providing green lawns for informal seating, encourages spontaneous activities and interactions among users. Well-designed water features, such as water fountain spouts and streams, often become the main attractions of an urban space that engage users actively, especially children. Finally, urban farming and community gardens tend to bond people and boost a sense of belonging and community through active interaction and caring for nature.

Why?

- Greenery contributes to people's overall physical and mental health, sense of well-being and happiness (CABE, 2010).
- Green spaces tend to reduce the subjective perception of density and crowd (Stone & Rodgers, 2001).
- Greenery and water features help to cut down air and noise pollution (Kellert & Wilson, 1993) and contribute to the alleviation of the urban heat phenomenon (Marcus & Francis, 1997).
- Interaction with greenery benefits physiological aspects of human beings (Shaftoe, 2008).

How?

Design Measures and Considerations

- Expose urban space users to substantial views of nature. Design facilities and amenities that encourage active uses or physical activity within green spaces, such as paths, running tracks, playgrounds, sports courts and drinking fountains (City of New York, 2010).
- Green spaces, along with sports facilities and children's playgrounds, should be provided within a three- to five-minute walk (250–400m) from the residential areas (Urban Design Compendium, 2007).

Reference to Good Practices

VISUAL ACCESS TO GREENERY: Being an integral part of a green connector, the pedestrian bridge ***Henderson Waves*** in Singapore (Figure 2.36) provides extensive **visual connection** to the surrounding greenery.

TALL TREES: Recently planted trees in ***Raffles Place Park*** in Singapore (Figure 2.37), together with a variety of seating amenities, are considered "quick-win" solutions for improving usage and encouraging dwelling in this green square in the middle of the very dense CBD area, even during the weekends.

INTERACTION WITH WATER BODIES: *Cheonggyecheon stream* in Seoul (Figure 2.38) is a truly interactive space with edges and details purposely designed to allow and encourage seamless and safe interaction with water.

URBAN SPACE QUALITY

19 Greenery: Form, Pattern and Diversity

What?

Design Principles
- Provide diversity in forms and patterns of greenery.
- Place greenery at different strategic locations.

Diversity in forms and patterns of green and water features is another key element that contributes to the creation of a vibrant urban space that is conducive to various types of passive and active uses. For instance, tall and low greenery may be used to demarcate pedestrian routes and direct pedestrian movement. Clustered tall trees provide soft shade, which creates conditions that are suitable for more intimate and relaxing activities, such as reading, chatting and resting. Open green lawns (shaded or otherwise by buildings or tall trees) provide secure areas to retreat from the busy city, and, if the scale allows, are suitable for large formal and informal activities, such as public events, concerts, festivals, temporary markets or simply picnicking.

Moreover, the careful arrangement and placement of greenery and water features at different locations of urban space, both horizontally and vertically (such as roof-tops, slopes, steps, semi-levels, covered or indoor areas, sunken or underground levels, etc.), can also help in distributing the intensity of activities. Opening up roof-top gardens and parks activates a space that would otherwise not be used, while offering different public space experiences, enriching the overall green footprint of the development and contributing to the alleviation of the urban heat phenomenon and energy saving.

Why?
- Various forms and patterns of greenery enrich users' perception (Marcus & Francis, 1997).
- Diversity of form and greenery patterns substantially contributes to the identity of an urban space (Marcus & Francis, 1997).
- Plantings can slow down wind velocity and contribute to regulate micro-climate (New York City Department of Design and Construction, 2008).

How?

Design Measures and Considerations

- Consider the combination of both natural and man-made elements as part of a larger green network. Identify areas on site with the highest ecological importance to be preserved, such as mature trees, and begin to develop the site on such a basis (Urban Design Compendium, 2007).

- Consider the provision and location of greenery (Handbook on Tree Conservation & Tree Planting Provision for Development Projects, 2005, ch. 4).

- Green features should be carefully chosen, particularly with regard to the specific local context and their impact on aesthetics and micro-climate of urban space (Hong Kong Planning Department, 2006).

Reference to Good Practices

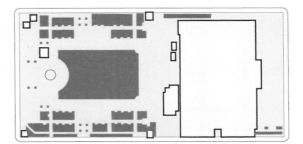

PATTERNS OF GREENERY: Different patterns of greenery may **stimulate** different **types of activity.** *Bryant Park* in New York (Figures 2.39a, top, and 2.39b, bottom) is a typical example of an open **green lawn** at the center of an urban space for more informal and occasional activities, while the rows of **tall trees** distributed on the periphery direct the movement and create spaces for more intimate activities under their shade.

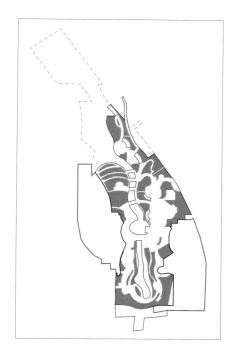

PATTERNS OF GREENERY: Vertical distribution of greenery is effective in very **high-built-density areas**, which also gives the **hierarchy** to urban space. In **Namba Park**, Osaka (Figure 2.40a, left, and 2.40b, right), green urban spaces are distributed vertically in the form of cascades, providing good visual and physical connection, while breaking down this extra-large-scale development into a set of more human-scale sub-spaces. The advantage of such a distribution is that activity nodes can be distinctively separated, while at the same time being part of a larger urban space.

URBAN SPACE QUALITY

20 Biodiversity

What?
Design Principles
• Encourage use of local flora species.
• Link greenery to a larger ecosystem.

The rapid expansion of cities and urban population has modified the ecology and features of the urban landscape. Among the ecological impacts of this urbanization are the fragmentation of open and natural areas, degradation of water resources, loss of natural vegetation, alteration of habitats and creation of new types of habitat (Benedict & Macmahon, 2002; Tratalos et al., 2007; Uslu & Shakouri, 2013).

Contemporary ecological paradigms have moved beyond focusing primarily on natural ecosystems, including people and artificially built environments, their social and cultural dynamics, as important parts of more sustainable urban ecosystems (Felson & Pollak, 2010). Urban biodiversity is defined as "the variety and richness of living organisms (including genetic variation and habitat diversity found in and on the edge of human settlements" (Muller et al., 2010, p. xvii). Urban environments are complex and dynamic ecological entities with unique internal rules of behavior, growth and evaluation, and can offer opportunities for improving biodiversity (Alberti et al., 2003; Savard et al., 2000). Green urban areas are important settings for interactions between people and nature, and preserving urban biodiversity is important in managing urban landscapes, especially in mega-cities (Qureshi & Breuste, 2010).

Habitat fragmentation caused by urbanization is one of the main challenges. Creating connections between urban parks through green corridors and establishing green infrastructure is seen as one of the key concepts for preserving and restoring biological diversity and the ecological process (Benedict & Macmahon, 2002). Urban spaces play an important role in this green network, and wherever possible should be linked to an existing larger ecosystem to enable ecological continuity.

Why?
• Urban biodiversity not only promotes species' richness, but also has a positive impact on human well-being, bringing a better quality of life for the urban residents (Uslu & Shakouri, 2013).
• Urban biodiversity enriches recreational areas within built environments, which is essential for residents' health (Niemelä, 1999).
• Local biological diversity also contributes to the character of urban space (Connery, 2009).

How?
Design Measures and Considerations
• Balance the needs between human access and biodiversity; for example, for a long strip of greenery configuration, keep a well-maintained area in the first 10 meters while leaving a "more messy" or unmaintained area for wildlife beyond (Urban Design Compendium, 2007).
• Consider combinations of grasses, flowers, shrubs and trees to attract a range of insects, birds and animals. Encourage hedge planting for nesting and hunting opportunities for birds and small mammals (Urban Design Compendium, 2007).
• Consider the advantages and disadvantages of certain flora species (Boo et al., 2006).
• Link urban space with nearby green spaces.
• Design facilities and amenities that encourage active uses or physical activity, such as paths, running tracks, playgrounds, sports courts and drinking fountains. Make such spaces safe and visible (City of New York, 2010).
• Nature conservation areas, sports facilities and children's playgrounds should be provided within a three- to five-minute walk (250–400m) from residential areas (Urban Design Compendium, 2007).

Reference to Good Practices

LOCAL FLORA SPECIES: Biodiversity creates rich local texture that enhances the **visual quality** of urban space, while inviting various species of fauna. Cherry blossoms are a unique natural feature in Japan and contribute considerably to the local **character** of *Roppongi Hills* in Tokyo (Figure 2.41).

LINK TO A LARGER ECOSYSTEM: *Henderson Waves* bridge (Figure 2.42) is a segment of a 9-kilometer-long **green connector** that stretches from West Coast Park to HarbourFront in the central south area of Singapore. It directly **connects two large green areas**, Telok Blangah Hill Park and Mount Faber Park, separated by the road, creating a safer corridor for various fauna (such as birds and monkeys) to move around. Moreover, this unique pedestrian bridge blends well into the natural surroundings due to its organic design and use of natural materials, which enhances the natural experience.

URBAN SPACE QUALITY

21 Environmentally Friendly Strategies

What?
Design Principles
- Employ diverse environmentally friendly strategies.
- Promote environmental awareness and environmentally friendly use of urban space.

Employing environmentally friendly strategies into design of urban spaces contributes to the environmental performance of urban space, including improvement of energy performance and reduction of urban heat phenomena and micro-climate betterment, but also raises the awareness of and care for the environment among users. Some examples of such strategies may include: providing a large number of tall plants to alleviate urban heat conditions; installing facilities for producing energy for local use (solar panels, water, wind, etc.); lowering energy consumption through the implementation of low-energy lighting batteries and sensor lights; employing water recycling systems; waste recycling

promotion (recycling waste bins, etc.); growing one's own food, etc.

Why?
- Environmental design strategies help to regulate the micro-climate of the space and enhance user comfort.
- Environmental design strategies promote recycling to preserve natural resources and reduce water and energy consumption, and thus contribute to environmental sustainability.

How?
Design Measures and Considerations
- Whenever possible, maximize vegetation for shade and cooling, storm water runoff mitigation, pollution mitigation, respite and habitat (New York City Department of Design and Construction, 2008).
- Whenever possible, implement water management techniques, for example, storm water management and water-efficient landscaping to control the use of water (New York City Department of Design and Construction, 2008).

Reference to Good Practices

ENVIRONMENTALLY FRIENDLY FEATURES: A giant canopy is a unique feature of **Clarke Quay** in Singapore (Figure 2.43). Apart from its strong visual identity, the canopy serves as a sophisticated micro-climate tool with the aim to improve users' comfort. It consists of connected transparent umbrella-like structures and so-called "whale fans" that allow natural sunlight and foster natural ventilation, which results in a slight decrease of air temperature (4°C).

URBAN SPACE QUALITY

22 Environmental Integration

What?

Design Principles

- Respect and preserve the existing natural environment where possible.
- Enhance the natural experience through landscaping design.

Whenever possible, urban space should respect the context of the existing natural environment through nature preservation. Such protection of natural and sensitive ecosystems in cities has traditionally been the focus of urban planners. However, urban planners and urban designers today are being increasingly challenged to demonstrate not only how new developments can protect but also improve the local ecology. The imperative is to design with nature and to enhance the natural experience. Instead of mimicking nature-like forms, design with nature rather refers to meaningful interaction between architecture and nature, as well as people and nature, while implementing processes commonly found in natural environments.

Reference to Good Practices

Why?

- The preservation of natural resources supports biodiversity, while enhancing the overall quality of the environment and users' comfort.
- Enhancing the natural experience through landscaping strengthens the natural identity of an urban place.

How?

Design Measures and Considerations

- Consider the combination of both natural and man-made elements as part of a larger green network. Identify areas on site with the highest ecological importance to be preserved, such as mature trees, and begin to develop the site on such a basis (Urban Design Compendium, 2007).
- Create linkages to existing urban areas and the wider landscape by an open space network that may join parks, road reserves, playing fields, private gardens, buffer planting and surface drainage corridors through linear elements such as natural streams, wooded belts or canals (Urban Design Compendium, 2007).
- Designing hard and soft landscape should involve the following considerations: appearance, suitability of materials, robustness, cleansing, avoiding clutter, concern for pedestrians, concern for people with disabilities, traffic and related matters (Carmona et al., 2010).

ENHANCING THE NATURAL EXPERIENCE: *Cheonggyecheon stream* is a result of the reconstruction of a former creak after an elevated highway was demolished in downtown Seoul (Figure 2.44). It is an interactive space which brings much-needed natural experiences into the surrounding concrete jungle.

PRESERVATION OF NATURE: Preservation of the existing mature trees in **Tokyo Midtown** (Figure 2.45) enhances the natural conditions of the context. More than 140 trees have been preserved and effectively transformed into a greenbelt area around this large-scale mixed-use development. As a result, its unique preserved nature brings a strong character to the developments and attracts locals and tourists, especially during the cherry blossom season which represents one of the distinguishing elements of Japan's national identity.

URBAN SPACE ATTRIBUTE
G USER COMFORT

User comfort is the prerequisite of a successful urban space. While comfort may be described as an intrinsically subjective category, without the minimum comfort level provided people would not dwell in an urban space. Comfort relates to environmental factors, such as exposure to sun, wind, noise and other external conditions, physical, social and psychological comfort (Carmona et al., 2010). Comfort also refers to a sense of security which can be enhanced by the adequate design and management of urban space.

URBAN SPACE QUALITY

23 Protection from Extreme Weather Conditions

What?
Design Principles
- Provide covered walkways.
- Provide larger covered areas.

An extensive amount of sunlight and rain may pose great challenges for sustaining activities in urban spaces. In the Singaporean context, for instance, due to its tropical climate characterized by high air temperature, high sun exposure, and high humidity and rainfall levels (especially during the rainy season), protection from extreme weather is one of the most basic conditions in order for an urban space to function well at different times of the day as well as during different seasons. Similar conditions may also apply to colder climates with excessive amounts of snow.

Pleasant walking-through conditions is a basic requirement for successful urban public spaces (see, e.g., Carmona et al., 2010; Gehl, 2010; Marcus & Francis, 1997; Shaftoe, 2008). In the context of Singapore, covered walkways are introduced on major paths that lead to important nodes for pedestrians, such as bus stops, schools and supermarkets. This interconnected pedestrian network, protected from excessive sun and rain, enables comfortable pedestrian mobility and improves accessibility and connectivity, while also encouraging optional and spontaneous activities within and around urban spaces.

In order to enhance the comfort and optimize the use of space at different times of the day and year and under various weather conditions, the design of urban space should provide large covered or enclosed areas that are suitable for more permanent activities, regardless of the weather conditions, with additional facilities, such as seating or playground amenities.

Why?
- Covered walkways allow necessary everyday activities in extreme weather conditions, such as commuting to bus stops, schools or supermarkets (Gehl, 1996).
- Shelters increase passive and active engagement with the environment (Marcus & Francis, 1997).
- Sidewalk coverage and continuity are associated with increased walking, thereby improving health.
- Well-designed shelters may contribute to the visual identity of urban spaces.

How?
Design Measures and Considerations
- Consider providing shelters along the main pedestrian routes that connect major activity nodes.

Reference to Good Practices

COVERED WALKWAYS:
Covered walkways at the **Marine Parade** in Singapore (Figure 2.46) form a porous pedestrian network which supports the **necessary daily activities** and the diversity of usage under different weather conditions. All housing precincts in Singapore provide a sheltered linkage to the nearest bus stop or subway station.

COVERED BRIDGE: *Garden Bridge* in Chinatown, Singapore (Figure 2.47) provides a sheltered connection between a shopping mall and a tourist district, while also encouraging various activities along the way and enriching **visual identity**.

LARGER COVERED AREAS: Larger covered areas support more stationary and long-term activities regardless of the weather conditions, such as seating, people-watching or large events. A sheltered seating area at the *Old Man Square* in Singapore (Figure 2.48a, center) provides a comfortable space for social interaction among the elderly users. An interactive LED screen at *The Place* in Beijing (Figure 2.48b, bottom) invites users to urban space, creating a theater-like experience for the public and enhancing its visual identity.

URBAN SPACE QUALITY

24 Variety of Shade/Sunlight Conditions

What?

Design Principles
- Provide a variety of shaded and sunlit areas.
- Provide adjustable shading means.

Designing for good shade is context specific. While direct sunlight may not be preferred in the tropical context, it may be quite the opposite in other climates. Neither context, however, namely excessive coverage and excessive exposure to sunlight, balances the amount of natural light and shade and, in such a way, reduces the comfort level and the diversity of use. Moreover, the amount of shade alone is an insufficient measure to ensure active use of space and social interaction. Other factors are of equal, if not greater, importance, including a variety of shaded and sunlit areas and provision of movable/adjustable means of shading.

The variety of shaded and sunlit areas enhances choice and user comfort. Different users have different preferences in urban space. Some prefer to enjoy the sunlight, while others do not. A variety of shade can be induced by implementing different means for shading—both hard and soft means. Hard means of shading include those that give solid and evenly distributed shade. Hard shade may be cast by the surrounding buildings or by additional built structures, such as opaque shelters or different types of canopies. Well-designed spatial layouts create different shading conditions during the day. Additional built structures are critical in providing shade around noon. Soft shade refers to more uneven

or "unstable" shade, such as that cast by tall trees, pergolas and transparent canopies. Soft shading offers protection from the direct sun while allowing some light to penetrate.

In addition to permanent hard and soft shading means, movable and adjustable means of shading, such as expandable tents and parasols, boost the comfort and sense of control and ownership, as they allow users to adjust the spatial properties according to their personal needs.

Why?
- A variety of shaded and sunlit areas enhances choice and stimulates different activities at different times of the day.
- Such a variety contributes to the regulation of micro-climate, improves user comfort, stimulates senses and brings positive psychological benefits (New York City Department of Design and Construction, 2008).
- Adjustable shading means enhanced spatial adaptability and allows dynamic use of urban space.

How?

Design Measures and Considerations
- Whenever possible, in continental climates, orientate building in a north–south direction to reduce sun exposure during extreme weather conditions and pinpoint south-facing sunny/ shaded areas for seating during the afternoons (Carmona et al., 2010; Urban Design Compendium, 2007).
- Consider using adjustable/retractable shading means, which can be opened during extreme weather and closed during comfortable weather conditions.

Reference to Good Practices

HARD SHADING MEANS: Tall buildings around the ***Raffles Place Park*** in Singapore (Figure 2.49) provide shady conditions in the **mornings** and **afternoons**.

SOFT SHADING MEANS: Soft shading provided by **tall trees** and **pergolas,** as at the *Meridian Roof Garden*, Singapore (Figure 2.50), enables activities during **noon** time.

SOFT SHADING MEANS: Transparent and semi-transparent canopies may be sufficient means that balance the penetration of sunlight into urban space, while also providing protection from the rain**,** as in *Clarke Quay*, Singapore (Figure 2.51).

ADJUSTABLE SHADING MEANS: Flexible means of **shading** help to **extend street activities** during **noon** time, when the surrounding buildings do not provide any shade. In *Albert Mall*, Singapore (Figure 2.52) the provision, maintenance and security of movable means of shading are managed and secured by the local community of street vendors.

URBAN SPACE QUALITY

25 Air Control and Optimization

What?
Design Principles
- Ensure good ventilation.
- Employ ways to enrich the air quality.

Urban space has to be a healthy environment. This includes good air quality and good ventilation available in space. Urban space should not be exposed to external air pollution, such as heavy traffic and unsavory smells. In case such conditions are unavoidable, the design needs to employ conscious and strategic measures to enrich the air quality (smell, temperature, humidity, etc.), some of which are water elements, fragrant plants, partitions and shelters, etc.

Why?
- Good natural ventilation enhances the experiential quality of urban space and contributes to physical and psychological health and the comfort of users (McIndoe et al., 2005).
- Non-visual qualities of space, such as distinct fragrance and positive sounds, contribute to a sense of place (Shaftoe, 2008).

How?
Design Measures and Considerations
- Tall buildings may create a wind tunnel effect, which is an uncomfortable condition for a public space. Whenever possible, buildings should not be arranged to form parallel lines, and sites should be divided into smaller segments to avoid long and linear site geometry. Irregular arrangements are preferred as they help to break the wind speed. Several rows of trees can also help to buffer wind velocity (Carmona et al., 2010; Hong Kong Planning Department, 2006; New York City Department of Design and Construction, 2008).
- Specifically in high urban density and hot and humid climate conditions, breezeways along the major wind directions should be provided in order to remove heat, gases and particulates in the air. Breezeways should be created in forms of major open ways at inter-linked open spaces and amenity areas (Hong Kong Planning Department, 2006).
- Shelter belts (trees, hedges, walls, fences, etc.) can provide a comfortable breeze when they are properly oriented with airflow permeability of around 40 percent. In such a way, the wind is diffused rather than hitting an obstruction, which prevents air turbulence (Carmona et al., 2010).
- Invite positive smells such as scent of flowers or food into urban space.
- Consider both advantages and disadvantages of certain flora species (Boo et al., 2006).

Reference to Good Practices

NATURAL VENTILATION: Voids in the three-dimensional pedestrian network of *Jianwai SOHO* in Beijing (Figure 2.53a, above) provide both **natural light** and **ventilation** to **underground** levels. **Spatial layout** of *Lassalle School of the Arts* in Singapore (Figure 2.53b, right) enables good **visual porosity** and **natural ventilation**.

ENRICHING AIR QUALITY: Water fountain at the central plaza in **Clarke Quay**, Singapore (Figure 2.54) brings moisture and helps in cooling down the air temperature.

URBAN SPACE QUALITY

26 Noise Control and Optimization

What?
Design Principles
- Protect the environment from noise pollution.
- Employ ways to enrich the aural quality.

Similar to air quality, urban space needs to ensure good sound quality. This involves protecting urban space from any external noise, such as heavy traffic or construction, through thoughtful spatial layout, building arrangements, various barriers and enclosures. Moreover, it also includes ensuring that the activities in space do not bring noise pollution to the surrounding areas, such as loud music or crowds, especially late at night. To alleviate the negative impacts of noise pollution the design of urban space needs to employ conscious and strategic measures to enrich the sound quality. These measures may include introducing positive sounds into urban space to override the external negative sounds, such as water fountains or "muzak" (elevator music), among others.

Why?
- Positive sounds (such as soft conversations, birdsong or children's voices) contribute to the vibrancy of urban space (Bacon, 1974; Shaftoe, 2008).

- Good aural quality enhances the psychological comfort of users and enriches the sensual aspect of convivial space (McIndoe et al., 2005; Shaftoe, 2008).

How?
Design Measures and Considerations
- Detach urban space from the source of noise pollution, such as traffic. This can be done by, for example, providing transition zones of greenery and built structures to buffer the noise, or elevating urban space from the road level.
- Consider implementing acoustic barriers that are visually unobtrusive. They could be incorporated into landscaping elements or be made of glass or other transparent materials (Hong Kong Planning Department, 2006).
- Instead of focusing solely on removing negative sounds, consider inviting positive sounds, such as waterfalls and fountains (Carmona et al., 2010; Lang, 1994). Background sounds of water streams, birds chirping or wind swirling through trees create an intimate feeling.
- Some sources of (not necessarily soft) sounds can generate a positive atmosphere and lively spaces, such as music and other audio-visual means of entertainment (Urban Design Compendium, 2007). Slower, more relaxed music tends to make people slow down and browse for longer.

Reference to Good Practices

NOISE PROTECTION: Making **sunken spaces**, as in the case of the ***Cheonggyecheon stream*** in Seoul (Figure 2.55), helps protect from external noise pollution.

ENRICHING AURAL QUALITY: The sounds of a water fountain in ***Civic Plaza***, Singapore (Figure 2.56) help to detract from the traffic noise.

HARDWARE QUALITIES OF URBAN SPACE: AN EXAMPLE

SHINONOME CODAN COURT, TOKYO, JAPAN

Intensified Residential Development

Project Information
Client: Urban Renaissance Agency.
Architects: Riken Yamamoto & Field Shop, Toyo Ito & Associates, Kengo Kuma & Associates and Research Institute of Architecture, Kenchiku Design Studio and Yamamoto Hori Architects General.
Contractor: JV of Maeda, Hazama, Haseko.

Project Brief
Primary Use: Residential.
Adjacent Use: Office, Commercial/Retail, Event Space, Infrastructural, Recreational.

2.57 Aerial view of Shinonome Codan Court, Tokyo, Japan.

Urban Space
Site Area: 48,090m².
Urban Space Area: 57 percent.
Gross Plot Ratio (GPR): 4.73.
Gross Floor Area (GFA): 227,682m².
Building Height: 47m.
Population Density: 1,518.92 people/ha.

400m Radius Context
Open Space: 77 percent.
Gross Plot Ratio (GPR): 4.06.
Gross Floor Area (GFA): 2,042,022m².

Project Description
Shinonome Codan Court is a large-scale high-density collective residential complex in Tokyo that introduces new concepts to public housing and combines dwellings with offices (SOHO), commercial facilities and public amenities in unconventional ways. It was completed in 2003/2005. Six residential blocks, up to 14 floors, with more than 2,000 dwellings, are designed by six groups of internationally well-known architects: Riken Yamamoto & Field Shop (Block 1), Toyo Ito & Associates (Block 2), Yama Architects & Partners, Kengo Kuma & Associates (Block 3), ADH Architects and Workstation, as well as Makoto Motokura, Keisuke Yamamoto and Keiji Hori. The project is constructed on a 16.4-hectare man-made island located about 5km away from Tokyo downtown. The development covers a total area of 4.81 hectares and has a GPR of 4.73. The vicinity of water, unique topography and a certain amount of isolation from the city has allowed for

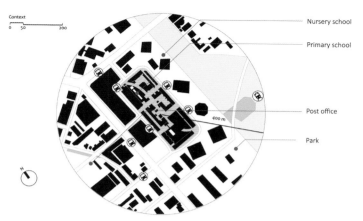

2.58 Surrounding context (400m radius).

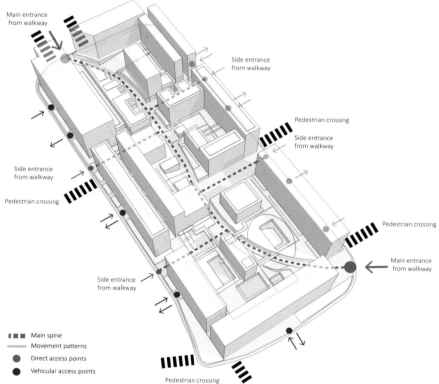

2.59 Accessibility and connectivity.

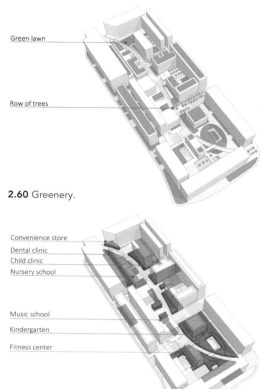

2.60 Greenery.

2.61 Programs within and around urban space.

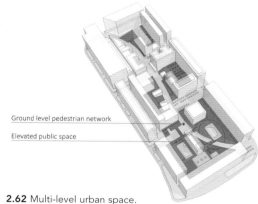

2.62 Multi-level urban space.

experimentation both in the design of individual block structures and in the public space between them. Investigation of the relations between inner and outer spaces, private and public realms is one of the most significant elements and the main quality of this project, which resulted in specific designs and intense use of semi-private spaces, the so-called outdoor living spaces (OLS). A curved (S-shaped) 10m-wide path crosses the middle of the site from south to north, anchored by a mall at one end and a subway station at the other. Six linear plazas that are inserted into the S-shaped avenue form the backbone of the OLS. Lined

with a variety of supporting spaces, such as children's facilities, communal buildings and commercial services, as well as small pocket-like parks providing views to the nearby Tatsumi Canal, this inner street offers a distinct spatial experience. This three-dimensional network of diverse public and semi-public spaces fosters intense activities and social interaction among inhabitants, accompanied by various community programs, such as occasional flea markets and communal urban farming on the roof gardens (of Kengo Kuma's block in particular).

In the following example of evaluation, • refers to the criteria (design principles) that are met by this urban space, while ○ marks those criteria that are not met.

HARDWARE

A Accessibility
1 Pedestrian Access Points
- The public network of Shinonome Codan Court is accessible via six clearly visible and easily reachable pedestrian access points from the surrounding roads (Figure 2.59).
- Two main access points are marked by the central pedestrian path that runs diagonally through the development (Figure 2.63). Four additional entrances are available from the lateral sides of the elongated rectangular site (Figure 2.66).

2 Universal Access
- The public spaces at the upper level of this three-dimensional pedestrian network are predominantly accessed via a number of staircases. The development is also well equipped with a number of universal access points (Figure 2.64).
- More than six universal access points are available.

3 Types and Distribution of Universal Access
- The development provides three types of universal access, namely elevators in residential blocks (Figure 2.64), additional moving platforms for the disabled from the central spine, and ramps.
- Universal access points are fairly and logically dispersed across the development.

4 Prioritizing Pedestrians
- Each of the six formal access points is accompanied by safe and well-marked pedestrian crossings.
- The central spine and the elevated spaces are completely pedestrianized (Figures 2.65 and 2.67). At the ground level, the vehicular traffic is clearly separated from the pedestrian traffic. The car park areas are located on the lateral sides of the pedestrian path and accessed from the side roads without coming into contact with pedestrians (Figure 2.69).

B Connectivity
5 Movement Patterns
- Direct and safe connections are established to dominant external pedestrian routes (Figure 2.66).
- Pedestrian spaces are well interconnected at all levels. A

central spine with side entrances creates a clear fish-bone pattern, with bridges logically positioned at the upper levels (Figure 2.68).

6 Node Connectivity
- The development supports transient activities. A curved S-shaped 10m-wide pedestrian path runs across the site in a south–north direction, anchored by important nodes at both ends, namely a mall at one end and a subway station at the other (Figures 2.58 and 2.59).
- Commercial and leisure facilities along the central path attract both residents and the general public, making this urban space an important public space destination (Figures 2.70, 2.73 and 2.74).

7 Sightlines and Way-Finding
- Urban space provides good visibility of horizontal and vertical directions within the development (Figures 2.65, 2.67 and 2.68).
- Although movement directions are clear, possibly due to the curved shape of the central spine, the main entrances and exits are not fully visible from all points of the three-dimensional network.

C Mobility Means
8 Bicycle-Friendly Design
- Space provides a fair amount of sheltered bicycle parking areas at the ground level of the development (Figure 2.71).
- The development promotes cycling at the ground level.

9 Public Transport
- The development is located close to (within 400m walking distance) at least one mode of public transportation (Figure 2.58).
- Only one type of public transportation (subway) is available within walking distance from the development.

10 Vehicular Access
- A sufficient number of parking facilities are provided within the development.
- Car park facilities are located at the ground level on both sides of the S-shaped path and are directly accessible from the surrounding roads (Figure 2.59).

11 Drop-Off and Taxi Stands
- The development provides safe drop-off points.
- A designated taxi stand is available in the vicinity.

2.63 The main entrance to the pedestrian spine.

2.64 Vertical universal access: elevator.

2.65 Central pedestrian path.

2.66 Side entrance.

2.67 Elevated pedestrian network.

2.69 Parking area separated from pedestrian flow.

2.68 Bridges connecting the elevated spaces.

2.70 Commercial and communal facilities along the spine.

2.74 Public "pocket" plaza.

2.73 Children's playground.

2.71 Bicycle parking facility.

2.72 Plazas and seating areas are differentiated from pedestrian paths.

2.75 Visual landmark: unique façade and lighting.

2.77 Way-finding facilities.

2.76 Recreational green area next to the Tatsumi Canal.

D Legibility and Edges

12 Spatial Layout

- The three-dimensional network has a clear layout, both at the ground level and at the upper levels. A good line of sight is established between and within all levels. Pedestrian walkways are clearly differentiated from other activity nodes (Figures 2.59 and 2.62).
- The hierarchy within the pedestrian network is well established. The major pedestrian walkway, the S-spine, is wider than the anchored pedestrian walkways. At the elevated level pedestrian routes and plazas are differentiated through varied shapes and pavements, primarily wood and grass (Figure 2.72).

13 Focal Points of Activity

- The development provides a fair amount of diverse and legible focal points of activity. The inner street is lined with a variety of supporting spaces and facilities, such as a children's playground (Figure 2.73), communal services, commercial activities (Figure 2.70) and a community garden on the roof of Kengo Kuma's block.
- Even though it provides clear layout and directions, the majority of the activity nodes cannot be seen from the main access points and from central points in the space. Better visibility of focal points of activity is available at the elevated levels.

14 Visual Landmarks

- The development has a number of visual landmarks.
- Apart from the unique façades of the surrounding buildings, the landmarks include well-lit staircases, a children's playground, green gathering spaces and memorable signage, among other features (Figures 2.75 and 2.77).

15 Permeability

- With a number of side entrances and elevated pocket-like parks that provide views to the nearby Tatsumi Canal, Shinonome Codan Court provides good visual connections with the surrounding area, creating a distinct and permeable spatial experience.
- The surrounding edges are either visually permeable or provide active and rich qualities, such as well-designed and colorful semi-private spaces at the inner façades of the residential blocks (Figure 2.75). These so-called outdoor living spaces (OLS) create active thresholds between public and private, inner and outer domains.

E Spatial Variety

16 Spatial Variety

- The space is well divided into a number of sub-spaces, enhancing users' spatial and perceptual experience.
- These sub-spaces, including plazas and small parks, vary in scale and proportion, types of greenery and paving materials.

17 Spatial Adaptability

- The development proves to be adaptable to various temporary programs such as occasional flea markets along the central spine.
- However, the development does not provide full flexibility. There are no implemented structural elements as means to change the arrangement of spaces and enclosure degree for temporary and future use(s).

F Environmentally Friendly Design

18 Greenery and Water: Availability and Access

- Although not extensive, the space provides a sufficient amount and a variety of greenery to enhance the users' perception and comfort (Figures 2.58 and 2.60). It is also situated close to Tatsumi Canal (Figure 2.76), which contributes to the natural and restorative experience within and around the development.
- Green features allow some level of interaction. Tables and flexible seating are implemented around the taller trees, while the community garden on the roof of Kengo Kuma's block provides space for communal farming and social interaction.

19 Greenery: Form, Pattern and Diversity

- The diverse greenery includes grass, taller shrubs, bushes and trees, used to form soft barriers and to delineate different sub-spaces.
- Greenery may be found at all levels of the development, including taller trees at the ground level and grass and bushes at the elevated levels (Figure 2.60).

20 Biodiversity

- The development is diverse in terms of local flora species, providing low (grass), medium (bushes) and high (trees) greenery to support biodiversity.
- However, the landscaped environment is man-made and somewhat fragmented, providing only poor ecological continuity in relation to a larger ecosystem in its surrounding area.

21 Environmentally Friendly Strategies
- The development employs green roofs that contribute to alleviation of the urban heat island effect and improve the comfort of the residents. The environmental comfort level is further enhanced by the passive design strategies with the spatial layout that is appropriate for the local climate. The development's night-time landscape is created by employing light sources that are energy conserving and long living (Figure 2.75). Finally, prefabrication of the balcony units reduced waste production during the construction of the development.
- In addition, the communal roof gardens and outdoor green spaces enhance the sense of community and care for the environment, and thus contribute to social sustainability.

22 Environmental Integration
- The development respects its surrounding context and creates good connections to a canal in its immediate vicinity.
- The design integrates landscaping features and natural materials, such as wood, that enhance the overall natural experience.

G User Comfort
23 Protection from Weather Conditions
- Only segments of the main pedestrian pathways are protected from the sun and rain.
- Larger covered spaces are provided to support public use in bad weather conditions.

24 Shade and Sunlight
- The development has a spatial layout that is appropriate to the local climate and provides a variety of shade and sunlight conditions, also supported by occasional canopies and tall trees.
- The development does not provide any flexible or adjustable means of shading to enhance users' comfort and choice.

25 Air Control and Optimization
- The space has good air quality and good ventilation during different seasons. It is not exposed to substantial external factors, such as heavy traffic or unsavory smells.
- Balanced spatial layout in terms of permeability creates open spaces with both good ventilation and protection from strong winds.

26 Noise Control and Optimization
- Space is free from both external and internal noise, such as heavy traffic or constant loud music, construction or industry.
- The inward-looking spatial arrangement protects the development from any excessive external noise, while wooden pavements and soft landscapes help absorb potential internal noise from users.

USE AND SOCIO-PERCEPTUAL VALUES OF URBAN SPACE

The SOFTware component encompasses the uses of a public space and its social and perceptual qualities (Figure 2.78). Its primary focus is on the positive relationships between the users and urban space as well as on social interaction among the users. Such relationships may result from the diversity and intensity of activities, user groups and facilities available in and around urban space, seating amenities, levels of interactivity and privacy, as well as the character, history and culture embedded within the urban space. Accordingly, this section discusses the ways in which places are populated by activities and users, and how people perceive and give meaning to urban spaces.

The social dimension of urban environments is one of the crucial elements of its sustainability. Social sustainability is somewhat ambiguous and often refers to a number of concepts in social sciences, such as "social exclusion" (see, e.g., Hills et al., 2002; Pierson, 2002), "social capital" and "social cohesion" (see, e.g., Forrest & Kearns, 2001; Glasson & Wood, 2009; Kearns & Forrest, 2000), "social equity" and "sustainability of community" (see, e.g., Bramley & Power, 2009; Dempsey et al., 2011; Sherlock, 1990). Moreover, the empirical knowledge focusing specifically on social sustainability in built environment disciplines is still sparse and uneven, and its influence on public space design is still quite weak (Lozano, 1990; Zhang & Lawson, 2009).

According to some authors, such as Bramley and Power (2009) and Dempsey and colleagues (2011), the main aspects that shape sustainable communities include: interactions among residents (social networks); active participation in formal and informal community activities; sense of place; long stability of residents' structure (versus frequent turnovers); and security.

The connection between users and their urban environment is an important factor in encouraging, initiating and maintaining various modes of human interaction. People's awareness and appreciation of the environment they inhabit contribute to building a stronger sense of place, while at the same time boosting self-awareness, self-identity and a sense of attachment and belonging. While the physical elements of space undoubtedly contribute to space identity, the character of space is shaped by its users, the activities they perform and the symbolic meanings they translate into space.

Lefebvre (1991) defines space as a complex social product, constantly being constructed and reconstructed through everyday lived experience, affecting spatial practices and perceptions.

A space is both a means of production for the social realm and a social product of that realm. Place is the result of often unspoken or taken-for-granted values, habits, tastes, practices and expectations that are attained through everyday lived experiences (Merleau-Ponty, 1962). Such an understanding is close to the notion of "habitus," which is defined as the mental structure or a set of internalized patterns through which people perceive, understand, appreciate and evaluate the external world (Bourdieu, 1990; Habermas, 1984, 1989). This is a two-way process in which people simultaneously internalize the external and externalize the internal world.

URBAN SPACE ATTRIBUTE
H DIVERSITY AND INTENSITY OF USE

Well-designed and diverse programs and amenities provided in urban space are crucial for its vitality. When there is nothing to do, space is empty and generally uninviting.

Jacobs (1961) identified four conditions that are required to generate diversity and activity in public space. Space must possess more than one primary function; surrounding edges must be permeable; it should consist of a mixture of building types, ages, sizes and conditions; and it must have a sufficiently dense concentration of people. The presence of people invites other people to dwell in a space, which results in a more vibrant public space while optimizing its use over time. A vibrant and intense urban space is the result of physical diversity and interconnections among available functions and adjacent uses, as well as the diversity of users and their time schedules.

Focusing on activities that happen "between the buildings," Gehl (1996) identified three types of activities that users generally engage in within the public realm, namely necessary, optional and social activities. Moreover, he draws strong links between the intensity of activities in a space and the quality of the spatial design itself.

Necessary activities include the compulsory activities of daily life, such as going to school or work, shopping, waiting for a bus and general everyday tasks. These activities are generally only marginally influenced by the physical aspects of the space; they are independent of seasons, weather and the exterior environment. On the other hand, optional activities refer to voluntary activities in which people engage only if they wish and if the time and place allow, such as strolling, sitting, sunbathing and various other recreational activities. These activities are dependent on external physical conditions, including weather. If spatial design is of poor quality and the weather conditions are unsuitable, only necessary and short-term outdoor activities are likely to occur.

URBAN SPACE FRAMEWORK

	Values:	Attributes:	Urban Space Quality:
SOFTWARE	**USE & SOCIO-PERCEPTUAL VALUE**	**H: DIVERSITY & INTENSITY OF USE**	27: Diversity of Activities: Within Urban Space
			28: Choice of Activities: Around Urban Space
		I: SOCIAL ACTIVITIES	29: Seating Amenities
			30: Seating: Condition and Variety
			31: Interactivity
			32: Intimacy and Exposure
		J: IDENTITY (IMAGE & CHARACTER)	33: Imageability
			34: History and Symbolic Value
			35: Art, Culture and Alternative Culture
			36: Unique Nature

2.78 Software urban space component.

URBAN SPACE QUALITY

27 Diversity of Activities: Within Urban Space

What?
Design Principles
- Provide at least one public amenity for specific active use within urban space.
- Provide a variety of well-integrated public amenities for specific passive and active uses within urban space.

According to Project for Public Spaces (2008), the more activities people have an opportunity to participate in, the better. However, such a quest should not necessarily be taken as an axiom. In fact, some single-use spaces prove to be highly vibrant and successful on various levels. The vitality of an urban environment is in fact more related to overlapping and interweaving activities rather than to their mere number (Montgomery, 1998).

Why?
- Provision of amenities attracts users to intensify and animate the space, which also enhances natural self-surveillance and safety, as the presence of "eyes on the street" acts as a deterrent to crime (Jacobs, 1961).
- Well-designed facilities enable optional activities; they invite people to stop, sit, eat and play in space, and thus create opportunities for social interaction (Gehl, 1996).

- Mixed and overlapping activities also boost local economic activity (Jacobs, 1961), increase convenience, choices and opportunities, and encourage walking and cycling, which results in health benefits and a higher sense of personal well-being (McIndoe et al., 2005).

How?
Design Measures and Considerations
To increase the choice of activities within urban space, consider providing the following:
- Public amenities for **non-specific activities**, such as large open spaces capable of accommodating more than one use, including both hardscape grounds and softscape areas (fields, lawns, etc.).
- Public amenities for **specific active uses**:
  - public amenities designated for ***sports and recreational activities***, including various sports grounds (badminton, football, basketball, etc.), alternative sports amenities (skate parks, etc.), jogging and/or cycling lanes, exercise areas for different age groups and playgrounds;
  - public amenities for ***events, larger gatherings and performances***, such as open, covered or enclosed stages and amphitheaters;
  - public amenities for community shared uses, such as communal gardening areas, TV areas, barbecue pits, communal storages, etc.

• Combine different types of amenities to increase choice and multi-generational interaction.

Reference to Good Practices

Roppongi Hills is one of the largest integrated developments in Japan, located within the Roppongi district in Tokyo, on a 109,000-square-meter site which amalgamated more than 400 smaller lots. This complex mixed-use development combines office space, apartments, shops, restaurants, cafés, movie theaters, a museum, a hotel, a major TV studio (Asahi), an outdoor amphitheater and a few parks.

Due to the specific configuration of the terrain, various levels are activated by providing a network of generous open spaces. Public spaces are accommodated with urban furniture and sculptures, as well as greenery and water elements that make the spaces interactive and socially engaging (Figures 2.79a and 2.79b). Roppongi Hills Arena is the central multi-purpose plaza sheltered by a giant retractable roof, hosting a variety of events, such as concerts, performances, fashion shows, festivals, parties, receptions, exhibitions and sales promotion events (Figure 2.80). O-YANE Plaza is another vast open space at the intersection of the Art Walk and West Walk, two major pedestrian arteries in Roppongi Hills. Art Walk leads to cultural facilities, while West Walk passes through shops and boutiques of the five-storey

Galleria atrium. Half covered by a transparent glass roof, this plaza offers year-round use, regardless of the weather conditions.

Roppongi Hills has a number of green spaces of different scales. Major green areas include Mohri Garden in typical Japanese style, green stretches along Keyakizaka Street, agricultural Keyakizaka Complex roof garden and Roppongi Sakura gardening club within the area of Roppongi Hills Residences (Figure 2.81). With the extensive provision of **multi-functional, well-connected, flexible and adjustable urban spaces**, community gardening, public art and innovative public furniture, Roppongi Hills sets good design examples for achieving a greater level of social sustainability in a high-density context.

Bryant Park is a privately managed public park in Manhattan, New York, well known for its attempts to solve social issues through quality urban design. In addition to an open library, the park provides a number of amenities for specific active use, such as a French-style carousel, Citi Pond, a boule board, chess tables, extensive gardens and seasonal planting displays, table tennis, the Bryant Park Grill, free wireless access, and an ice-skating rink during winter (Figures 2.82 and 2.83). Being the only large-scale public park in midtown Manhattan, Bryant Park is an attractive location for various public and private **events**, such as concerts, performances, exhibitions, fashion shows, literary events and product launches.

2.79a and **2.79b** A variety of open public spaces: ***Roppongi Hills***, Tokyo, Japan.

2.80 Roppongi Hills Arena, central multi-purpose plaza, Roppongi Hills, Tokyo, Japan.

2.81 A variety of green spaces: *Roppongi Hills*, Tokyo, Japan.

2.82 A variety of amenities for specific activities: ping-pong tables—***Bryant Park***, New York, USA.

2.83 In winter, the lawn becomes a large ice-skating rink—***Bryant Park***, New York, USA.

URBAN SPACE QUALITY

28 Choice of Activities: Around Urban Space

What?
Design Principles
- Provide synergetic activities in the immediate surroundings of urban space.
- Provide a diversity of activities in the immediate surroundings of urban space.

High-quality urban spaces are neither singular nor independent entities. The edge of urban space and the immediate surrounding areas are equally important as the activities, design and management available in the space itself. Their vitality and vibrancy results from the synergy with the activities provided in their immediate vicinity. The surrounding activities are magnets that bring people to urban space and encourage its use. According to many authors (see, e.g., Alexander et al., 1977; Bentley et al., 1985; Gehl, 1996), a considerable number and intensity of activities occur at the edges of outdoor spaces. These activities may sometimes be understood as secondary uses. On their way to a specific destination, people may engage in other activities and dwell in space for a longer period of time. Seamless interaction between inside and outdoors

and active frontages of the surrounding structures are crucial for creating the synergy.

Why?
- Dense edges of activity, such as retail, commercial, cultural or community uses, contribute to a sustainable number of users and the active use of urban space, while providing the users with a feeling of enclosure, privacy and direction.
- The diversity of activities in the areas surrounding the public space supports its use during varying times of the day.

How?
Design Measures and Considerations
- In New York's *Current Public Plaza Standards* (New York City Department of Planning, 2009), public plaza standards require at least 50 percent of a building's frontage facing a public plaza to be occupied by retail and commercial activities, such as restaurants, supermarkets and clothing stores. On the other hand, certain adjacent uses are defined as incompatible and are thus prohibited. These, among others, include banks and offices, parking, car servicing and showrooms.
- Use the public space to anchor nearby successful destinations and public transportation nodes.

Reference to Good Practices

MULTIPLE ACTIVITIES AT DIFFERENT LEVELS: The *BasketBar* at the University Campus of Utrecht (Figure 2.84) is an innovative example of a compact, multi-functional, multi-leveled and intensely used urban space. The project is a bookstore extension that includes a café and a sunken barrier-free mini-amphitheater with an elevated basketball court on its roof. The middle circle of the basketball court is made out of glass, establishing, in such a way, a direct visual connection between the two levels.

ACTIVITIES AROUND URBAN SPACE: *Times Square* in New York (Figure 2.85a, top) and *Shinjuku Station* in Tokyo (Figure 2.85b, bottom) are some of the busiest places in the world, providing a range of different programs and activities such as cafés, bookshops, entertainment, retail and offices.

ACTIVITIES AROUND URBAN SPACE: The open space of **Albert Mall** in Singapore (Figure 2.86) is surrounded by a number of local shops and restaurants, street vendors and temples, which serve as magnets for a variety of activities and users.

URBAN SPACE ATTRIBUTE

I SOCIAL ACTIVITIES

According to Gehl's (1996) classification of activities, social activities include all those that depend on the presence of other people in space, such as children at play, greetings and conversations, and communal activities, as well as passive activities, such as people-watching. They happen spontaneously, often as a result of better environmental conditions of necessary and optional activities. Activities may have various intensities, from passive contacts, chance contacts, acquaintances, friends and close friendships, depending on the context in which they occur. Accordingly, social activities in city centers are often more passive and superficial than those occurring in residential neighborhoods, for instance.

According to Whyte's (1980) rule of "triangulation," the adequate arrangement and linkage of programs and amenities in space can substantially contribute to the intensity of its use and of social interaction. If elements in a space are positioned in such a way that they form a triangle, they increase the possibility for activities and human interactions to occur. For instance, a bench,

a trash bin and a telephone booth placed adjacent to each other at a bus stop create a condition of synergy which may trigger more interactions than when these elements stand alone.

URBAN SPACE QUALITY

29 Seating Amenities

What?
Design Principles
- Provide sufficient formal seating amenities.
- Provide sufficient informal seating amenities.

Numerous research studies recognize seating as one of the key elements in creating successful urban public space (e.g., Carmona et al., 2010; Gehl, 2010; Marcus & Francis, 1997; Shaftoe, 2008). The provision of well-designed and comfortable seating amenities is crucial for inviting people to linger and dwell within urban spaces. Seating encourages gatherings and face-to-face contact, and thus increases opportunities for social interaction (Carmona et al., 2010; Gehl, 1996).

Sufficient provision of seating has become a common recommendation by numerous researchers and guidelines. As argued by William Whyte (1988, p. 110), "people tend to sit most where there are places to sit." According to New York's *Active Design Guidelines* (City of New York, 2010), seating as well as other complementary amenities (such as drinking fountains or restrooms) support the frequency of people walking around a particular public space as well as the duration of the walk, especially considering elderly users.

The provision of informal or secondary seating is another crucial aspect in making urban spaces more approachable and animated. Secondary seating elements, such as steps, raised platforms, lawns, planter boxes, sculptures, wooden floors, fences or low walls to sit or lean on, invite people to have either a short break or linger in urban space in a more informal way.

Why?
- Seating amenities invite people to dwell in space, providing comfortable resting points, supporting both transient and people-watching, as well as long-term activities, such as reading, relaxing and lingering.
- Informal seating increases the capacity and choice while providing a variety of means for observation and informal communication (Shaftoe, 2008).

- Informal seating promotes the inclusiveness of urban space and helps to reduce the "empty feel" of large urban spaces.

How?
Design Measures and Considerations
- Provide different vantage points for informal seating, for example, seating steps, balconies and upper levels, to avoid direct eye contact between sitters and passers-by. Informal seating should look inviting, and should not look abandoned when not in use (Carmona et al., 2010).
- The height of informal seating should be between 40 and 75cm. Most of the public plazas in New York limit informal seating to a maximum 50 percent of total seating provided (Marcus & Francis, 1997).
- Wherever possible, seating should be provided at 100m intervals along the pedestrian route (DfT, 2007; Newton & Ormerod, 2007). In areas of high intensity of activity, it is desirable to provide access to seats every 50 meters (Urban Services, n.d.).
- New York City's *Street Design Manual* (New York City Department of Transportation, 2009) suggests that benches should not be longer than 6 feet and, if longer than 4 feet they should be designed to discourage people from reclining on them.

Reference to Good Practices

FORMAL AND INFORMAL SEATING: *Ion Orchard* at Orchard Road in Singapore (Figures 2.87a, left, and 2.87b, right) provides plenty of formal and informal seating along its main pedestrian path, such as fixed and movable benches, steps and planter boxes.

SEATING VARIETY AND CAPACITY: The *High Line Park* in New York (Figures 2.88a, top, and 2.88b, bottom) is a plausible example of well-designed seating amenities along the linear parkway, providing a variety of views to the city, public art and ongoing activities. In 2013 the park attracted almost five million visitors.

URBAN SPACE QUALITY

30 Seating: Condition and Variety

What?
Design Principles
• Provide a variety of seating conditions.
• Provide a choice of types of seating amenities.

Seating provision might be one of the basic preconditions to enable social activities in urban space, but the capacity alone is insufficient to ensure the quality of social interactions. Social activities result from numerous factors, some of which are directly related to the quality of design of the urban environment. Only when a certain level of comfort within the environment is achieved do people tend to interact with space and with other people. According to Shaftoe (2008), the main problem related to seating amenities in public space is not the lack of provision, but rather the unsuitable or insufficient diversity of seating facilities, their placement, orientation, layout, availability of shelters and the level of flexibility.

Placing seating amenities beneath shade or a shelter may considerably improve users' comfort and appreciation of space, especially in tropical climates and around noon. On the other hand, in non-tropical climates more sunlight may be preferred. However, in both contexts, it is advisable to provide seating in a variety of sunlit and shaded areas, rather than aiming for a homogeneous condition and limited choices. In addition, seating in landscaped settings offers restorative effects through sensory stimulation and distraction from stress. In addition to sun and shade, and for increasing users' choice and comfort during night-time, the diversity of well-lit and dimmed conditions is important.

Different groups of people demand different ways to sit, and there is no such thing as "one thing fits all" (Marcus & Francis, 1997; Shaftoe, 2008). Thus, providing different types of seating in urban space is highly advisable.

While designing quality formal seating amenities, four key characteristics should be considered: arrangement and orientation, flexibility and adjustability, comfort, and additional furniture. Arrangement refers to the provision of different seating amenities for a variety of single uses (such as resting or sunbathing) and group uses, including passive people-watching or waiting and more active social interactions, such as having a conversation or playing a board game. Adjustability involves the consideration of both movable and fixed seating. Movable and adjustable seating amenities can improve the choice and variety of seating conditions, in terms of comfort (ergonometric, shade, etc.), sociability and

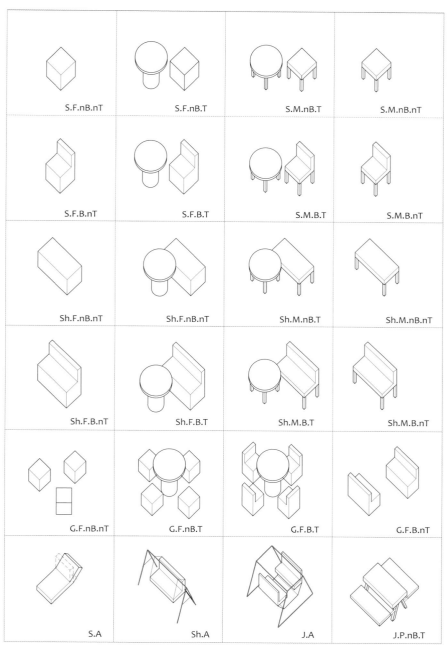

S.F.nB.nT	S.F.nB.T	S.M.nB.T	S.M.nB.nT
S.F.B.nT	S.F.B.T	S.M.B.T	S.M.B.nT
Sh.F.nB.nT	Sh.F.nB.nT	Sh.M.nB.T	Sh.M.nB.nT
Sh.F.B.nT	Sh.F.B.T	Sh.M.B.T	Sh.M.B.nT
G.F.nB.nT	G.F.nB.T	G.F.B.T	G.F.B.nT
S.A	Sh.A	J.A	J.P.nB.T

LEGEND

S	: SINGLE	F	: FIXED
Sh	: SHARED	M	: MOVABLE
G	: GROUP	A	: ADJUSTABLE
J	: JOINT	p	: PORTABLE
nB	: without BACKREST	nT	: without TABLE
B	: with BACKREST	T	: with TABLE

2.89 Types of Seating Amenities.

interaction (rotating, swinging, rocking-chairs, etc.). Seats without backrests and armrests are less comfortable and do not promote longer dwelling in space, especially for elderly users and young children. Finally, additional elements, such as tables and parasols, contribute to higher comfort level, and encourage dwelling and social activities. Based on the combinations of these characteristics, 24 possible types of seating are distinguished, as shown in Figure 2.89. In addition to these types, amphitheaters, planter ledges, low walls and steps are all variations of fixed group seating.

Why?
- The diversity of seating conditions increases users' choice and comfort. It enables the use of urban space at different times of the day and increases the variety of activities.
- Various seating types support different levels of social interaction (Marcus & Francis, 1997).
- The variety of dimensions, locations and configurations of seating helps facilitate interaction among different groups of users (New York City Department of Planning, 2009).

How?

Design Measures and Considerations

- New York's *Current Public Plaza Standards* (New York City Department of Planning, 2009) recommends a variety of dimensions, locations and configurations of seating to facilitate interaction among different groups of users. It proposes six types of seating for a public plaza, namely: movable seating, fixed benches, seat walls, fixed individual seating, planter ledges and seating steps. It is advisable for every downtown plaza to have at least two types of seating. For plazas with an area of 450 to 900 m², three types of seating are required.
- Tables/seats should be constructed from durable materials and be easy to clean and maintain. At least part of the table should provide access for people in wheelchairs (Urban Services, n.d.).

Reference to Good Practices

SEATING VARIETY: About 650 movable chairs with around 250 tables and parasols, as well as the red stage seating on top of the TKTS booth, quickly became iconic interactive features of the recently pedestrianized ***Times Square*** in New York (Figures 2.90a, top, and 2.90b, bottom). In addition, low walls, planter boxes and benches are also provided, increasing the choice and comfort for pedestrians in this busy and intensively used urban space.

SEATING VARIETY: In 2013, from mid-March until mid-May, as part of the National Parks Board's (NParks) series of initiatives to commemorate five decades of greening Singapore, ***Raffles Place Park*** (Figure 2.91) was the first setting of a roving exhibition, named "Playsets of Yesteryears." The exhibition provided visitors with an overview of the history of 12 Singaporean parks and included interactive installations featuring new trees and a collection of unusual benches and play equipment from the 1970s and 1980s. Unique types of seating, such as swings, sculptural benches and joint portable tables retained after the exhibition, dramatically enriched the variety of seating within the park and attracted different user groups, such as the elderly and youth, and not only the office crowd working in the CBD.

SEATING VARIETY: Seating amenities in ***Toa Payoh***, a pedestrian commercial street in a public housing context in Singapore (Figure 2.92), are diverse in type, including fixed individual and grouped benches and chairs, and amphitheater seating. The majority of seats, as is demanded by the tropical context, are placed in shady areas and are well integrated with the greenery.

URBAN SPACE QUALITY

31 Interactivity

What?
Design Principles
- Provide flexible/movable seating and/or tables.
- Provide interactive elements in urban space.

Movable and flexible seating amenities and interactive elements, such as sculptures, installations, fountains, interactive displays, swings and game facilities (chess tables, hopscotch, mini-golf, etc.), are highly recommended by many recent urban design reviews and guidelines (see, e.g., Marcus & Francis, 1997; New York City Department of Planning, 2009; Shaftoe, 2008). With high arrangement capacity allowing different configurations of seating (individual or group), movable seating improves spatial adaptability and flexibility while increasing users' choice and comfort level, encouraging greater social interaction and boosting a sense of control and ownership. Interactive elements animate the space while also serving as landmarks and bringing unique character to urban spaces.

Reference to Good Practices

Why?
- Movable seating invites people to manage the space on their own and possibly establish a stronger sense of belonging to a place.
- Interactive elements provide varying degrees of engagement with and disengagement from the space, while also increasing opportunities for spontaneous contact and social interaction (Carmona et al., 2010).

How?
Design Measures and Considerations
- Provision of movable seating is one of the three required types for New York's plazas with an area larger than 900 m² (New York City Department of Planning, 2009).
- Consider the use of different interactive elements to engage different user groups. For instance, while interactive water features, game facilities and sculptures tend to attract children, chess tables and interactive displays may also engage older user groups.

INTERACTIVE ELEMENTS IN URBAN SPACE: During the NParks' "Playsets of Yesteryears" exhibition in 2013, a variety of nostalgic playsets, including old school swings, merry-go-rounds and seesaws, were brought to **Raffles Place Park** from various playgrounds around town (Figure 2.93). Additional smaller games, such as hopscotch and board games, were also implemented which enabled users to relive their childhood memories of playing in parks. The exhibition proved to be very successful, not only among the young and the elderly, but also among the park's regular users, mostly the office crowd. The overall quality of Raffles Place Park in Singapore dramatically improved after the introduction of new interactive and movable seating and greenery. Most of these unique furniture features were retained in the park after the exhibition as permanent fixtures, which contributed to sustaining the vibrancy of this green space.

INTERACTIVE ELEMENTS IN URBAN SPACE: *Superkilen* in Copenhagen (Figure 2.94) provides a number of interactive urban features designed with a specific ethnic touch, including swing chairs, sculptures and playground amenities, among others, making this linear park an enjoyable and sociable setting for all ages and ethnic groups.

INTERACTIVE GAMES: Chess-playing tables increase interaction among the elderly users at the *Old Man Square* in Singapore (Figure 2.95).

URBAN SPACE QUALITY

32 Intimacy and Exposure

What?
Design Principles
- Provide both exposed seating arrangements and inward-looking arrangements.
- Provide adjustable filters to create physical or visual barriers.

Different kinds of seating arrangements enable different types of interaction among users. While some people find it sufficient to just passively engage with the place and other people, others seek for more direct contact (Carr et al., 1992). Good public space caters to both involvement in and withdrawal from social activities (see, e.g., Carmona et al., 2010; Shaftoe, 2008; Yeang, 2000).

Different seating arrangements may be used as means of defining pedestrian movement patterns and spatial subdivision. In addition, the provision of flexible, soft and semi-permeable barriers enables users to adjust the exposure and intimacy level and, thus, improves comfort and self-management.

Why?
- Provision of both exposed seating arrangements for people-watching and inward-looking layouts for more intimate interaction is thus critical for balanced social interaction and level of privacy.

- Provision of semi-transparent and/or adjustable filters, such as low and medium greenery, semi-transparent walls and fences, rocks and fountains, among others, enhances choices of different privacy and intimacy levels, and boosts different levels of social contact.

How?
Design Measures and Considerations
- Whenever possible, provide different seating arrangements and at different strategic locations, such as on the edge looking out, on the edge looking in, around the center of urban space, on an island, or in more secluded niches and pocket spaces (Marcus & Francis, 1997)
- Seating should be provided not only inside urban space, but also at the edge of urban space near entrances to attract users. New York's *Current Public Plaza Standards* (New York City Department of Planning, 2009) provides very precise recommendations. Seating amenities at the edge of urban space should be located up to 0.5m from the sidewalk. The minimum amount of "edge seating" is 1 linear meter of seating for every 2 linear meters of a building façade. Moreover, half of such seating should have backrests and half of the seating with backrests should be exposed to the sidewalk.
- Adjustable filters can be part of other amenities; for example, they can be integrated with seating, planting and building façades, or retractable internal devices such as blinds or curtains.

INTIMACY AND EXPOSURE: Specific design elements can improve users' comfort and increase choice in urban space by creating a variety of intimacy and enclosure levels. For instance, a group seating wooden bench, semi-enclosed by low walls at the *SCAPE Event Space* in Singapore (Figures 2.96a, left, and 2.96b, right), clearly demarcates the "private territory" while maintaining a visual connection to the surroundings. Seating on steps, on the other hand, offers greater exposure.

URBAN SPACE ATTRIBUTE

J IDENTITY (IMAGE AND CHARACTER)

The discussion about users' perception of an urban setting inevitably calls for Kevin Lynch and his theories regarding the "environmental image" of a space. Lynch (1960, p. 6) defines an environmental image as the result of "a two-way process between observer and environment," between what the environment objectively suggests and what the observer subjectively filters from it. It requires three elements: identity, structure and meaning. However, Lynch's mental mapping method only captures whether an environment is memorable or forgettable, through the perceptual recognition of its physical form, while failing to capture its meaning and its symbolical and emotional values (Carmona et al., 2010).

In response, a number of authors focus on meaning and symbolic values of a space, often described as "sense" or "spirit" of place (see, e.g., Canter, 1977; Casey, 2001; Crang, 1998; Day, 2002; Lefebvre, 1991; Relph, 1976). "Sense of place" or *genius loci* is often discussed as the experience beyond physical or sensory properties of place, but rather involves people's feeling about place (Jackson, 1998), which also encompasses emotional attachment, a sense of belonging, and the personalization and appropriation of space (Carmona et al., 2010). Territoriality is often used as a basis to develop "social milieux" whereby people could structure themselves as a group and recognize insiders and outsiders. These milieux then "mold the attitudes and shape the behavior of their inhabitants" (Knox & Pinch, 2000). Yet, both a place's character and users' sense of identity are not static notions, physically grounded and socially fixed, but rather are dynamic and temporary phenomena (Amin, 2002; Gaffikin et al., 2010).

URBAN SPACE QUALITY

33 Imageability

What?
Design Principles
- Provide unique and memorable spatial features.
- Retain or add to characteristics that are well known by a wider public.

In his book *The Image of the City* (1960, p. 9), Kevin Lynch coins the term "imageability" and defines it as the:

> quality in a physical object which gives it a high probability of evoking a strong image in any given observer. It is that shape, color, or arrangement which facilitates the making of vividly identified, powerfully structured, highly useful mental images of the environment.

A more positive perceptual experience comes from the ability to process the information more fluently (Halberstadt, 2006; Reber et al., 2004). In other words, spaces that possess information that is easy to understand and remember foster a better reaction and sense of appreciation in users.

Places with distinctive physical features distinguish themselves from the larger surrounding context. They become memorable landmarks and are easily identifiable in comparison to spaces of a similar type. They are also places that are well known to a wider public, being either important meeting points for the local users or tourist attractions.

Why?
- Unique spatial features are memorable and attract visitors (Shaftoe, 2008).
- Easily distinguishable spatial elements create strong mental images of the environment, enhance legibility and way-finding while bringing identity to a place (Lynch, 1960).

How?
Design Measures and Considerations
- Employ distinctive form, color, scale (monumental space), unique green features, artwork and other design means to instill the memorable image of a place.
- Instead of focusing simply on place differentiation, urban designers should focus on enhancing the distinctiveness of urban space, which often comes from carefully looking at the potentials within the space itself. Superficial place theming and reinforcement of false identities should be avoided (Carmona et al., 2010).
- Where possible, urban spaces should respect and build upon the existing tangible and intangible characteristics, such as historic values, important events, monuments, historical plazas, unique natural character or distinct streetscapes and building façades.

Reference to Good Practices

ICONIC FEATURES: Distinct architectural features, such as the durian-shaped theater building and expressive performance stage, accompanied by the immediate vicinity of the Singapore River and grand views to Singapore's cityscape, provide memorable quality to ***Esplanade Promenade*** that attracts large numbers of visitors daily (Figure 2.97).

URBAN SPACE QUALITY

34 History and Symbolic Value

What?
Design Principles
- Preserve tangible traces of historical/cultural heritage.
- Retain or add quality that is associated with history, important historical events and/or people and culture.

Tangible (and intangible) traces of historical, cultural and religious heritage form an invaluable repository of experiential and symbolic knowledge and collective memory (Gathorne-Hardy, 2004). It is an invaluable monument of changes in time and the source of collective identity. Such traces may include historic buildings and ruins, monuments, sacred spaces, religious objects and practices, among others. Cultural heritage evokes a sense of place and strengthens the sense of attachment and belonging to a place, while also catering to specific user groups associated with history,

cultural and religious practices. It is, thus, important to preserve heritage for the enjoyment of future generations.

Heritage features are often important landmarks in the city and considerably affect the overall urban design at both local and intermediate levels (Hong Kong Planning Department, 2006). Moreover, apart from preserving historical structures and features, non-tangible local characteristics should be retained and nurtured, including daily activities, customs and ways of living through urban design (Chan & Lee, 2007).

Conservation, preservation, restoration, renovation and reuse of historical sites and buildings are often matters of higher planning decisions and may not be in the domain of direct influence of the urban designer. However, it is important that designers show high sensitivity to and respect for the heritage on site and in its surrounding context. Providing new monuments, cultural and religious programs or employing architectural styles that are clearly associated with local culture and history are some of the ways designers could employ to enrich the cultural and symbolic value of an urban space.

Why?

- Historical and cultural heritage positively contributes to the character of place (Shaftoe, 2008).
- Well-preserved heritage is often a tourist attraction and may also stimulate the local economy within and around urban space (McIndoe et al., 2005).

How?

Design Measures and Considerations

- It is highly advisable to conserve historic buildings when they have high aesthetic value, provide architectural and environmental diversity and contrast, improve functional diversity, enable the continuity of cultural memory and heritage, and possess economic and commercial value (Carmona et al., 2010, pp. 245–246; Hong Kong Planning Department, 2006; Tiesdell & Adams, 1995).
- Consider different conservation policies and strategies. These, among others, include: preservation, which involves individual buildings and structures; conservation, which refers to managing the alterations of many buildings; and revitalization, which enables a building or site to be protected through being actively used and economically developed, in respect to the existing sense of place (Carmona et al., 2010; Hong Kong Planning Department, 2006).
- Wherever possible, the design of new developments should support views to the heritage features and respect their height (Hong Kong Planning Department, 2006).
- Consider the adaptability of historical buildings and sites, to allow the capacity for change while balancing the past and the present (Carmona et al., 2010).
- In addition, where possible and appropriate, new developments may consider creating a sense of history through architectural forms, materials and artwork that relate to the local context (Hong Kong Planning Department, 2006).

Reference to Good Practices

PRESERVING MATERIAL HERITAGE: *Old Man Square* (Figure 2.98) is a partially sheltered urban space between Buddha Tooth Relic Temple built in the Tang dynasty's architectural style and Chinatown Complex in Singapore's historic and touristic downtown area. The square is well known for chess playing and especially attracts elderly users, who also bring a strong identity to this place. The style of the event stage also resembles local culture. The stage is an important node for performances and events during various local festivals, such as the Lantern Festival or Lunar New Year. The Old Man Square is an important social and historic node that sustains a strong local identity and a community flavor in a rapidly changing high-density urban context.

RE-EMPLOYING MATERIAL HERITAGE: The *High Line Park* in New York (Figure 2.99) is a good example of adaptive reuse and preservation of the old rail tracks that are now an integral part of landscape design. The High Line Viaduct was opened to trains in 1934 and stopped operating in 1980. Since its first section was opened to the public in 2009, this elevated urban park has made a substantial positive social and economic impact on its neighborhood while revamping and enriching its aesthetic and historic value.

ASSOCIATION WITH HISTORY: Meaning "prosperous harbor" in Chinese, the name of Sengkang was derived from a small road called Lorong Sengkang. Prior to this, the area was also known as Kangkar (Gang Jiao) or "foot of the port" as there was once a fishing port located along Sungei Serangoon. Fishing villages and rubber and pepper plantations flourished in the area in the old days. Accordingly, the design of the *Sculpture Park* in Sengkang (Figure 2.100), Singapore depicts the fishing village and marine theme. While contemporary in appearance, the interactive fish and wave-like sculptures metaphorically evoke the past of this residential area and contribute to its strong identity.

URBAN SPACE QUALITY

35 Art, Culture and Alternative Culture

What?
Design Principles
- Provide art- and culture-related programs.
- Cater to subcultures.

Good urban spaces encourage various user groups to dwell in such spaces while benefiting from their presence and spontaneous practices. Certain programmed or non-programmed activities may attract specific user groups with particular common interest(s), which often results in the creation of a unique, often temporary, character. Such a character is spontaneously created by people and their practices, rather than by the physical and programmatic order imposed by the design and management. Such a character is closely related to spontaneous, non-planned and creative urban developments, territoriality, negotiation and appropriation of space by particular subcultures, often (but not necessarily) minorities, ethnic communities, artists, and youth, among others.

Particular user groups involved in specific sports or performing activities, such as rollerblading, skateboarding or pantomime, can contribute to the temporary character of urban space (Zepf, 2000). The presence of the performers on a regular basis in the urban space often encourages other people to watch or even participate.

According to Cohen (1996, p.92), territoriality relates to the process through which:

environmental boundaries (and foci) are used to signify group boundaries (and foci) and become invested with a sub-culture value. Sub-culture is not only a way of living, a collective behavior, but also the way of becoming rooted in the situation of the community.

Why?
- Public art plays an important role in the process of cultural regeneration (Wansborough & Mageean, 2000).
- Cultural enhancement and renewal strategies are strongly linked to the economic enhancement of an urban setting (McIndoe et al., 2005).
- Exposure to arts and artistic experiences is beneficial to psychological health and well-being (Ulrich et al., 1991).

Reference to Good Practices

- The presence of subcultures contributes to the character of place and promotes social inclusion.

How?
Design Measures and Considerations
- Public art should be easy to understand and attractive. Artworks should be structurally sound, designed to minimize maintenance and resist vandalism (Urban Services, n.d.).
- Consider animating the space by allowing and regulating street entertainment through organized events or the provision of designated areas for self-initiated and self-managed performances (Shaftoe, 2008).
- Consider including appropriate spaces for young people to hang out, such as youth shelters and sports systems, which maintain a balance between not too exposed and not too isolated; adventure playgrounds, which encourage young people to experiment under supervision; and skateboarding spaces (Shaftoe, 2008).
- Design facilities that give excitement to young people, yet minimize danger and victimization. One way to do this is to include young people in the planning, design and management of public spaces (Shaftoe, 2008; Whyte, 1988).

PUBLIC ART: Public spaces are great venues for showcasing local art and promoting cultural activities. With an idea to create a new cultural center in Tokyo and bring arts and culture closer to the public, apart from the Mori Museum and various exhibition spaces, a number of sculptures and sculpture-like urban furniture may be found all around the **Roppongi Hills** complex in Tokyo (Figure 2.101) as part of a public art project.

SUBCULTURES: Unique design features and ambience with themed sub-spaces and arts- and crafts-related shops at *Insadong Ssamziegil* in Seoul (Figures 2.102a, top, and 2.102b, bottom) particularly attract young and creative users.

SUBCULTURES: Specific sport and entertainment amenities, accompanied by graffiti, are specifically designed to appeal to younger crowds, as in ***SCAPE Event Space*** in Singapore (Figures 2.103a, top, and 2.103b, bottom).

URBAN SPACE QUALITY

36 Unique Nature

What?
Design Principles
- Provide unique natural features.
- Preserve natural elements with strong links to preservation, history or religion.

Unique natural features contribute to the visual identity of a public space. Apart from visual character, preserving nature with strong links to history or religion, such as national parks and reserves, sacred landscapes and shrines, brings historical, cultural and symbolic meaning to a place.

Why?
- Unique natural features enrich the aesthetic and symbolic value of urban spaces.
- Preserved nature enhances a sense of place and belonging to a place.
- It tends to reduce density and is valuable for conserving local biodiversity (Stone & Rodgers, 2001).

- A tangible physical record is a repository of knowledge (Gathorne-Hardy, 2004).

How?
Design Measures and Considerations
- For hard and soft landscapes, eight considerations are suggested: *appearance, suitability of materials, robustness, cleansing, avoiding clutter, concern for pedestrians and for people with disabilities, and traffic and related matters* (English Heritage, 2000, in Carmona et al., 2003, p. 164).
- Provide natural elements that enhance vision, hearing, smell and touch. Instead of focusing on removing negative sound, consider inviting positive sounds, such as waterfalls and fountains (Lang, 1994, pp. 226–227).
- Consider the continuity of urban narrative, which may relate to: *obsolescence*—the inability of urban structures and locations to adapt to change; *time frames of change*—understanding certain things that change over time and things that stay the same; *resilience and robustness*—the ability to resist and to accommodate change, respectively (Carmona et al., 2003, pp. 193–210).

Reference to Good Practices

UNIQUE NATURAL FEATURES: Unique landscape design of the water body is the most memorable feature of the **Skypark at VivoCity** in Singapore (Figure 2.104).

PRESERVED NATURAL FEATURES: Hinokicho Park in *Tokyo Midtown*, Tokyo (Figure 2.105) preserves the landscape elements from the Japanese Edo period.

SOFTWARE QUALITIES OF URBAN SPACE: AN EXAMPLE

SKYPARK AT VIVOCITY, SINGAPORE

Elevated Recreational Space

Project Information
Client: Mapletree Investments.
Architects: Toyo Ito Architects, Japan General.
Contractor: Penta-Ocean Construction Co. Ltd.

Project Brief
Primary Use: Recreational.
Adjacent Use: Commercial/Retail, Infrastructural, Urban Center.

2.106 Skypark at VivoCity, Singapore.

Urban Space
Site Area: 89,140m².
Urban Space Area: 105 percent.
Gross Plot Ratio (GPR): 1.54.
Gross Floor Area (GFA): 137,400m².
Building Height: 15m.

400m Radius Context
Open Space: 77 percent.
Gross Plot Ratio (GPR): 0.92.
Gross Floor Area (GFA): 462,210m².

Project Description
Hyped as Singapore's largest retail and lifestyle destination and designed by the renowned Japanese architect Toyo Ito, VivoCity represents a new model for shopping and public space experience. This commercial development successfully links the important urban nodes in its surroundings, namely the HarbourFront subway station, HarbourFront Shopping Centre and St James Power Station. Wide and open spaces are organic in shape and are designed in response to the waterfront to offer relaxation, entertainment and attractive views to the sea and Sentosa Island, one of the major tourist attractions in Singapore. The key urban space is the roof-level Skypark which has proven to be a very popular urban retreat venue among locals and tourists alike, especially during weekends. This multi-level roof park is equipped and anchored by a number of uses and facility

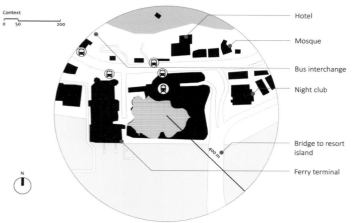

2.107 Surrounding context (400m radius).

Context
0 50   200

Hotel

Mosque

Bus interchange

Night club

Bridge to resort island

Ferry terminal

N

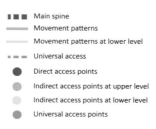

■ ■ ■ Main spine
──── Movement patterns
──── Movement patterns at lower level
▪ ▪ ▪ Universal access
● Direct access points
● Indirect access points at upper level
○ Indirect access points at lower level
● Universal access points

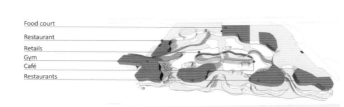

Green lawn
Shallow pond
Trees
Sculpture
Unique geometry

2.109 Greenery and identity.

Amphitheater
Interactive pond
Children's playground
Outdoor café
Viewing deck

2.110 Programs within urban space.

Food court
Restaurant
Retails
Gym
Café
Restaurants

2.111 Programs around urban space.

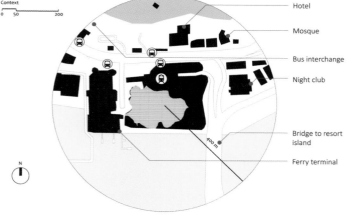

Entrance from mall

Covered walkway

Side entrance from adjacent ferry terminal

Entrance from mall

Entrance from waterfront

2.108 Accessibility and connectivity.

points to sustain a healthy use pattern, with substantial and diverse groups and social interaction. These include a restaurant and a food court, a department store, a sheltered amphitheater, a shallow wading pool and a children's playground at the lower level. The development covers an area of 89,140m² and has four levels, including the basement and the roof-top park.

129

In the following example of evaluation, • refers to the criteria (design principles) that are met by this urban space, while ○ marks those criteria that are not met.

SOFTWARE

H Diversity and Intensity of Use
27 Diversity of Activities: Within Urban Space
- The Skypark provides a number of facilities for specific active use, which attract a wide variety of different user groups. In 2014 VivoCity won AsiaOne's People's Choice Awards for the best family-friendly mall in Singapore.
- Urban space provides a diversity of well-integrated public amenities for specific active and passive uses. Such amenities include an amphitheater with additional multi-purpose open space for occasional outdoor events, a children's playground at the lower level and a shallow pond which encourages safe interaction with water (Figures 2.110, 2.112, 2.113 and 2.114).

28 Choice of Activities: Around Urban Space
- The elevated park is bounded by retail, dining and recreational activities (gym) provided at the roof level (Figures 2.111, 2.115 and 2.116).
- It also connects a number of important nodes in its neighborhood, mainly transportation, retail and office nodes, such as the HarbourFront subway station, HarbourFront Centre (shopping and office) and St James Power Station (dining and club destination) (Figure 2.107).

I Social Activities
29 Seating Amenities
- Skypark provides a sufficient amount of formal seating next to major activity nodes and shelters, including benches and amphitheater seating (Figures 2.114 and 2.117).
- Since the floor is paved in wooden planks, almost the entire space is often used for informal seating, especially in areas at the edge of the shallow pool and those providing direct views to the waterfront and Sentosa Island. In addition, staircases, planter boxes and grass patches are used for informal gatherings (Figure 2.120).

30 Seating: Condition and Variety
- A variety of sunlit, shaded and sheltered conditions are provided for the seating amenities, which enhances the choice and comfort of users.
- Three types of seating amenities are available, including fixed benches without backrests (Figure 2.117), movable plastic chairs in the children's playground area (Figure 2.118) and

amphitheater seating (Figure 2.114), as well as extensive informal seating on the timber deck (Figure 2.119).

31 Interactivity
- Plastic chairs in the sunken children's playground courtyard are movable, which facilitates flexibility, adjustability and interaction (Figure 2.118). The rest of the seating amenities at the main park level are fixed.
- The entire development allows for rich interaction with spatial elements and among users. The timber deck, shallow water feature (Figure 2.113) with a number of interactive sculptures at the roof level and a jumping water fountain in the children's playground (Figure 2.121) are the key elements in space that provide a number of opportunities for physical and social interaction.

32 Intimacy and Exposure
- Although fixed, the seating arrangements at the Skypark are fairly varied to support different levels of interaction. This is enhanced by the provision of informal seating and movable chairs, additionally supporting different seating arrangements and exposure (Figure 2.122).
- Occasional shelters and greenery provide means for creating more intimate settings.

J Identity (Image and Character)
33 Imageability
- The unique organic geometry and location of the entire development next to the harbor makes it very distinctive and memorable in comparison to the surrounding context and other shopping and leisure destinations (Figure 2.123).
- Skypark at VivoCity is very popular among both local users and foreign visitors. Accordingly, it is a well-known meeting destination.

34 History and Symbolic Value
○ The development does not have links with historical or cultural heritage.
○ Except for the fluid geometry responding to the nearby water, the design of VivoCity does not have any clear associations with local history and culture.

35 Art, Culture and Alternative Culture
- Having been a supporter of the Singapore Biennale 2006, VivoCity incorporates a series of interesting and interactive artworks by six international artists, including "Vivo Punch" sculptures (Figure 2.124), a snowman (Figure 2.125), a giant flower and a hanging acrobat, among others, some of which

2.112 Sunken children's playground at level 2.

2.113 Shallow pond at the roof-top level.

2.114 Amphitheater at the roof-top level.

2.116 Retail, café and recreational activities bounding urban space at the skypark.

2.115 Retail and café spaces at multiple levels.

are in the Skypark. These sculptures make the roof garden highly interactive and bring an exceptional touch of the arts to everyday life. In addition, the roof garden is a venue for occasional events, performances and festivals.

• With its diverse amenities, the Skypark caters to diverse user groups, and particularly to young children and families (Figure 2.126).

36 Unique Nature

• The unique water feature that spans the area of four Olympic-sized swimming pools mimics the beach environment and considerably contributes to the identity of the roof garden (Figure 2.113).

○ Landscape design of the Skypark at VivoCity does not have any links to environmental preservation, local history or religion.

2.117 Formal seating: fixed benches along a sheltered walkway.

2.118 Movable chairs next to the children's playground area.

2.120 Informal seating on the timber deck and staircases.

2.119 Informal seating on the timber deck.

2.121 Interactive elements in the children's playground area.

2.122 More intimate setting is created by the shelter.

2.123 Unique organic form and location.

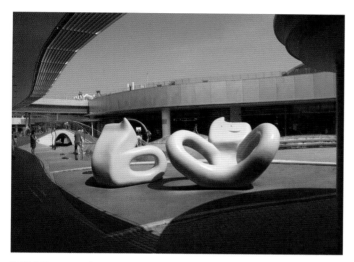

2.124 "Vivo Punch" interactive sculptures.

2.125 Snowman.

2.126 Multi-generational setting: young children, their parents and grandparents.

ORGWARE:

OPERATIONAL AND MANAGEMENT VALUE OF URBAN SPACE

ORGware refers to the operational and management aspects of public space, including the provision and maintenance of amenities and supporting services (healthcare, eldercare, childcare, etc.), safety and security, access, time and use regulations, affordability, and equity (Figure 2.127). While there may be a clearer differentiation between HARDware and SOFTware components, in many aspects ORGware overlaps with both HARDware and SOFTware and at the same time links the two components and achieves their full capacities.

Operational and management value of urban space is often seen in respect of ownership, which is considered one of the major indicators of how public the public space is. For instance, in their "star model," Varna and Tiesdell (2010) have recognized three key dimensions of publicness, namely legal, managerial and design-oriented, further broken down into five interdependent subcategories: control, civility (managerial), ownership (legal), physical configuration and animation (design-oriented). Németh and Schmidt (2011) identified four combinations of ownership and operation, including publicly owned and operated; privately owned and publicly operated; publicly owned and privately operated; and privately owned and operated. Finally, in his study, Marcuse (2005) goes even further in differentiating six levels of ownership, ranging from fully public to completely private, considering the difference between function and use: namely public ownership—public function—public use (streets, squares, etc.); public ownership—public function—administrative use; public ownership—public function—private use (spaces leased to commercial activities, such as café terraces, events, etc.); private ownership—public function—public use (airports, public transport stations, etc.); private ownership—private function—public use (commercial developments, such as cafés, bars, restaurants, shops, etc.); and private ownership—private use (home).

"Civility" is another term used to define ways in which public spaces are managed and maintained, as well as the cultivation of a positive and welcoming ambience. Lynch and Carr (1979) identified four key management tasks, namely distinguishing between "harmful" and "harmless" activities; increasing the tolerance toward free use while establishing a broad agreement on what is permissible; separating (in time and space) groups and activities with a low tolerance of each other; and providing "marginal" places for free behavior. Civility involves the awareness

of and respect for other users of public space (e.g., Boyd, 2006; Brain, 2005; Fyfe et al., 2006). Freedom of action in public space is thus a "responsible" freedom, which is defined by Carr and colleagues (1992, p. 152) as "the ability to carry out the activities that one desires, to use a place as one wishes but with the recognition that a public space is a shared space." Such a view is in concurrence with the concept of "convivial space" which emphasizes the ethical, political and negotiating aspects of public spaces (Harries, 1997; Illich, 1985). For Lofland (1998), the public realm operates as the center of communication and the "practice of politics"—in other words, agreements and conflicts—while also allowing for solitude and passive individual integrity. Urban public space is a human-constructed common that in high-density, high-complexity, high-diversity and high-intensity conditions turns into a congestible good that generates rivalry and conflict (Dietz et al., 2002; Neuts, 2011; Poklembovái et al., 2012). In such a context, public space and users' interactions are constantly renegotiated.

While discussing the political economy perspective of public space, Carmona (2010a, 2010b) identifies the two poles of critiques of public space today: one inclining toward under-management and the other toward over-management. One group of critiques argue that certain qualities (or rather deficiencies) of the environment could increase a tendency toward uncivil behavior, crime, littering, vandalism and antisocial behavior, and thus degrade the environment and the community (Loukaitou-Sideris, 1996; Newman & Hogan, 1981). The other side criticizes the overly managed public space, as it leads to privatization, commodification and homogenization of the space (Loukaitou-Sideris & Banerjee, 1998; Sorkin, 1992; Zukin, 1995). However, Carmona (2010a, 2010b) argues that under-management and over-management may in fact represent two sides of the same coin, as they directly or indirectly contribute to each other. He argues that the poorly designed and managed public space by the public sector encourages individuals and smaller community groups to manage the public space privately. On the other hand, the increasing act of privatization and moving facilities to the periphery enhance the "cracks" in urban fabrics and neglect the space between developments.

This section elaborates on provisions, safety, management and regulation as the key attributes that contribute to the operational and management performance of urban spaces. Accordingly, some of the principles may belong to a realm of higher decision-making, rather than under the direct influence of urban designers.

URBAN SPACE FRAMEWORK

Values:	Attributes:	Urban Space Quality:
ORGWARE / **OPERATIONAL VALUE**	**K: PROVISION OF AMENITIES & SERVICES**	37: Hygiene Facilities 38: Lighting 39: Information Facilities 40: Healthcare and Social Services
	L: SAFETY & SECURITY	41: Safety and Image 42: Security
	M: MANAGEMENT & REGULATIONS	43: Rules and Regulations 44: Access Regulation and Management 45: Time & Program Regulation and Management 46: Permissions and Management 47: Affordability and Equality

2.127 Orgware urban space component.

URBAN SPACE ATTRIBUTE

K PROVISION OF AMENITIES, SERVICES, PUBLIC FACILITIES AND INFRASTRUCTURE

Urban amenities include the goods, infrastructure and services that form an important and integral part of life in any community. The sufficient provision of quality amenities and services within the community are vital to the satisfaction and overall quality of life of its members. Users' ability to fully grasp and experience the meaning in urban public space can be sometimes reduced by the issues of limited access, mobility and quality of social resources (Lloyd & Auld, 2003). Some basic public amenities, such as electricity, drinking water, sanitation, healthcare facilities and solid waste management are critical determinants of the quality of urban living and should be distributed equally and be accessible by all user groups (Aderamo & Aina, 2011; Bhagat, 2010). Social and community amenities, such as schools, healthcare centers, recreational and sports facilities, post offices, shops, markets and police stations, among others, are essential for everyone's well-being and provide opportunities for social connections (Chan & Lee, 2007; Parry et al., 2012). Social infrastructure and amenities refer to a range of activities, organizations and facilities that are accessible to all and support the formation, development and maintenance of social relationships, including public, private, community and voluntary services (Young Foundation, 2009). It has been proved that poor design and lack of adequate public amenities have long-term, health, economic and social costs, including isolation and mental health, among others (Young Foundation, 2009).

Amenities in urban spaces comprise features that provide necessary comfort for their users and support different uses and user groups, such as lighting, garbage bins, drinking fountains, public toilets, seating amenities, roadside barriers, acoustic barriers, signage, flagpoles, clock towers, telephones, ATMs and healthcare facilities, among others. The provision and maintenance of amenities, services, public facilities and infrastructure have a strong impact on the use of public space, way-finding, security and users' overall quality of life (Hong Kong Planning Department, 2006; Marcus & Francis, 1997; Németh & Schmidt, 2007; Oc & Tiesdell, 1999; WHO, 2007; Whyte, 1980).

URBAN SPACE QUALITY

37 Hygiene Facilities

What?
Design Principles
- Keep the space in clean and good physical condition.
- Provide sufficient amount and diversity of hygiene amenities.

Good urban spaces should be kept in good physical condition, regularly cleaned and maintained to ensure a high level of hygiene and safety. A sufficient amount of well-kept hygiene amenities, such as public restrooms, trash bins, drinking water fountains, water supply for cleaning and watering plants, among others, enhances users' comfort and convenience, and encourages longer dwelling in space. The evidence of maintenance should be present to increase the attractiveness of the place, such as mown lawns, pruned shrubs, emptied trash bins, dog mess and graffiti removed (Newton & Ormerod, 2007). Users will care more for an environment if the space is well and regularly maintained (Marcus & Francis, 1997).

Why?

- Regular maintenance increases the durability of urban space, and improves hygiene, and mental and physical well-being (CABE, 2010; Marcus & Francis, 1997; McIndoe et al., 2005; Németh & Schmidt, 2007; Shaftoe, 2008; WHO, 2007; Whyte, 1980).
- Well-maintained spaces encourage positive social behavior and reduce crime and violence (Wilson & Kelling, 1982).
- Amenities support the increased frequency and duration of public space use, as well as physical activity (City of New York, 2010).
- Community participation in maintenance enhances a sense of belonging, pride and achievement.

How?

Design Measures and Considerations

- Consider providing communal storage for cleaning equipment on site or in its immediate vicinity to ease maintenance and encourage community participation.
- Consider using materials that are easy to clean and paint, as well as dark-colored surfaces, where appropriate, to discourage graffiti (Marcus & Francis, 1997).

- Hygiene amenities should be easily accessible by everyone, located along accessible paths and frequently used areas (such as those close to food shops and stalls, seating areas, public transport, etc.) and distributed throughout the site for convenience, so that garbage would not have to be carried over long distances, for instance (Levine, 2003).
- Consider providing heavy-duty trash cans that will resist potential violence and misuse (Marcus & Francis, 1997).
- In urban plazas, where food can be purchased and consumed, consider providing all those facilities that are available in a restaurant, especially drinking fountains and public restrooms (Marcus & Francis, 1997).
- In urban spaces with high activity levels, such as retail centers or recreation spaces, trash cans are normally placed at 30-meter intervals (Urban Services, n.d.).
- Automatic public toilets must allow a minimum clear path of 8 feet (about 2.4m) in width (New York City Department of Transportation, 2009).
- Provide drinking fountains or bubblers in areas of intensive use along the edge of the main pedestrian traffic (Urban Services, n.d.).
- The location and design of some facilities, such as roadside barriers, road signs, rubbish bins or acoustic barriers, should be chosen with care, considering their visual impacts on the overall urban space aesthetics (Hong Kong Planning Department, 2006).

Reference to Good Practices

CLEANING AND MAINTENANCE: Public cleaning and maintenance to ensure good physical conditions in *Times Square*, New York (Figure 2.128a, left) is done regularly by the Times Square Alliance. The *High Line Park* in New York (Figure 2.128b, above) is maintained by the Friends of the High Line, a non-profit company that provides over 90 percent of the High Line's annual operating budget and is responsible for maintenance, operations and public programming.

HYGIENE FEATURES: The provision of hygiene amenities, such as trash bins and public toilets, at accessible locations and frequented pedestrian routes encourages maintaining good physical condition of the space. Unique designs of hygiene amenities, such as tulip-shaped cans in **Bryant Park**, New York (Figures 2.129a, top, and 2.129b, bottom), make them also look aesthetically pleasing and approachable, and promote environmental awareness and recycling. Public restrooms within urban space enhance convenience and promote dwelling. Public toilets in Bryant Park, New York were ranked the best in the world in 2011.

URBAN SPACE QUALITY

38 Lighting

What?
Design Principles
- Provide adequate lighting along main pathways and activity nodes.
- Provide ambient and/or adjustable lighting.

Good lighting is a prerequisite for night-time visibility, security and safety in public spaces. However, the design often emphasizes security, which results in a tendency to over-light public spaces. In fact, too much lighting may be just as inappropriate as insufficient lighting. Adequate lighting should relate to the type and intensity of night-time activities in public spaces and contribute to the creation of a balanced and inviting environment. Creative and innovative use of ambient lighting enhances the aesthetic qualities of space, creates attractive ambiences and a sense of drama, and thus contributes to the unique character of urban spaces.

Different lighting strategies and illumination effects can be implemented through landscape design, retail displays, architectural details, signage, and formal and informal urban furniture (benches, handrails or staircases, for instance), while paying special attention to transit stops, entrances, edges, main pedestrian paths and focal points of activities.

Why?
- Lighting design can also transform the perception of public space.

- Adequate lighting invites users to use the space and extends hours of urban life and activity in surrounding buildings (City of New York, 2010; Marcus & Francis, 1997)
- Flexible and adjustable lighting contributes to users' sense of belonging, interaction and privacy; it may also contribute to lower energy consumption.
- Well-lit focal points, such as buildings, fountains or sculptures, and good night signage improves way-finding (Levine, 2003).

How?
Design Measures and Considerations
- It is suggested that pedestrian street lighting be spaced evenly along the sidewalk; lamp-posts should be consistent in height and offer adequate light coverage (City of New York, 2010).
- In general, lighting along circulation paths should be positioned at a lower level to focus the light spread and prevent excessive lighting and glare.
- The spacing of lamp-posts depends on several factors, including the height of the pole, space width, the amount of light the fixture provides, and the lighting levels necessary for the particular space use; more closely spaced lamp-posts create a stronger edge along the urban space (New York City Department of Transportation, 2009).
- Consider using different types and levels of lighting at entrances and landmarks to enhance safety, way-finding and identity (Levine, 2003).
- Consider the use of solar bulbs, sensor-sensitive or low-energy-consuming lighting to contribute to environmental sustainability.
- Consider lighting that can be adjusted by users.

Reference to Good Practices

AMBIENT LIGHTING: Lighting of the major pedestrian spine and staircases in ***Shinonome Codan Court*** in Tokyo (Figures 2.130a, top, and 2.130b, bottom) improves visibility and safety during the late night hours. Innovative ambient lighting of façades as well as lighting integrated with urban furniture (such as chairs, way-finding features and staircases) also creates an inviting and memorable setting.

AMBIENT LIGHTING: While enhancing visibility and safety along the main pedestrian routes, the imaginative use of lighting may create different effects, such as inviting a dramatic atmosphere surrounding the ***Cheonggyecheon stream*** in Seoul (Figure 2.131).

INTERACTIVE LIGHTING: The innovative use of ambient lighting can initiate and foster **interaction**, such as the LED displays in *The Place* in Beijing (Figure 2.132a, left) and at *Ion Orchard Plaza* in Singapore (Figure 2.132b, right). Ambient lighting is successfully used as means of decoration, communication and user interaction.

URBAN SPACE QUALITY

39 Informational Facilities

What?
Design Principles
- Provide public communicational facilities.
- Provide good signage and way-finding facilities.

The provision of accessible, well-positioned and user-friendly communicational and informational facilities, such as public phones, bulletin and advertisement boards, Wi-Fi internet, info-kiosks, site maps and signage, among others, are important elements of increasingly complex urban space developments.

Why?
- User-friendly informational facilities enhance spatial use and orientation, while supporting active aging and inclusiveness of urban space (WHO, 2007).
- Good way-finding facilities enhance safety, especially in case of emergencies (Passini, 1984).

- The provision of a variety of way-finding means ensures effective communication with all users regardless of their sensory abilities, intellectual abilities, literacy levels, languages and physical stature (Levine, 2003).
- Communicational facilities provide a chance for social interaction.

How?
Design Measures and Considerations
- Consider the use of adequate signage, such as multilingual signage, adequate font size, familiar symbols, color codes, light and floor signage, as well as verbal communication to enhance communication and good way-finding (Passini, 1984).
- Place informational amenities at strategic locations, along accessible paths and frequently used areas (Passini, 1984).
- Consider using lighting design to enhance visibility of entrances and landmarks and to ease internal circulation (Levine, 2003).
- Provide Wi-Fi free of charge, wherever possible, to enable different uses in space and to attract different user groups.

Reference to Good Practices

ILLUMINATED SIGNAGE AND INTEGRATED LIGHTING: In the housing complex *Shinonome Codan Court* in Tokyo (Figure 2.133) illuminated site maps and signage are well-integrated into urban furniture which also contributes to space identity at night-time (see also Figure 2.130b).

WAY-FINDING FACILITIES: Clear layout and visual connection to surroundings with strategically located site maps and signage enhance way-finding in large-scale complex urban developments, such as *Taikoo Li Sanlitun* in Beijing (Figure 2.134a, top) and *Jianwai SOHO* in Beijing (Figure 2.134b, bottom).

URBAN SPACE QUALITY

40 Healthcare and Social Services

What?
Design Principles
• Provide affordable general healthcare service for all age groups.
• Provide affordable social services specifically catering to "vulnerable" user groups.

The provision of affordable and accessible healthcare and social services within walking distance from urban spaces increases convenience and invites different user groups to dwell in spaces. Such services include general healthcare, as well as a variety of social services specifically catering to "vulnerable" user groups, including the elderly, small children and the disabled, among others, such as senior centers, counseling services, day-care centers, family centers, etc. While such a principle may not be under the direct influence of urban designers it is important to address health and equality through various means of design.

Why?
• The provision of general healthcare facilities helps in maintaining and restoring health for all and supports active aging (CABE, 2010; WHO, 2007).
• The provision of affordable healthcare and social facilities embraces the social mix and balanced communities, supports community bonding, and promotes social inclusion and equality (CABE & DETR, 2001; WHO, 2007).

How?
Design Measures and Considerations
• Position healthcare services at convenient locations, accessible by all means of transport (WHO, 2007).
• Use attractive and inviting design for open spaces around healthcare and social amenities to help remove common institutional and stigmatized attitude toward healthcare environments.

Reference to Good Practices

DAY-CARE FACILITIES: The provision of local day-care facilities, such as several kindergartens and nursery schools in **Shinonome Codan Court**, Tokyo (Figure 2.135), increases convenience and promotes social interaction and empathy among the residents.

URBAN SPACE ATTRIBUTE

L SAFETY AND SECURITY

Carmona and colleagues (2010) relate security to the protection of people, and of individual and common property. From the management perspectives, safety and security are generally discussed in relation to "hard" and "soft" control and security mechanisms. Hard mechanisms include measures of territorial control, such as fences, gates and the presence of guards, among others, while soft mechanisms refer primarily to surveillance and self-policing.

As suggested by Van Melik and colleagues (2007), the recent trends toward increased safety, programmed events and entertainment spaces have led to the creation of two types of public places: secured spaces and themed spaces. In this respect, they provide somewhat different interpretations of hard and soft control mechanisms. According to them, the secured public spaces are characterized by hard control mechanisms that include the surveillance, the enforcement of appropriate activities, and the exclusion of undesirable behaviors and unwanted user groups (Carmona et al., 2003; Newman, 1995; Shaftoe, 2008). On the other hand, themed public spaces use the soft control mechanism of inclusion, by creating ambience and stimulating activities, in order to attract people and encourage self-policing (Jacobs, 1961; Shaftoe, 2008).

URBAN SPACE QUALITY

41 Safety and Image

What?
Design Principles
- Employ adequate design measures to prevent physical injuries.
- Employ design strategies that make space appear approachable, inviting—and thus safe.

The most direct relationship between spatial design and safety refers to the implementation of different measures to prevent users from having accidents and sustaining physical injuries, and to enable them to react efficiently in case of emergencies. Moreover, public space that is well designed, attractive, clean, well maintained and well lit, without traces of obvious vandalism (Wilson & Kelling, 1982), appears more approachable and inviting, as it emits a stronger sense of a safe environment.

Why?
- Adequate safety measures influence users' decision whether to linger in public space (Shaftoe, 2008).
- Inclusive space promotes urban security (Shaftoe, 2008), as more "eyes on the street" enhance safety and natural self-surveillance (Jacobs, 1961).

How?
Design Measures and Considerations
- Clearly demarcate areas that accommodate different activities to prevent potential conflicts and physical injuries.
- Use safe (non-slippery, unbreakable, etc.) materials and avoid sharp edges.
- Provide adequate fences where level changes occur and add pavement leaders for the blind.
- Provide good lighting (City of New York, 2010; Levine, 2003).
- Clearly highlight main and emergency exits (Passini, 1984).
- Provide good porosity to ensure clear visual connection to external spaces; avoid tall, opaque surfaces for urban space edges, gates and intrusive surveillance to increase the level of inclusiveness (Carmona et al., 2010; Jacobs, 1961).
- Enable overlapping activities in space and time to ensure the presence of people and enhanced self-surveillance (Jacobs, 1961).

Reference to Good Practices

SAFETY MEASURES: Fences prevent physical injuries and increase walking comfort (*Pinnacle at Duxton*, Singapore; Figure 2.136a, top). Being also informal means for leaning, additional signage to alert users in case of inappropriate use may be needed (*Jianwai SOHO*, Beijing; Figure 2.136b, bottom).

INVITING ENVIRONMENT: Attractive design and the presence of people create an image of a safe environment (**Superkilen,** Copenhagen; Figure 2.137).

URBAN SPACE QUALITY

42 Security

What?
Design Principles
- Employ security measures.
- Employ passive and non-intrusive means of security.

Good security is an essential element of every neighborhood and urban space. A lack of security threatens even successful urban designs. It is important that urban space employs adequate and meaningful security measures to prevent crime, violence and thievery, as people generally prefer to stay in a safe and secured environment where thieves, burglars or vandals are absent (Corbett & Corbett, 2000). However, over-control and over-security do not contribute to the vibrancy and inclusiveness of public space (Loukaitou-Sideris & Banerjee, 1998; Newman, 1995; Shaftoe, 2008; Zukin, 1995). Physical barriers with controlled access, security guards and police may emit a strong feeling of unease and loss of privacy. Hard control mechanisms prevent "unwanted" behavior and increase security, but also exclude unwanted user groups (Carmona et al., 2003). Accordingly, the

more passive and less aggressive and intrusive means of security should be encouraged, such as the presence of civilian guards, well-marked surveillance and alarm systems.

Why?
- Reasonable levels of security and soft control mechanisms encourage people to use the space and interact, while fostering self-policing (Jacobs, 1961; Shaftoe, 2008).
- Electronic surveillance forces users to be responsible and conscious of their own behavior (Shaftoe, 2008).
- The presence of people and natural surveillance ensures safety while maintaining a sense of privacy and freedom in space (Jacobs, 1961; Shaftoe, 2008).

How?
Design Measures and Considerations
- Consider less intrusive security measures, such as well-marked surveillance cameras, alarm systems, lockers for personal belongings, civilian guards, self-surveillance, clearly marked rules of behavior, to ensure quality security levels (Carmona et al., 2003; Newman, 1995; Shaftoe, 2008).
- Self-surveillance alone is not a sufficient security measure.

Reference to Good Practices

HARD SECURITY MEASURES: Hard security measures are sometimes justified, as in the case of residential developments that are open to public access. Security check gates at the *Pinnacle at Duxton*, Singapore (Figure 2.138a, top) prevent those without entry tickets from entering the sky bridge, as well as non-residents from entering the more private areas. Opaque fences and secured gates filter the "unwanted" user groups to access *Dangdai Moma* in Beijing (Figure 2.138b, bottom), which in fact may reduce accessibility.

SOFT SECURITY MEASURES: Visible CCTV cameras are sometimes needed to limit "unwanted" behavior. Any electronic surveillance mechanisms employed in place should be well notified in order to respect users and their privacy, as in the *Raffles Place Park*, Singapore (Figure 2.139).

URBAN SPACE ATTRIBUTE

M MANAGEMENT AND REGULATIONS

Management refers to ways in which public spaces are controlled and managed, and specifically relates to the methods used by owners to indicate appropriate uses, users and behaviors (Németh & Schmidt, 2011). To assess the management of public spaces, Németh and Schmidt (2007) developed a methodology, based on site visits, literature reviews, and interviews with users and managers of spaces. The result is an index that shows the presence and intensity of management techniques. The index includes four major dimensions, namely: (1) laws and rules governing the space; (2) the presence of surveillance and policing in space; (3) employment of image techniques to literally or symbolically dictate appropriate behavior; and (4) the presence of access restrictions and territorial separations.

Carmona (2010a, 2010b) identifies the two poles of critiques of public space today: one inclining toward under-management and the other toward over-management. While one side argues that certain qualities (or rather deficiencies) of the environment could increase tendency toward uncivil behavior, crime, littering, vandalism and antisocial behavior, and thus degrade the environment and community (Loukaitou-Sideris, 1996; Newman & Hogan, 1981), the other side criticizes the overly managed public space as it leads to privatization, commodification and homogenization of the space (Loukaitou-Sideris & Banerjee, 1998; Sorkin, 1992; Zukin, 1995). However, Carmona (2010a, 2010b) argues that under-management and over-management may in fact represent two sides of the same coin, as they directly or indirectly contribute to each other. He argues that the poorly designed and managed public space by the public sector encourages individuals and smaller community groups to manage the public space privately. On the other hand, the increasing act of privatization and moving facilities to the periphery enhances the "cracks" in urban fabrics and neglects the space between developments. Kilian (1998) suggests that all spaces are both public and private and express power relationships between public and private spheres; as a result they all contain restrictions, whether explicit or implicit.

It is obvious that in public space provision today contractual relationships, such as public–private partnerships, play an increasingly important role (De Magalhães, 2010). Although, at present, the predominant ways of public space governance, provision and management are still traditional, the gradual transfer of responsibilities for public space governance from public to private sectors through various types of contracts are inevitable.

Management and regulations are inevitable negotiating mechanisms to indicate appropriate uses, users and behaviors in highly dense and intense residential urban space, as well as to optimize the use of space over time, ranging from laws, rules and restrictions to more inclusive and less intrusive regulatory frameworks.

URBAN SPACE QUALITY

43 Rules and Regulations

What?
Design Principles
* Promote inclusion and prevention through management, regulations and provision.
* Employ ways to encourage users' participation in space management.

Good public space promotes inclusion and prevention through management, regulations and provision, rather than the exclusion of unwanted behaviors through restrictions of people, animals and activities, unless they target realistic risks and dangers. Users' participation in space management through education, voluntary job opportunities and community cleaning, for example, is highly desirable, as it enhances a sense of attachment and belonging.

Why?
* Social inclusiveness increases the vitality and safety of public spaces (Carmona, 2010a).
* An equal and inclusive environment contributes to a more democratic and tolerant society (CABE, 2008).
* Users' participation develops a greater sense of ownership and belonging of community and local democracy; it increases social interaction while reducing social conflict (McIndoe et al., 2005).

How?
Design Measures and Considerations
* Limit the number of restrictions to necessary and reasonable ones.
* Regulate spatial uses and behaviors, rather than simply restricting or eliminating them, by providing spaces for animals, smokers, potentially conflicting activities (such as playing with balls and other requisites, or skateboarding, etc.).
* Employ strategies for users' participation in space management, especially in designated communal spaces.

Reference to Good Practices

RULES AND REGULATIONS: Certain rules and regulations, and sometimes restrictions and prohibitions, are reasonable, as they prevent physical injuries, and ensure hygiene and safety for all users of public space. Clearly marked rules and restrictions prevent undesirable behavior, as in *Pinnacle at Duxton*, Singapore (Figure 2.140a, top). However, too many of such restrictions may make the public space feel uninviting and aggressive, as in *Qianmen Street* in Beijing, for instance (Figure 2.140b, bottom). Regulations, on the other hand, not only restrict but also invite certain activities.

USERS' PARTICIPATION IN MANAGEMENT ACTIVITIES: Volunteering activities, such as tour guiding, greeting, assistance in gardening, event management or cleaning and promotion through photography are only some of the ways to facilitate users' participation in management and maintenance of the **High Line Park** in New York (Figure 2.141).

URBAN SPACE QUALITY

44 Access Regulation and Management

What?
Design Principles:
- Allow partial 24-hour access to space (passing through).
- Allow 24-hour access and use.

Access for all is what guarantees the free spatial and temporal circulation of persons and goods in a public space, and is one of the main indicators of its levels of openness, "publicness" and

inclusiveness. Inclusive public spaces are ideally characterized by four mutually supportive qualities of access that should also be understood in relation to the temporal dimension, namely physical access, social or symbolic access, access to activities and access to information (Akkar, 2004). However, such ideal inclusive qualities are rarely attained in practice.

Allowing segments of space or the entire space to be accessible 24 hours for passing through or for any other public use is crucial in the process of negotiation over space use, especially in the context of high-density environments. Various contemporary examples of privately owned public spaces challenge the legal and normative conventions about the openness and accessibility of public space.

Why?

- 24-hour access extends the use of public space, and generates urban life and activities of surrounding buildings (Shaftoe, 2008).
- 24-hour access promotes non-restricted movement during night-time and may have economic outcomes.

How?

Design Measures and Considerations

- Provide adequate lighting to enhance visibility and safety during late hours.
- If possible, provide adjacent 24-hour use (such as night bars or 24-hour stores).
- Consider specific regulations and design measures for late night use, due to potential negative outcomes, such as noise, littering, violence, etc.

Reference to Good Practices

24-HOUR ACCESS: 24-hour accessible passages allow safe connection and movement during night-time, although the surroundings may not offer any night-time activities. Twenty-four-hour access through privately owned public space developments, such as ***Skypark at VivoCity*** in Singapore (Figure 2.142), further challenges the common understanding of "publicness."

LATE NIGHT USE: *Clarke Quay* in Singapore (Figure 2.143) is a setting that allows and encourages late night use, without imposing any restrictions or loud sound control.

URBAN SPACE QUALITY

45 Time and Program Regulation and Management

What?
Design Principles
- Provide means for occasional events.
- Facilitate regular events.

Urban spaces have always been venues of important social events, such as cultural and political gatherings, festivals, celebrations, markets and exhibitions, among others. Setting and supporting occasional and regular programs of events, with adequate safety and use regulations, make urban spaces livelier and more attractive, with a capacity to strengthen the identity of the community.

Accommodating multiple uses for different user groups also brings challenges and the designers must consider the ways in which such different users would share the space and how such various uses would affect the areas surrounding urban space (Carr et al., 1992). Rather than causing tensions among different user groups, the design of urban space should foster their peaceful

coexistence (Loukaitou-Sideris, 1996). Careful planning for specific activities and specific user groups at different times has the ability to resolve such a time management issue.

Why?
- Regular cultural and entertainment programs encourage people to visit, use and linger in urban spaces (Carmona et al., 2003).
- Occasional events invite positive density and intensity in urban life, activate economic activities in surrounding buildings and may contribute to the temporary identity of urban space (Shaftoe, 2008).

How?
Design Measures and Considerations
- Employ a design that is flexible in adopting different programs and capacities (Brand, 1994; Shaftoe, 2008).
- Provide means and human resources to facilitate events.
- Overlap activities to maximize the use of space over time and to cater to different age, ethnic and gender user groups.

Reference to Good Practices

OCCASIONAL EVENTS: *Schouwburgplein* in Rotterdam (Figure 2.144) is a large, adaptable space that provides means for managing and facilitating various occasional and regular events.

OCCASIONAL EVENTS: The *High Line Park* in New York (Figure 2.145) offers a series of regular and occasional programs, events and workshops related to arts, history, culture, design and nature, involving a number of volunteers.

REGULAR EVENTS: Regular events, such as the weekly flea markets, make *SCAPE Event Space* in Singapore (Figure 2.146) a regular destination for youth, enabling them to showcase their creativity.

URBAN SPACE QUALITY

46 Permissions and Management

What?
Design Principles
- Permit, manage and facilitate non-designed activities.
- Allow informal activities without permission.

Lefebvre's phrase "the right to the city" (Lefebvre, 1968) captures people's basic rights not only of physical access to public spaces but also of the rights for spontaneous gatherings and interaction, including political participation.

Good urban spaces not only allow programmed activities but also permit spontaneous non-designed uses at any time of the day, with or without providing adequate permissions or imposing a fee and other regulatory measures, including limiting numbers of users, regulating late night activities, occasional private events and political gatherings, etc. In ideally democratic public spaces such informal activities are allowed without any permission or strict regulations. However, this is very rare, if not completely nonexistent, in practice.

Perhaps the "terrain vague," term coined by the architect Manuel de Solà-Morales (1992), possesses the characteristics that are the closest to this condition of "ideal and liberating democracy." "Terrain vague" refers to almost forgotten, seemingly obsolete or dysfunctional sites that punctuate the otherwise cohesive and over-designed urban tissue. Offering room for spontaneous, creative appropriation and informal uses that would otherwise have trouble finding a place in public spaces subjected increasingly to the demands of commerce, the "terrain vague" allows certain resistance to emerge, creating alternative ways of experiencing the city. The idea is not to favor the temporary or unplanned over the permanent and planned, but to aim for an active amalgamation of heterogeneous components that broaden the terms of the urban experience. Similarly, Franck and Stevens (2007) recognize "loose spaces" that confront the aesthetically and behaviorally over-controlled and homogeneous environments of leisure and consumption that have lost any sense of unpredictability and surprise. "Loose spaces" allow for the chance, the spontaneous and the discovery of the unexpected.

Why?
- Non-designed activities bring alternative cultures and plural temporary identities to urban spaces.
- Non-designed activities invite diverse user groups and encourage social interaction (Gehl, 1996; Shaftoe, 2008).
- Informal use of space and flexible regulation animate public space and increase intensity of space (Carmona et al., 2003; Shaftoe, 2008).

How?
Design Measures and Considerations
- Provide adequate, flexible spaces and amenities (such as informal seating, shade, lighting, etc.) to stage different informal activities at different times of the day.
- Consider specific regulations related to late night use or capacity, when necessary.

Reference to Good Practices

NEGOTIATED SPACE: Imposed rules of an underground passage in Singapore, *Esplanade Underpass Square* (Figure 2.147a, top), are negotiated by youth. Non-designed creative activities performed by break-dancers, jugglers and skateboarders, among other user groups, bring life to otherwise empty and underused large spaces during weekends and late at night, and attract considerable audiences. Similar activities occur informally in *Dhoby Ghaut Green* in Singapore (Figure 2.147b, bottom).

URBAN SPACE QUALITY

47 Affordability and Equality

What?
Design Principles
- Provide a variety of public programs, services or facilities that are free of charge.
- All public programs, services or facilities are free of charge.

Commercial events and activities occurring in urban space must not diminish its essentially public and inclusive nature. Events in public spaces should be staged for the public good rather than for private gain. Programs, services and facilities provided in urban space should remain accessible to all users for free, or at affordable prices.

Why?
- Affordable or free cultural and entertainment programs encourage people to visit, use and linger in urban spaces (Carmona et al., 2003), and promote equality (WHO, 2007).
- Equal and inclusive environments contribute to a more democratic and tolerant society (CABE, 2008).
- Inclusive environments are more economically resilient, and socially diverse and vibrant (CABE, 2008).

How?
Design Measures and Considerations
- Consider providing free-of-charge entrance to space, activities and events, free-of-charge seating, public toilets, parking, Wi-Fi, etc.

Reference to Good Practices

REGULAR FREE-OF-CHARGE EVENTS: An outdoor theater designated for regular entertainment events and performances at the **Esplanade Promenade** in Singapore (Figure 2.148) attracts a number of passers-by and increases the livability of this urban space and its surroundings. All events are free of charge for all visitors. When there are no events going on, this sheltered space is used as an attractive social node.

AFFORDABLE AND FREE-OF-CHARGE ACTIVITIES: The sky bridge at *Pinnacle at Duxton* in Singapore (Figure 2.149a, top) is accessible by the public at affordable prices. A limited number of free tickets is provided to its residents. For special events, such as watching the New Year's Eve's fireworks, a bidding system is established that awards free tickets to 200 visitors, due to the limited capacity of the space. *Bryant Park* in New York (Figure 2.149b, bottom) provides a number of game and sports amenities for users for free, depending on the weather conditions and the event calendar. Some of the amenities are chess, backgammon and ping-pong tables, and mini-golf courses.

ORGWARE **QUALITIES OF URBAN SPACE: AN EXAMPLE**

DANGDAI MOMA (LINKED HYBRID), BEIJING, CHINA

Intensified Residential Development

Project Information
Client: Modern Green Development Co., Ltd., Beijing.
Architects: Steven Holl Architects.
General Contractor: Beijing Construction Engineering Group.

Project Brief
Primary Use: Residential.
Adjacent Use: Recreational, Commercial/Retail, Event Space, Educational, Art & Culture.

2.150 Dangdai Moma, Beijing, China.

Urban Space
Site Area: 59,300m².
Urban Space Area: 61 percent.
Gross Plot Ratio (GPR): 3.73.
Gross Floor Area (GFA): 221,000m².
Building Height: 73.5m.

400m Radius Context
Open Space: 85 percent.
Gross Plot Ratio (GPR): 2.10.
Gross Floor Area (GFA): 1,055,040m².

Project Description
Dangdai Moma, also known as "Linked Hybrid," is an integrated residential development in Beijing, designed by Steven Holl Architects. It became famous for its unusual aesthetics and sky bridges, and is particularly acclaimed for its integration of geothermal energy for cooling or heating. The design aims to promote interaction through its porous and generous urban public space around, within and above the development. Through a mix of commercial, educational, residential and recreational uses at different levels, it aims to bring in people from the surrounding areas and to generate a micro-urbanism that would be in contrast with the dominating privatized urban developments in China. The sky bridge is a unique ring of bridges and public spaces that links all the eight residential towers together, from the twelfth to the eighteenth floors. The sky lounge programs include bar, restaurant, gallery,

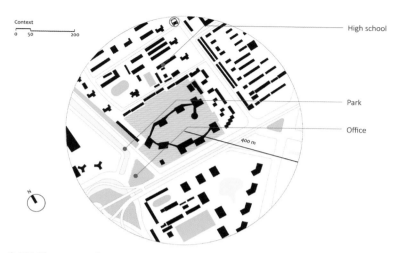

2.151 The surrounding context (400m radius).

Context
0 50 200

High school

Park

Office

400 m

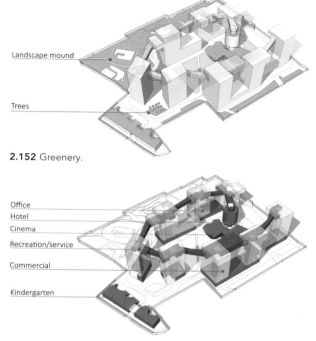

Landscape mound

Trees

2.152 Greenery.

Office
Hotel
Cinema
Recreation/service
Commercial
Kindergarten

2.153 Programs within urban space.

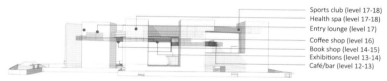

Sports club (level 17-18)
Health spa (level 17-18)
Entry lounge (level 17)
Coffee shop (level 16)
Book shop (level 14-15)
Exhibitions (level 13-14)
Café/bar (level 12-13)

2.155 Programs within elevated urban space.

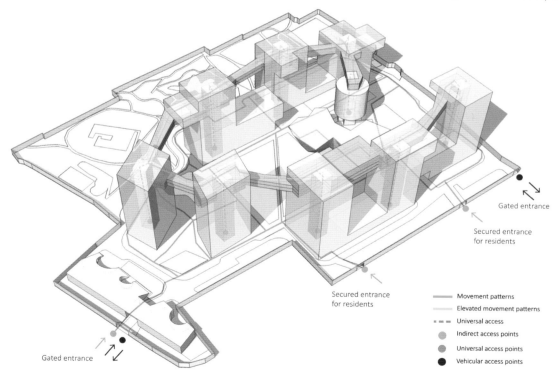

2.154 Accessibility and connectivity.

Gated entrance

Secured entrance
for residents

Secured entrance
for residents

Gated entrance

—— Movement patterns
—— Elevated movement patterns
- - - Universal access
● Indirect access points
● Universal access points
● Vehicular access points

bookstore, lounge, swimming pool, sauna, gym, spa and shops. The development is spread over the site area of 59,300m² and has high built density, with Gross Plot Ratio (GPR): 3.73. Although not entirely successful in practice, Dangdai Moma represents an example of emerging hybrid gated communities which are partially open to the general public, with innovative spatial typology.

In the following example of evaluation, • refers to the criteria (design principles) that are met by this urban space, while o marks those criteria that are not met.

ORGWARE

K Provision of Amenities, Services, Public Facilities and Infrastructure

37 Hygiene Facilities

- The publicly accessible space of Dangdai Moma is clean and well maintained by the development's management (Figure 2.156).
- The development provides a fair amount of trash cans (Figure 2.157) and public toilets to support cleanliness and good maintenance. In addition, grey water from all apartments is recycled and reused for irrigation, toilet flushing and water ponds provided at ground level.

38 Lighting

- The main pathways and activity nodes are well lit to ensure good lighting levels at night.
- The urban space employs ambient lights which, in synergy with the colorful façades and bridges, create a unique and attractive atmosphere during the evening hours.

39 Informational Facilities

- A gallery at the bridge level with the physical model of the entire development serves to inform the residents and visitors about its unique design (Figure 2.159).
- In addition, the development provides good signage and way-finding facilities.

40 Healthcare and Social Services

- o No general healthcare service is provided within the development or in walkable distance.
- o No affordable public social services are available on site or in its vicinity, except for a private Montessori school and kindergarten.

L Safety and Security

41 Safety and Image

- The design of urban space employs adequate measures to prevent physical injuries, including ramps and fences at all critical points. Motorized vehicles are only allowed around the development (Figure 2.158).
- o The urban space itself is attractive, with active and porous edges (Figures 2.160 and 2.161). However, while there is a general feeling of safety due to fences around the development and the presence of security guards at the main gate, the space does not appear very welcoming to the general public.

Note: In comparison, Dangdai Moma's "twin sister" in Chengdu, Sliced Porosity Block or Raffles City, also designed by Steven Holl, provides a more inviting setting. An elevated podium public space in the middle of this mixed-use residential development is accessible from street level and through the shopping mall beneath, and appears cozier and more user-friendly (Figures 2.162 and 2.163).

42 Security

- The security guards are present at the main gate and the entire development is under surveillance (Figures 2.164 and 2.165).
- o However, security gates, guards and CCTV surveillance are somewhat aggressive security measures that make the space over-controlled.

Note: Sliced Porosity Block in Chengdu also employs high security measures, including security patrols and surveillance cameras (Figure 2.166). However, the absence of gates at the three entrances to urban space makes it appear more approachable. In addition, positioned as it is in the middle of the development, urban space encourages self-surveillance from the adjacent residential blocks (Figure 2.167).

M Management and Regulations

43 Rules and Regulations

- o The urban space employs a number of restriction measures to control unwanted behaviors, activities and user groups.
- o Space does not clearly encourage active users' participation in space management.

Note: Sliced Porosity Block in Chengdu also employs rules and restrictions, but in a somewhat less intrusive manner. The public space is used intensively, especially during weekends (Figure 2.169). Among other user groups, one can at the same time see elderly men sleeping on available benches and even groups of teenagers drinking beer, which are activities often marked as unwanted and, thus, excluded. It seems that Holl's concept of porous "micro-urbanism" finds its more comprehensive implementation in this project, in comparison to *Dangdai Moma* complex.

44 Access Regulation and Management

- o Accessibility to Dangdai Moma is heavily reduced due to only one gate being manned by security guards and is limited to working hours of public programs and services available (Figures 2.159 and 2.172). The park is limited to residents' use only and is controlled electronically by the residents' cards (Figure 2.171).

○ The urban space is not accessible by the general public at night.

Note: Public elevated plazas of the Sliced Porosity Block are loosely connected to the street level on three sides of the block and are accessible 24 hours, also supported by the presence of a hotel in one of the blocks. In addition, the attractive lighting installations, one of the highlights of this project, support and encourage late evening activities.

45 Time and Program Regulation and Management

○ Except for indoor gallery spaces, the development is not a setting for occasional public events.
○ There are no regular public events staged in Dangdai Moma.

Note: The Light Pavilion at the Sliced Porosity Block is used as a setting for light shows, including displays for traditional Chinese festivals (Figure 2.170).

46 Permissions and Management

○ Dangdai Moma does not support or manage informal gatherings and events.
○ Activities are strictly regulated.

Note: Some informal activities are present at the Sliced Porosity Block. However, larger gatherings and events are arranged by the management team and need appropriate permissions.

47 Affordability and Equality

• Most of the public facilities can be used free of charge by all social groups.
○ Some spaces and services are restricted to residents only or an entrance fee is charged.

Note: Public areas and available facilities at the *Sliced Porosity Block* are used free of charge. Some additional services and commercial uses charge a fee.

2.156 Clean and well-maintained water pond and public space (Dangdai Moma).

2.157 Available trash bins next to water pond (Dangdai Moma).

2.159 Gallery space at the bridge level (Dangdai Moma).

2.158 Motorized vehicles allowed around the development only (Dangdai Moma).

2.160 Visual porosity (Dangdai Moma).

2.161 Central public space (Dangdai Moma).

2.162 Main entrance (Sliced Porosity Block).

2.163 Access to public podium via shopping mall (Sliced Porosity Block).

2.164 Approaching Dangdai Moma.

2.165 Security gate (Dangdai Moma).

2.166 Security patrol (Sliced Porosity Block).

2.167 Central urban space (Sliced Porosity Block).

2.168 Central green plaza (Sliced Porosity Block).

2.169 Relaxing next to water (Sliced Porosity Block).

2.172 Café (Dangdai Moma).

2.171 Residents' park (Dangdai Moma).

2.170 Part of light installation: daytime (Sliced Porosity Block).

QUALITIES OF URBAN SPACE: AN EXAMPLE OF FULL ANALYSIS

TREELODGE@PUNGGOL, SINGAPORE

Intensified Residential Development

Project Information
Client: HDB (Housing and Development Board, Singapore).
Architects: Surbana Corporation Pte. Ltd.
General Contractor: Kay Lim Construction & Trading Pte. Ltd.

Project Brief
Primary Use: Residential.
Adjacent Use: Recreational, Commercial, Educational, Religious.

2.173 Aerial view of Treelodge@Punggol, Singapore.

Urban Space
Site Area: 29,500m².
Urban Space Area: 46 percent.
Gross Plot Ratio (GPR): 3.16.
Gross Floor Area (GFA): 93,276m².
Building Height: Max. 248m.

400m Radius Context
Open Space: 83 percent.
Gross Plot Ratio (GPR): 1.68.
Gross Floor Area (GFA): 844,670m².

Project Description
Treelodge@Punggol (previously known as Treetops@Punggol) is Singapore's First Green Mark Platinum Award Public Housing Project. The eco-precinct was launched in March 2007 under the Build-To-Order (BTO) HDB (Housing and Development Board) Scheme (a responsive system that offers flexibility for flat buyers in terms of choice of preferred location and timing). It was completed in 2010. This public housing development is located in Punggol New Town, close to Punggol MRT/LRT Station, Damai LRT Station and the Punggol Bus Interchange. This eco-precinct comprises seven residential 16-storey building blocks with a total of 712 dwelling units. The Treelodge@Punggol received a number of local and international awards for its green and sustainable design, including the Green Good Design Award in 2010, the Chicago Athenaeum International Architecture Award in 2010 and the Futurac Green Leadership award in 2011.

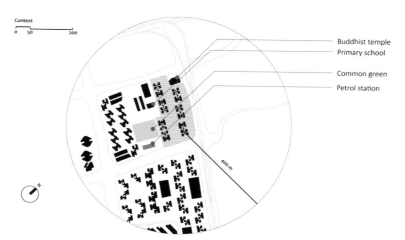

2.174 Surrounding context (400m radius).

Buddhist temple
Primary school
Common green
Petrol station

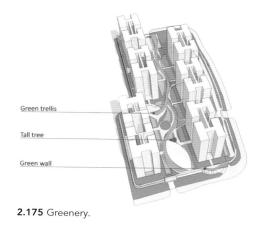

2.175 Greenery.

Green trellis
Tall tree
Green wall

Fitness corner
Community facilities
Jogging path
Playgrounds
Community garden
Pavilions

2.176 Programs within and around urban space.

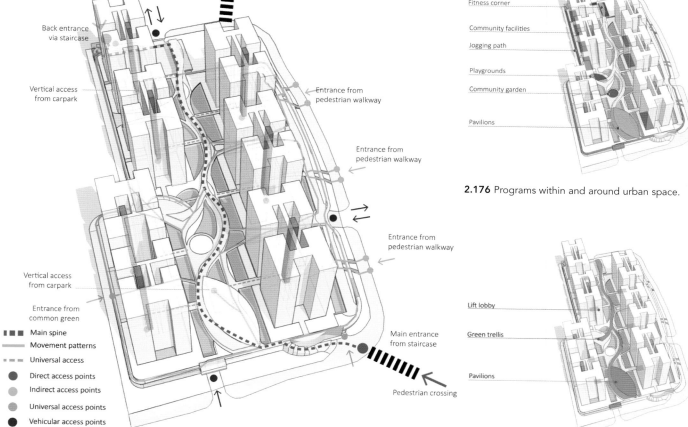

Pedestrian crossing
Back entrance via staircase
Vertical access from carpark
Entrance from pedestrian walkway
Entrance from pedestrian walkway
Entrance from pedestrian walkway
Vertical access from carpark
Entrance from common green

- Main spine
- Movement patterns
- Universal access
- Direct access points
- Indirect access points
- Universal access points
- Vehicular access points

Main entrance from staircase
Pedestrian crossing

2.178 Accessibility and connectivity.

Lift lobby
Green trellis
Pavilions

2.177 Weather protection.

It has a podium car park, and generous provision of green spaces at the elevated precinct level. The development itself provides recreational facilities for its residents, including a sheltered space for mass gatherings (precinct pavilion), seating amenities, a community garden, a children's playground, an exercise station for the elderly and an elevated jogging path around the block. Other facilities, such as a primary school, Chinese temple, petrol station with convenience store and common green area, are situated in the development's immediate surroundings. The entire development covers a total area of 2.95 hectares and has a GPR of 3.16.

In the following examples of evaluation, • refers to the criteria (design principles) that are met by this urban space, while ○ marks those criteria that are not met.

HARDWARE

A Accessibility
1 Pedestrian Access Points
- Elevated urban space is accessible via 10 vertical access points (by foot) from the main ground road level (Figure 2.178).
- The main access points are well distinguished by monumental stairs and ramps, while additional access leads through the car park immediately beneath the elevated public space podium (Figures 2.179, 2.180 and 2.182).

2 Universal Access
- In addition to staircases, space provides ramps and elevators as alternative means of universal access (Figures 2.181 and 2.183). However, the connection between the ground level and the elevated level within the urban space is limited to elevators only. The elevators are hidden in the car park area, which reduces visibility and overall ease of access for the disadvantaged user groups.
- Four universal access points are available within the development (Figure 2.178).

3 Type and Distribution of Universal Access
- Space provides two types of universal access, namely ramps (from the street level and throughout the space when level changes occur) and elevators (from the car park beneath the elevated public space platform) (Figure 2.183).
- Universal access points are evenly distributed across the development.

4 Prioritizing Pedestrians
- A large number of safe and well-marked pedestrian crossings are available around the development (Figure 2.178).
- Vehicular traffic is clearly separated from pedestrian traffic. The car park is located beneath the main fully pedestrianized level. Vehicular entrance to the car park itself is well marked for the ease and safety of pedestrian movement (Figures 2.184 and 2.185).

B Connectivity
5 Movement Patterns
- ○ Although connected to the surrounding roads, this elevated urban space seems to be somewhat isolated. Direct access is provided via staircases only and the space does not lead to major urban nodes in its surroundings.

- The development has well-interconnected internal pathways leading to key activity nodes on site (Figure 2.186).

6 Node Connectivity
- ○ Urban space does not support transient activities. As a result, it is not used as a connecting space between the activity nodes in its immediate surroundings.
- ○ The facilities for long-term activities (such as precinct pavilion, children's playground and elderly fitness corner) attract residents only and do not make this urban space an important public space destination for the larger urban context.

7 Sightlines and Way-finding
- Urban space provides relatively good visibility of horizontal and vertical directions within the development.
- ○ However, the main entrance and exit points are not fully visible from all areas within the development, which reduces its way-finding performance.

C Mobility Means
8 Bicycle-friendly Design
- Space provides a large amount of bicycle parking facilities within the car park area at the ground level of the development.
- ○ However, cycling is not allowed within the development.

9 Public Transport
- The development is located in close proximity (within 400m walking distance) to public transportation (Figure 2.174).
- Two public transportation modes are available, namely buses and trains, which increases users' choice and convenience.

10 Vehicular Access
- A sufficient number of parking facilities are provided within the development, including those with wheelchair access.
- Parking facilities are well integrated within the development, without creating conflict with pedestrian movement (Figures 2.184 and 2.185).

11 Drop-offs and Taxi Stands
- The development provides sheltered lobbies for safe drop-offs.
- ○ There are no designated taxi stands in the surrounding areas.

D Legibility and Edges
12 Spatial Layout
- Urban space has a clear layout. Major pedestrian space is located in the middle of the development, while the jogging lane traverses around the residential block (Figures 2.173, 2.178 and 2.186). The pedestrian network is visible and clearly

differentiated from the spatial nodes designed for more static and space-defined activities (Figure 2.188).

- The hierarchy of the pedestrian network is well established. Major and minor pedestrian routes are differentiated through varied widths, shapes, pavement colors and textures, as well as protecting trellises (Figure 2.188).

13 Focal Points of Activity

- The space features a fair distribution of diverse and legible nodes and focal points of activities. Activity nodes include amenities specifically designed for particular activities, such as event and gathering space, children's playground or community garden, among others (Figures 2.176 and 2.187).
- The majority of activity nodes may be seen from the main access points and from central points in urban space.

14 Visual Landmarks

- The precinct pavilion is the obvious visual landmark of the development (Figure 2.189).
- The elevated deck, however, is lacking in clear diversity of additional visual landmarks, possibly due to its moderate scale and somewhat uniform design of amenities.

15 Permeability

- The development provides good visual connections between the inner public space and the immediate surrounding area.
- The majority of the surrounding surfaces at the elevated pedestrian level are porous. The edge is additionally activated by the designated jogging lane and greenery.

E Spatial Variety
16 Spatial Variety

- The main pedestrian space is subtly divided into a number of sub-spaces, mostly associated with various activity nodes provided within the development, creating a variety of experiential settings for users. Low barriers such as fences, plants and benches, shelters and canopies, pavement patterns and textures are some of the elements employed to enhance spatial variety.
- Sub-spaces are subtly differentiated through aesthetic and experiential qualities, such as variation in scale and proportion, types of greenery, colors and materials of the surrounding surfaces, different levels of sunlight exposure, and in such a way evoke the perception of rich variety in spatial quality (Figure 2.191).

17 Spatial Adaptability

- Although relatively small in scale, the precinct pavilion with adjacent uncovered areas is occasionally used to accommodate temporary programs under different weather conditions, such as community events, weddings and funerals.
- The design is lacking in flexible layout and adjustable structural elements to enhance the capacity of creating and changing spatial arrangements, partitioning or enclosure when needed.

F Environmentally Friendly Design
18 Greenery and Water: Availability and Access

- Treelodge@Punggol is well known for its generous and diverse provision of greenery, which is the development's unique feature.
- The variety of greenery creates an inviting and sensory-rich setting that enlivens users' perceptions, comfort and interaction with nature. One such interactive feature is the community garden for communal gardening activities, which also promotes a sense of cohesiveness within the relatively new resident community.

19 Greenery: Form, Pattern and Diversity

- Greenery appears in various forms and patterns throughout the development, including grass patches, planter boxes, green trellises and tall trees.
- Greenery is introduced at all levels of the development, including the elevated eco-deck, roof-tops, façades and selected columns. The "Green Spine," with its green trellises, cuts through the middle of the precinct connecting various amenities, while the 650-meter-long "Green Path" runs around the development. Larger trees are planted at the car park level and grow up through the air wells into the eco-deck. In addition, planter boxes and green balconies are provided in various units, further promoting home gardening and vertical greening (Figures 2.175, 2.190 and 2.192).

20 Biodiversity

- The eco-deck contains a variety of carefully selected local flora species, including low (grass), medium (bushes) and high (trees) greenery. These plants need little sunlight and relatively low maintenance.
- The landscaped urban space is strategically located next to a common green area and in close proximity to the larger green ecosystems, including the nearby Town Park and My Waterway@ Punggol. In such a way, it serves as a green connector and contributes to the biodiversity of the larger region.

21 Environmentally Friendly Strategies

- The enhanced provision of greenery in Treelodge@Punggol contributes to alleviation of the urban heat island effect. Green roofs reduce heat absorption and enhance the comfort of residents (Figure 2.196).

- In addition, the development employs a number of environmentally friendly strategies that are suitable for Singapore's tropical climate, including passive design strategies and energy-efficient technologies to help optimize energy use, water and waste management, and reduce maintenance costs. Energy-saving lights are implemented along the common corridors and in the car park area, while motion sensors are introduced on staircases. Solar panels installed on the roof generate energy used for lift operation and lighting in the eco-deck. Rainwater is collected and used for communal corridor washing and irrigation. This system is designed in such a way that it does not need additional energy use. Each residential block is equipped with a centralized recyclable refuse chute which also helps in waste collection. The playgrounds and their elements are made of recycled materials, plastics, steel and aluminum, and environmentally friendly paints (Figure 2.193).

22 Environmental Integration

- Urban space is sensitively inserted into its context.
- The design integrates unique landscaping features that are appropriate to the context and enhance the natural experience. Besides the green eco-deck, roofs and façades, the development also introduces greenery within the lift lobbies at the car park level, creating landscaped thematic courtyards (Figure 2.194).

G User Comfort

23 Protection from Weather Conditions

- The main pedestrian pathways through the development are appropriately protected from the excessive sun and rain, to support comfortable movement (Figures 2.177 and 2.192).

- The precinct pavilion is a larger covered space that sustains public activities in bad weather conditions, which enhances users' comfort and optimizes the use of space at different times of the day and under different weather conditions (Figures 2.177 and 2.189).

24 Shade and Sunlight

- The space layout is oriented and designed to receive optimum sunlight and to provide a variety of shaded and sunlit conditions to enhance users' choice and comfort. Apart from buildings and hard shelters it employs additional means of soft shading, such as trees and green trellises, which reduce heat and glare.
- The development does not provide flexible or adjustable shading means, such as adjustable umbrellas, and moving or adjustable roofs and canopies.

25 Air Control and Optimization

- The space has good air quality and good ventilation.
- Employing a passive design strategy, the layout of Treelodge@ Punggol is strategically oriented to face northeast and southwest wind directions and maximize natural cross-ventilation. In such a way, a wind tunnel through the central spine of the eco-deck is created, and, together with lush landscaping, it creates a cooler and more conducive built environment (Figure 2.195).

26 Noise Control and Optimization

- Urban space is free from both external and internal noise pollution.
- The aural quality is also sustained through the provision of lush greenery that absorbs environmental noise and thus contributes to creating a quiet environment.

SOFTWARE

H Diversity and Intensity of Use
27 Diversity of Activities: Within Urban Space
- The elevated eco-deck provides amenities for specific active recreational activities for its residents.
- These well-integrated amenities for multi-generational use include a sheltered multi-purpose space for mass gatherings (Figure 2.189), a children's playground (Figure 2.198), an exercise station for the elderly (elderly fitness corner, Figure 2.203), a community garden (Figure 2.190), and a jogging path around the block (Figure 2.197).

28 Choice of Activities: Around Urban Space
- The development is surrounded by a primary school, a Chinese temple, a petrol station with convenience store (Figure 2.202) and a common green, which is a larger recreational area (Figure 2.199).
- However, these activities do not contribute to intensity of use within the precinct. Moreover, direct connections to these activities are not fully established, except for the common green recreational area. However, the current state may not be entirely representative, as Punggol is a relatively new estate and the neighborhood experiences constant transformations and new developments.

I Social Activities
29 Seating Amenities
- Public urban space provides a sufficient amount of formal seating, such as benches at gathering points, lift lobbies and around major activity nodes (Figure 2.200).
- Informal seating amenities are provided in the form of low walls and staircases throughout the development.

30 Seating: Condition and Variety
- Seating amenities are strategically located in either sheltered (or well-shaded) areas, or in spots exposed to sunlight in order to increase the convenience, choice and comfort of residents (Figure 2.200).
- Two types of seating amenities are provided, including benches of different shape and length, with and without backrests, as well as additional low walls for informal seating.

31 Interactivity
- All seating amenities are fixed and made of sturdy materials, which reduces the level of flexibility, adjustability and interaction.
- Except for the children's playground, elderly fitness corner and community garden, the space is lacking in its provision of interactive elements in space, such as interactive sculptures, installations, fountains or interactive displays, built-in games (chess tables, hopscotch, etc.), for instance, to promote greater interaction with space and social interaction among residents.

32 Intimacy and Exposure
- The development provides a variety of seating arrangements to promote different levels of interaction, from passive and solitary seating to inward-looking arrangements for conversations and larger gatherings (Figure 2.201).
- Seating amenities are placed and arranged to offer different levels of intimacy and exposure. Additional soft and permeable barriers in the form of low walls, fences and greenery help create niches and reduce exposure.

J Identity (Image and Character)
33 Imageability
- The place has distinctive and memorable physical and natural features that distinguish it from the larger surrounding context and other developments of similar type.
- The urban space does not possess characteristics that are well known to a larger public.

34 History and Symbolic Value
- Recently built, the development does not have traces of historical and cultural heritage, except for a Chinese temple in its vicinity.
- Design of the development does not have elements that associate it with local history and culture.

35 Art, Culture and Alternative Culture
- The development does not provide any art- and culture-related programs.
- While catering to local residents, the urban space does not clearly cater to any particular subculture.

36 Unique Nature
- The extensive greenery is a unique and memorable feature of Treelodge@Punggol.
- Landscape design does not have strong links to preservation, history or religion.

ORGWARE

K Provision of Amenities, Services, Public Facilities and Infrastructure

37 Hygiene Facilities

- Space is clean and kept in good physical condition.
- The development provides facilities that encourage and support good maintenance, such as trash bins (Figure 2.204) and water supply for cleaning communal areas and watering plants.

38 Lighting

- Adequate lighting is provided along the main pathways and activity nodes to ensure good lighting levels at night.
- Space is well equipped by the ambient and sensor lights on staircases that are activated by users when needed.

39 Informational Facilities

- The development provides boards that inform users about the unique features of its design and environmental performance (Figure 2.209).
- Good signage, way-finding and other informational facilities are available within the development.

40 Healthcare and Social Services

- o No general healthcare service is provided within the development or in walkable distance.
- Social services, such as childcare, student care centers and residents' committees, are available within its vicinity.

L Safety and Security

41 Safety and Image

- The design of urban space employs adequate measures to prevent physical injuries and promote safety. Being an elevated space, these measures primarily include adequate fences at all critical points, such as staircases, ramps and holes, and providing natural lighting to car park areas beneath the public space (Figure 2.208).
- Urban space avoids tall, opaque surfaces and, with lush greenery, good lighting and no traces of vandalism, it represents an inviting and approachable setting that enhances the perception of safety.

42 Security

- o The development does not provide obvious security measures, apart from self-surveillance.
- o No additional security measures are provided.

M Management and Regulations

43 Rules and Regulations

- Urban space promotes inclusion through regulations and provisions, rather than restriction and exclusion of unwanted behaviors, activities or user groups. Some activities, such as playing football or cycling, are not allowed (Figures 2.205 and 2.206).
- Urban space encourages environmental awareness, environmentally friendly behavior and self-regulation, through the provision of adequate and accessible amenities and overlapping activities (Figure 2.207).

44 Access Regulation and Management

- There are no restrictions for accessing the eco-deck 24 hours for either passing through or any other public use.
- Good lighting generally supports quiet night activities.

45 Time and Program Regulation and Management

- o The development does not manage occasional events, even though it is sometimes visited as the first eco-precinct in Punggol.
- o There are no regular events facilitated in Treelodge@Punggol.

46 Permissions and Management

- Urban space is open to all users and for various kinds of safe public activities with adequate permissions and proper self-regulation.
- o The development does not promote or allow informal activities without permission.

47 Affordability and Equality

- Space provides a variety of public amenities, services and facilities that can be used free of charge by all social groups.
- All available services and facilities may be used free of charge by everyone.

2.179 Main pedestrian access to elevated space.

2.180 Additional access.

2.182 Access from car park level.

2.181 Wheelchair-accessible setting.

2.183 Lifts at housing blocks.

2.184 Vehicular access.

2.185 Fully pedestrianized space.

2.186 Interconnected pathways.

2.188 Hierarchy of pedestrian network enhanced by trellises.

2.187 Focal points of activity.

2.189 Precinct pavilion: visual landmark.

2.191 Sub-spaces differentiated by pavement and greenery.

2.190 Interaction with greenery: community garden.

2.192 Green spine trellises.

2.197 Green path: jogging lane.

2.196 Green roofs.

2.193 Playground made of recycled materials.

2.194 Green car park.

2.195 Design based on air flow studies.

2.198 Children's playground.

2.199 Surrounding functions: common green recreational area.

2.203 Elderly fitness corner.

2.200 Fixed benches.

2.202 Surrounding functions: petrol station.

2.201 Inward-looking seating arrangement.

2.204 Trash bins positioned at convenient locations.

2.205 Restrictions.

2.209 Info-boards about the unique design features of Treelodge@ Punggol.

2.206 Regulations: dogs allowed with proper care.

2.208 Safety measures: fences positioned at critical points.

2.207 Regulations: encouragement of environmentally conscious behavior.

NOTES

1 In the original research, "design principles" were named as "criteria" which have an intrinsic positive value, with the aim of both describing and positively assessing urban spaces.

2 See http://www.pps.org/great_public_spaces/one?public_place_id=918&type_id=2.

REFERENCES

Aderamo, A. J., & Aina, O. A. (2011). Spatial Inequalities in Accessibility to Social Amenities in Developing Countries: A Case from Nigeria. *Australian Journal of Basic and Applied Sciences, 5*(6), 316–322. Retrieved from: http://ajbasweb.com/old/ajbas/2011/june-2011/316-322.pdf.

Akkar, M. (2004). New-generation Public Spaces—How "Inclusive" Are They? Paper presented at the OPENSpace—People Space Conference, Edinburgh, Scotland. Retrieved from: http://www.openspace.eca.ed.ac.uk/conference/proceedings/PDF/Akkar.pdf.

Alberti, M., Marzluff, J. M., Shulenberger, E., Bradley, G., Ryan, C., & Zumbrunnen, C. (2003). Integrating Humans into Ecology: Opportunities and Challenges for Studying Urban Ecosystems. *BioScience, 53*(12), 1169–1179.

Alexander, C. (1965). A City is Not a Tree. *Architectural Forum, 122*(1), 58–62.

Alexander, C., Ishikawa, S., & Silverstein, M. (1977). *A Pattern Language.* New York: Oxford University Press.

Alexander, C., Neis, H., & Anninou, A. (1987). *A New Theory of Urban Design.* New York: Oxford University Press.

Amin, A. (2002). Ethnicity and the Multicultural City: Living with Diversity. *Environment and Planning A, 34*(6), 959–980. doi:10.1068/a3537.

Andersen, L. B., Schnohr, P., Schroll, M., & Hein, H. O. (2000). All-cause Mortality Associated with Physical Activity During Leisure Time, Work, Sports, and Cycling to Work. *Archives of International Medicine, 160*(11), 1621–1628.

Bacon, E. (1974). *Design of Cities.* London: Thames & Hudson.

Benedict, M. A., & Macmahon, E. T. (2002). *Green Infrastructure: Smart Conservation for the 21st Century.* Washington, DC: Sprawl Watch Clearing Monograph Series. Retrieved from: http://www.sprawlwatch.org/greeninfrastructure.pdf.

Bentley, I., Alcock, A., Murrain, P., McGlynn, S., & Smith, G. (1985). *Responsive Environments: A Manual for Designers.* London: Architectural Press.

Bhagat, R. B. (2010). Access to Basic Amenities in Urban Areas by Size Class of Cities and Towns in India. International Institute for Population Sciences, Mumbai-400088.

Boo, C. M., Omar-Hor, K., & Ou-Yang, C. L. (2006). *1001 Garden Plants in Singapore* (2nd edn). Singapore: National Parks Board.

Bourdieu, P. (1990). *The Logic of Practice.* Cambridge: Polity Press.

Boyd, R. (2006). The Value of Civility? *Urban Studies, 43*(5/6), 863–878. doi:10.1080/00420980600676105.

Brain, D. (2005). From Good Neighbours to Sustainable Cities: Social Science and the Social Agenda of New Urbanism. *International Regional Science Review, 28*(2), 217–238.

Bramley, G., & Power, S. (2009). Urban Form and Social Sustainability: The Role of Density and Housing Type. *Environment and Planning B: Planning and Design, 36*(1), 30–48. doi:10.1068/b33129.

Brand, S. (1994). *How Buildings Learn: What Happens After They're Built.* New York: Viking/Penguin.

Buchanan, P. (1988). What City? A Plea for Place in the Public Realm. *Architectural Review, 1101* (November), 31–41.

CABE. (2004). *The Value of Public Space—How High Quality Parks and Public Spaces Create Economic, Social and Environmental Value.* CABE.

Retrieved from: https://www.designcouncil.org.uk/sites/default/files/asset/document/the-value-of-public-space.pdf.

CABE. (2008). *Inclusion by Design: Equality, Diversity and the Built Environment.* London: Commission for Architecture and the Built Environment.

CABE. (2010). *Community Green: Using Local Spaces to Tackle Inequality and Improve Health.* London: Commission for Architecture and the Built Environment.

CABE, & DETR. (2001). *The Value of Urban Design.* London: Commission for Architecture and the Built Environment. Retrieved from: http://webarchive.nationalarchives.gov.uk/20110118095356/http://www.cabe.org.uk/files/the-value-of-urban-design.pdf.

Canter, D. (1977). *The Psychology of Place.* London: Architectural Press.

Carmona, M. (2010a). Contemporary Public Space: Critique and Classification, Part One: Critique. *Journal of Urban Design, 15*(1), 125–150. doi:10.1080/13574800903435651.

Carmona, M. (2010b). Contemporary Public Space, Part Two: Classification. *Journal of Urban Design, 15*(2), 265–281. doi:10.1080/13574801003638111.

Carmona, M., & De Magalhães, C. (2008). *Public Space: The Management Dimension.* London: Routledge.

Carmona, M., Heath, T., Oc, T., & Tiesdell, S. (2003). *Public Places Urban Spaces: The Dimensions of Urban Design.* London: Architectural Press.

Carmona, M., Tiesdell, S., Heath, T., & Oc, T. (2010). *Public Places Urban Spaces: The Dimensions of Urban Design* (2nd edn). London: Architectural Press.

Carr, S., Francis, M., Rivlin, L. G., & Stone, A. M. (1992). *Public Space.* Cambridge, England; New York: Cambridge University Press.

Casey, E. S. (2001). Body, Self, and Landscape: A Geophilosophical Inquiry into the Place-World. In P. C. Adams, S. Hoelscher & K. E. Till (eds), *Textures of Place: Exploring Humanist Geographies* (pp. 403–425). Minneapolis: University of Minnesota Press.

Chan, E. H. W., & Lee, G. K. L. (2007). Critical Factors for Improving Social Sustainability of Urban Renewal Projects. *Social Indicators Research: An International and Interdisciplinary Journal for Quality-of-Life Measurement.* doi:10.1007/s11205-007-9089-3.

Chapman, D. (2011). Engaging Places: Localizing Urban Design and Development Planning. *Journal of Urban Design, 16*(4), 511–530. doi:10.1080/13574809.2011.585840.

Childs, M. C. (2004). *Squares: A Public Place Design Guide for Urbanists.* Albuquerque: University of New Mexico Press.

City of New York. (2010). *Active Design Guideline: Promoting Physical Activity and Health in Design.* Retrieved from: http://centerforactivedesign.org/dl/guidelines.pdf.

Cohen, A. K. (1996). A General Theory of Subcultures. In K. Gelder & S. Thornton (eds), *The Subcultures Reader* (pp. 44–54). New York: Routledge.

Connery, K. (2009). Biodiversity and Urban Design: Seeking an Integrated Solution. *Journal of Green Building, 4*(2), 23–38.

Corbett, J., & Corbett, M. (2000). *Designing Sustainable Communities: Learning from Village Homes.* Canada: Island Press.

Crang, M. (1998). *Cultural Geography.* London; New York: Routledge.

Cullen, G. (1961). *Townscape.* London: Architectural Press.

Cullen, G. (1968). *Notation: The Observant Layman's Code for his Environment.* London: Alcan.

Day, C. (2002). *Spirit & Place: Healing Our Environment, Healing Environment.* Oxford; Woburn, MA: Architectural Press.

De Magalhães, C. (2010). Public Space and the Contracting-out of Publicness: A Framework for Analysis. *Journal of Urban Design, 15*(4), 559–574. doi:10.1080/13574809.2010.502347.

De Solà-Morales, M. (1992). Public and Collective Space: The Urbanisation of the Private Domain as a New Challenge. In K. Frempton (ed.), *A Matter of Things* (pp. 17–30). Reprint. Rotterdam: NAi Publishers.

Dempsey, N., Bramley, G., Power, P., & Brown, C. (2011). The Social Dimension of Sustainable Development: Defining Urban Social Sustainability. *Sustainable Development, 19*, 289–300.

Development and Building Control Division. (2011). *Code of Practice on Vehicle Parking Provision in Development Proposals*. Singapore: Land Transport Authority. Retrieved from: http://www.lta.gov.sg/content/dam/ltaweb/corp/Industry/files/VPCOP2011.pdf.

DfT. (2007). *Manual for Streets*. London: Thomas Telford Publishing. Retrieved from: http://www.dft.gov.uk/pgr/sustainable/manforstreets/.

Dietz, T., Dolšak, N. E., Ostrom, E., & Stern, P. C. (2002). The Drama of the Commons. In E. Ostrom, T. Dietz, N. Dolšak, P. C. Stern, S. Stronich, & E. U. Weber (eds), *The Drama of the Commons* (pp. 3–35). Washington, DC: National Academy Press.

Dittmar, H., & Ohland, G. (2003). *The New Transit Town: Best Practices in Transit-oriented Development*. Washington, DC: Island Press.

Felson, A. J., & Pollak, L. (2010). Situating Urban Ecological Experiments in Public Space. In M. Mostafavi with G. Doherty (eds), *Ecological Urbanism* (pp. 356–363). Baden, Switzerland: Lars Müller.

Forrest, R., & Kearns, A. (2001). Social Cohesion, Social Capital and the Neighbourhood. *Urban Studies, 38*(12), 2125–2143. doi:10.1080/00420980120087081.

Franck, K. A., & Stevens, Q. (eds). (2007). *Loose Space: Possibility and Diversity in Urban Life*. London; New York: Routledge.

Frank, L., & Engelke, P. (2001). The Built Environment and Human Activity Patterns: Exploring the Impacts of Urban Form on Public Health. *Journal of Planning Literature, 16*(2), 202–218.

Fyfe, N., Bannister, J., & Kearns, A. (2006). (In)civility and the City. *Urban Studies, 43*(5/6), 853–861. doi:10.1080/00420980600676063.

Gaffikin, F., Mceldowney, M., & Sterrett, K. (2010). Creating Shared Public Space in the Contested City: The Role of Urban Design. *Journal of Urban Design, 15*(4), 493–513. doi:10.1080/13602365.2011.547015.

Gathorne-Hardy, F. (2004). *Recharging the Power of Place: Valuing Local Significance*. London: Campaign to Protect Rural England, National Trust and Heritage Link. Retrieved from: http://www.theheritagealliance.org.uk/docs/power.pdf.

Gehl, J. (1996). *Life between Buildings: Using Public Space*. Copenhagen: Arkitektens Forlag.

Gehl, J. (2010). *Cities for People*. Washington, DC: Island Press.

Gehl, J., & Gemzoe, L. (2001). *New City Spaces*. Copenhagen: Danish Architectural Press.

Glasson, J., & Wood, G. (2009). Urban Regeneration and Impact Assessment for Social Sustainability. *Impact Assessment and Project Appraisal, 27*(4), 283–290. doi:10.3152/146155109X480358.

Greenwald, M. J., & Boarnet, M. G. (2001). Built Environment as a Determinant of Walking Behaviour: Analyzing Non-work Pedestrian Travel in Portland, Oregon. *Transportation Research Record, 1780*, 33–42. doi:10.3141/1780-05.

Habermas, J. (1984). *The Theory of Communicative Action*. Cambridge: Polity Press.

Habermas, J. (1989). *The Structural Transformation of the Public Sphere*. Cambridge, MA: MIT Press.

Halberstadt, J. (2006). The Generality and Ultimate Origins of the Attractiveness of Prototypes. *Personality and Social Psychology Review, 10*(2), 166–183. doi:10.1207/s15327957pspr1002_5.

Handbook on Tree Conservation & Tree Planting Provision for Development Projects. (2005). Retrieved from: http://www.nparks.gov.sg/cms/index.php?option=com_content&view=article&id=36&Itemid=150#Handbook.

Handy, S. L., Boarnet, M. G., Ewing, R., & Killingsworth, R. E. (2002). How the Built Environment Affects Physical Activity: Views from Urban Planning. *American Journal of Preventive Medicine, 23*(2), 64–73. doi:10.1016/S0749-3797(02)00475-0.

Harries, K. (1997). *The Ethical Function of Architecture*. Cambridge, MA: MIT Press.

Heath, G. W., Brownson, R. C., Kruger, J., Miles, R., Powell, K. E., & Ramsey, L. T. (2006). The Effectiveness of Urban Design and Land Use and Transport Policies and Practices to Increase Physical Activity: A Systematic Review. *Journal of Physical Activity and Health, 3*(Suppl. 1), S55–S76.

Hillier, B. (1996a). *Space is the Machine*. Cambridge: Cambridge University Press.

Hillier, B. (1996b). Cities as Movement Systems. *Urban Design International, 1*(1), 47–60.

Hillier, B., & Hanson, J. (1984). *The Social Logic of Space*. Cambridge: Cambridge University Press.

Hills, J., Le Grand, J., & Piachaud, D. (2002). *Understanding Social Exclusion*. Oxford: Oxford University Press.

Hirtle, S. C. (2008). Wayfinding, Landmarks. In S. Shekhar & H. Xiong (eds), *Encyclopaedia of Geographic Information Science* (pp. 1246–1248). New York: Springer.

Hong Kong Planning Department. (2006, July edn). Urban Design Guidelines. In *Hong Kong Planning Standards and Guidelines* (ch. 11), The Government of the Hong Kong Special Administrative Region. Retrieved from: http://www.pland.gov.hk/pland_en/tech_doc/hkpsg/full/ch11/pdf/ch11.pdf.

Illich, I. (1985) (c. 1973). *Tools for Conviviality*. London: Boyars.

Jackson, P. (1998). Domesticating the Street: The Contested Spaces of the High Street and the Mall. In N. R. Fyfe (ed.), *Images of the Street: Planning, Identity, and Control in Public Spaces* (pp. 176–191). London: Routledge.

Jacobs, A. and Appleyard, D. (1987). Towards an Urban Design Manifesto: A Prologue. *Journal of the American Planning Association, 53*(1), 112–120. doi:10.1080/01944368708976642.

Jacobs, J. (1961). *The Death and Life of Great American Cities*. New York: Random House.

Kearns, A., & Forrest, R. (2000). *Social Cohesion and Multilevel Urban Governance*. *Urban Studies, 37*(5–6), 995–1017. doi:10.1080/00420980050011208.

Kellert, S. R., & Wilson, E. O. (eds). (1993). *The Biophilia Hyphothesis*. Washington, DC: Island Press.

Kilian, T. (1998). Public and Private, Power and Space. In A. Light and J. M. Smith (eds), *The Production of Public Space* (pp. 115–134). Lanham, MD; Boulder, CO; New York; Oxford: Rowman & Littlefield.

Knox, P., & Pinch, S. (2000). *Urban Social Geography: An Introduction*. Harlow: Prentice Hall.

Lang, J. (1994). *Urban Design: The American Experience*. New York: Van Nostrand Reinhold.

Lefebvre, H. (1968). *Le Droit à la ville* [The right to the city] (2nd edn). Paris: Anthropos.

Lefebvre, H. (1991). *The Production of Space* (trans. D. Nicholson-Smith). Oxford; Cambridge, MA: Blackwell.

Levine, D. (2003). *Universal Design New York 2*. New York: City of New York Department of Design and Construction in partnership with The Mayor's Office for People with Disabilities. Retrieved from: http://www.nyc.gov/html/ddc/downloads/pdf/udny/udny2.pdf.

Lloyd, K., & Auld, C. (2003). Leisure, Public Space and Quality of Life in the Urban Environment. *Urban Policy and Research, 21*(4), 339–356.

Lofland, L. H. (1998). *The Public Realm: Exploring the City's Quintessential Social Territory*. Hawthorne, NY: Aldine de Gruyter.

Lopez, R. P., & Hynes, H. P. (2006). Obesity, Physical Activity, and the Urban Environment: Public Health Research Needs. *Environmental Health, 5*, 25. doi:10.1186/1476-069X-5-25.

Loukaitou-Sideris, A. (1996). Cracks in the City: Addressing the Constraints and Potentials of Urban Design. *Journal of Urban Design, 1*(1), 91–103. doi:10.1080/13574809608724372.

Loukaitou-Sideris, A., & Banerjee, T. (1998). *Urban Design Downtown: Poetics and Politics of Form*. Berkeley, CA: University of California Press.

Lozano, E. E. (1990). *Community Design and the Culture of Cities: The Crossroad and the Wall*. New York: Cambridge University Press.

Lynch, K. (1960). *The Image of the City*. Cambridge, MA: MIT Press.

Lynch, K. (1981). *A Theory of Good City Form*. Cambridge, MA: MIT Press.

Lynch, K., & Carr, S. (1979). Open Space: Freedom and Control. In T. Banerjee & M. Southworth (eds), *City Sense and City Design: Writings and Projects of Kevin Lynch* (pp. 413–417). Cambridge, MA: MIT Press.

Marcus, C. C., & Francis, C. (eds). (1997). *People Places: Guidelines for Urban Open Space*. New York: Van Nostrand Reinhold.

Marcuse, P. (2005). The "Threat of Terrorism" and the Right to the City. *Fordham Urban Law Journal, 32*(4), 767–785.

Mayer, I. S., & Seijdel, R. (2005). Collaborative Decisionmaking for Sustainable Urban Renewal Projects: A Simulation–Gaming Approach. *Environment and Planning B: Planning and Design, 32*, 403–423. doi:10.1068/b31149.

McIndoe, G., Chapman, R., McDonald, C., Holden, G., Howden-Chapman, P., & Sharpin, A. B. (2005). The Value of Urban Design: The Economic, Environmental and Social Benefits of Urban Design. Ministry for the Environment, Manatū Mō Te Taiao, Wellington. Retrieved from: http://www.mfe.govt.nz/sites/default/files/value-of-urban-design-full-report-jun05_0.pdf.

Merleau-Ponty, M. (1962). *Phenomenology of Perception*. London: Routledge.

Montgomery, J. (1998). Making a City: Urbanity, Vitality and Urban Design. *Journal of Urban Design, 3*(1), 93–116. doi:10.1080/13574809808724418.

Moudon A. V., & Lee, C. (2003). Walking and Bicycling: An Evaluation of Environmental Audit Instruments. *American Journal of Health Promotion, 18*, 21–37. http://dx.doi.org/10.4278/0890-1171-18.1.21.

Muller, N., Werner, P., & Kelcey, J. G. (eds). (2010). *Urban Biodiversity and Design*. New York: Wiley-Blackwell.

Németh, J., & Schmidt, S. (2007). Towards a Methodology for Measuring the Security of Publicly Accessible Spaces. *Journal of the American Planning Association, 73*, 283–297. doi:10.1080/01944360708977978.

Németh, J., & Schmidt, S. (2011). The Privatization of Public Space: Modelling and Measuring Publicness. *Environment and Planning B: Planning and Design, 38*(1), 5–23. doi:10.1068/b36057.

Neuts, B. (2011). Determining the External Social Costs of Public Space Crowding: Life in a Tourist Ghetto. Retrieved from: http://dlc.dlib.indiana.edu/dlc/handle/10535/7324.

New York City Department of Design and Construction. (2008). *Sustainable Urban Site Design Manual*. Retrieved from: http://www.nyc.gov/html/ddc/downloads/pdf/ddc_sd-sitedesignmanual.pdf.

New York City Department of Planning. (2009). *Privately Owned Public Spaces (Current Public Plaza Standards)*. Retrieved from: http://www.nyc.gov/html/dcp/html/pops/plaza_standards.shtml.

New York City Department of Transportation. (2009). *Street Design Manual*. Retrieved from: http://www.nyc.gov/html/dot/downloads/pdf/sdm_lores.pdf.

Newman, O. (1995). Defensible Space—A New Physical Planning Tool for Urban Revitalization. *Journal of the American Planning Association, 61*(2), 149–155.

Newman, P., & Hogan, T. (1981). A Review of Urban Density Models: Toward a Resolution of the Conflict Between Populace and Planner. *Human Ecology, 9*(3), 270–302. doi:10.1007/BF00890739.

Newton, R., & Ormerod, M. (2007). *I'DGO Inclusive Design for Getting Outdoors*. Retrieved from: http://www.idgo.ac.uk/design_guidance/factsheets/seating.htm.

Niemelä, J. (1999). Ecology and Urban Planning. *Biodiversity and Conservation, 8*(1), 119–131. doi:10.1023/A:1008817325994.

Norman, G. J., Nutter, S. K., Ryan, S., Sallis, J. F., Calfas, K. J., & Patrick, K. (2006). Community Design and Access to Recreational Facilities as Correlates of Adolescent Physical Activity and Body-mass Index. *Journal of Physical Activity and Health, 3*(Supplement 1), S118–S128.

Oc, T., & Tiesdell, S. (1999). The Fortress, the Panoptic, the Regulatory and the Animated: Planning and Urban Design Approaches to Safer City Centres. *Landscape Research, 24*(3), 265–286.

Parry, J. A., Ganaie, S. A., Nengroo, Z. A., & Bhat, M. S. (2012). Spatial Analysis on the Provision of Urban Amenities and their Deficiencies—A Case Study of Srinagar City, Jammu and Kashmir, India. *Research on Humanities and Social Sciences, 2*(6), 192–219. Retrieved from: http://www.iiste.org/Journals/index.php/RHSS/article/download/2393/2392.

Passini, R. (1984). *Wayfinding in Architecture*. New York: Van Nostrand Reinhold.

Pierson, J. (2002). *Tackling Social Exclusion*. London: Routledge.

Poklembovái, V., Kluvánková-Oravskáii, T., & Finkaiii, M. (2012). Challenge of New Commons—Urban Public Spaces. Paper presented at the 1st Global Thematic IASC Conference on the Knowledge Commons, Louvain-la-Neuve, Belgium, September. Retrieved from: http://biogov.uclouvain.be/iasc/doc/full%20papers/Poklembova.pdf.

Project for Public Spaces (PPS), & Metropolitan Planning Council. (2008). *A Guide to Neighborhood Placemaking in Chicago*. Retrieved from: http://www.placemakingchicago.com/cmsfiles/placemaking_guide.pdf.

Punter, J. (1991). Participation in the Design of Urban Space. *Landscape Design, 200*, 24–27.

Queensland University of Technology (QUT), & Institute for Sustainable Resources (ISR). (2009). *High-density Liveability Guide*. Brisbane, Qld, Australia: School of Design, QUT: QUT Institute for Sustainable Resources. Retrieved from: http://www.highdensityliveability.org.au/index.php.

Qureshi, S., & Breuste, J. H. (2010). Prospects of Biodiversity in Mega City of Karachi, Pakistan: Potentials, Constraints and Implications. In N. Muller, P. Warner, & J. G. Kelcey (eds), *Urban Biodiversity and Design* (pp. 497–517). Oxford: John Wiley & Sons.

Reber, R., Schwartz, N., & Winkelman, P. (2004). Processing Fluency and Aesthetic Pleasure: Is Beauty in the Perceiver's Processing Experience? *Personality and Social Psychology Review, 8*(4), 364–382. doi:10.1207/s15327957pspr0804_3.

Relph, E. (1976). *Place and Placelessness*. London: Pion.

Salingaros, N. A. (1998). Theory of the Urban Web. *Journal of Urban Design, 3*, 53–71. doi:10.1080/13574809808724416.

Salingaros, N. A. (1999). Urban Space and Its Information Field. *Journal of Urban Design, 4*(1), 29–49. doi:10.1080/13574809908724437.

Salingaros, N. A. (2000). Complexity and Urban Coherence. *Journal of Urban Design, 5*(3), 291–316. doi:10.1080/713683969.

Salmen, J. (1996). Universal Design and the Recreation Environment. *Trends, 33*(1), 14–19.

Sandercock, L., & Dovey, K. G. (2002). Pleasure, Politics and the "Public Interest": Melbourne's Riverscape Revitalization. *Journal of the American Planning Association, 68*(2), 151–164. doi:10.1080/01944360208976262.

Savard, J-P. L., Clergeau, P., & Mennechez, G. (2000). Biodiversity Concepts and Urban Ecosystems. *Landscape and Urban Planning, 48*(3–4), 131–142.

Schmidt, S., & Németh, J. (2010). Space, Place and the City: Emerging Research on Public Space Design and Planning. *Journal of Urban Design, 15*(4), 453–457. doi:10.1080/13574809.2010.502331.

Shaftoe, H. (2008). *Convivial Urban Spaces: Creating Effective Public Spaces*. London: Earthscan.

Shehayeb, D. (1995). The Behavioural Opportunities Approach: An Explanatory and Narrative Approach to Urban Public Space. In A. Seidal (ed.), *Banking on Design: Proceedings of the 25th Environmental*

Design Research Association (EDRA) Conference (pp. 208–215). San Antonio: EDRA.

Sherlock, H. (1990). *Cities are Good for Us: The Case for Close Knit Communities, Local Shops and Public Transport.* London: Paladin.

Sitte, C. (1965). *City Planning According to Artistic Principles.* London: Phaidon Press.

Song, Y., & Knaap, G-J. (2004). Measuring Urban Form: Is Portland Winning the War on Sprawl? *Journal of the American Planning Association, 70,* 210–225. doi:10.1080/01944360408976371.

Sorkin, M. (ed.). (1992). *Variations on a Theme Park: The New American City and the End of Public Space.* New York: Hill & Wang.

Southworth, M., & Ben-Joseph, E. (1997). *Streets and the Shaping of Towns and Cities.* New York: McGraw-Hill.

Stone, B., & Rodgers, M. (2001). Urban Form and Thermal Efficiency: How the Design of Cities Influences the Urban Heat Island Effect. *Journal of the American Planning Association, 67*(2), 186–198.

Talen, E. (2011). Sprawl Retrofit: Sustainable Urban Form in Unsustainable Places. *Environment and Planning B: Planning and Design, 38,* 952–978. doi:10.1068/b37048.

Tiesdell, S., & Adams, D. (1995). *Revitalising Historic Urban Quarters.* Oxford: Architectural Press.

Tratalos, J., Fuller, R. A., Warren, P. H., Davies, R. G., & Gaston, K. J. (2007). Urban Form, Biodiversity Potential and Ecosystem Services. *Landscape and Urban Planning, 83*(4), 308–317.

Ulrich, R., Simons, R., Losito, B., Fiorito, E., Miles, M., & Zelson, M. (1991). Stress Recovery During Exposure to Natural and Urban Environments. *Journal of Environmental Psychology, 11,* 201–230.

Urban Design Compendium. (2007). Retrieved from: http://www.homesandcommunities.co.uk/sites/default/files/book/udc/community-engagement/1110_udc1_final_artwork_120306-optimized.pdf.

Urban Services. (n.d.). Design Standards for Urban Infrastructure. Retrieved from: http://www.tams.act.gov.au/__data/assets/pdf_file/0007/396880/ds19_bbq.pdf.

Urry, J. (2007). *Mobilities.* Cambridge: Polity Press.

Uslu, A., & Shakouri, N. (2013). Urban Landscape Design and Biodiversity. In M. Ozyavuz (ed.), *Advances in Landscape Architecture.* InTech, doi:10.5772/55761. Retrieved from: http://www.intechopen.com/books/advances-in-landscape-architecture/urban-landscape-design-and-biodiversity.

Van Melik, R., Van Aalst, I., & Van Weesep, J. (2007). Fear and Fantasy in the Public Domain: The Development of Secured and Themed Urban Space. *Journal of Urban Design, 12*(1), 25–42. doi:10.1080/13574800601071170.

Varna, G., & Tiesdell, S. (2010). Assessing the Publicness of Public Space: The Star Model of Publicness. *Journal of Urban Design, 15*(4), 575–598. doi:10.1080/13574809.2010.502350.

Wall, A. (1999). Programming the Urban Surface. In J. Corner (ed.), *Recovering Landscape: Essays in Contemporary Landscape Architecture* (pp. 244–247). New York: Princeton Architectural Press.

Wansborough, M., & Mageean, A. (2000). The Role of Urban Design in Cultural Regeneration. *Journal of Urban Design, 5*(2), 181–197. doi:10.1080/713683962.

Whyte, W. H. (1980). *The Social Life of Small Urban Spaces.* Washington, DC: Conservation Foundation.

Whyte, W. H. (1988). *City: Rediscovering the Centre.* New York: Anchor/Doubleday.

Williams, K., & Green, S. (2001). *Literature Review of Public Space and Local Environments for the Cross Cutting Review: Final Report.* Oxford Centre for Sustainable Development, Oxford Brookes University. Retrieved from: https://www.academia.edu/attachments/31676195/download_file?st=MTQyMjY0NDA3Mywx MzcuMTMyLjQ3Ljc%3D&s=popover.

Wilson, J. Q., & Kelling, G. L. (1982). The Police and Neighbourhood Safety. *Atlantic Monthly, 249,* 29–38.

World Health Organization (WHO). (2007). *Global Age-Friendly Cities: A Guide.* WHO. Retrieved from: http://www.who.int/ageing/publications/Global_age_friendly_cities_Guide_English.pdf.

Yeang, L. D. (2000). *Urban Design Compendium.* English Partnerships. Retrieved from: http://www.made.org.uk/images/uploads/urban_design_compendium_1.pdf.

Young Foundation. (2009). *Amenities and Social Infrastructure.* Retrieved from: http://www.futurecommunities.net/socialdesign/amenities-and-social-infrastructure.

Zepf, M. (2000). Dialectical Identity in Urban Public Spaces. *Landscape Design, 295*(2000), 40–41.

Zhang, W., & Lawson, G. (2009). Meeting and Greeting: Activities in Public Outdoor Spaces Outside High-density Urban Residential Communities. *Urban Design International, 14*(4), 207–214. doi:10.1057/udi.2009.19.

Zukin, S. (1995). *The Cultures of Cities.* Oxford: Blackwell.

Chapter 3

Assessing the Quality of Urban Space

The Urban Space Framework establishes an integrated mechanism for more empirical urban space analysis. This chapter provides a set of simple tools for the systematic documentation and assessment of key urban space properties and performances, including classification and evaluation instruments, as well as a scoring system, based on the outlined Urban Space Framework. An integrated computational tool developed to assist in documentation, classification, evaluation, analysis and speculation of urban spaces—the Tool for Urban Space Analysis (TUSA)—is also introduced. While not being necessary for the analysis proposed in this book, the TUSA fully reflects high flexibility and adaptability of this research and research framework, as well as its practical application in various stages of urban space design and decision-making.

> *How to Document Urban Spaces?*
> *How to Classify Urban Spaces?*
> *How to Qualitatively Assess Urban Spaces?*
> *How to Analyze Urban Space Performances?*
> *TUSA—Tool for Urban Space Analysis*

RESEARCH PROCESS

Assessing the quality of urban space is a dynamic, cyclic, non-linear and non-exhaustive process, resulting from the dynamic and ever-changing relations between the urban environment and its users. The recent tendencies in urban design demonstrate shifts from centralized top-down to more decentralized bottom-up approaches, from master planning to strategic planning, from design solutions to design processes, from linear to non-linear thinking, from obsession with perfection, control and equilibrium to acknowledgment and (even) embracement of vulnerability, spontaneity and change (Batty, 2005; Ellin, 2006; Meredith et al., 2008). As a consequence, the designer of today acquires the role of a "tactician," seeking voids within hybridized and temporary socio-spatial fabric in order to foster diverse, resilient and socially sustainable developments.

In order to fully understand the dynamics and complexities that characterize emerging hybrid urban spaces in high-density contexts and to guide their sustainable development, embracing more inclusive, open, flexible, integrated and holistic approaches to urban space design and analysis is an imperative. This includes more speculative and qualitative temporal dimensions simultaneously, with the main focus on complex relationships between spatial typologies and programs, as well as ways of utilization and management, rather than on individual and static dimensions.

This research was carried out in three parallel phases, namely: the development of a research framework, the documentation of case studies and analysis, followed by continuous refinement of the framework and the research instrument, as illustrated in the research process diagram (Figure 3.1). Analysis mainly consisted of three sub-phases: classification and qualitative assessment, derived from the Urban Space Framework, and synthesis.[1] Synthesis included comparative qualitative and quantitative analysis, using the Tool for Urban Space Analysis (TUSA), an integrated computational tool developed to systematically classify, evaluate, analyze, speculate and guide the decision-making in the design and planning of emerging complex urban space configurations in high-density conditions.

A set of tools to document, classify, evaluate and analyze the qualities of hybrid urban spaces proposed in this chapter results from such a continuous research process. These tools are only temporary—and undoubtedly not entirely perfect—examples that may be used as simple means of initial systematic understanding, investigation, design and redesign of urban spaces.

HOW TO DOCUMENT URBAN SPACE

A number of techniques may be used to gather comprehensive data about spatial design characteristics and performances of urban spaces, as well as to investigate their capabilities to improve living conditions and to contribute to environmentally and socially sustainable high-density development.

Preselection of Case Studies

In preselecting case studies, the main criteria stem from the objectives of our study. Apart from the high-density condition, the main criteria for selecting case studies were the emerging

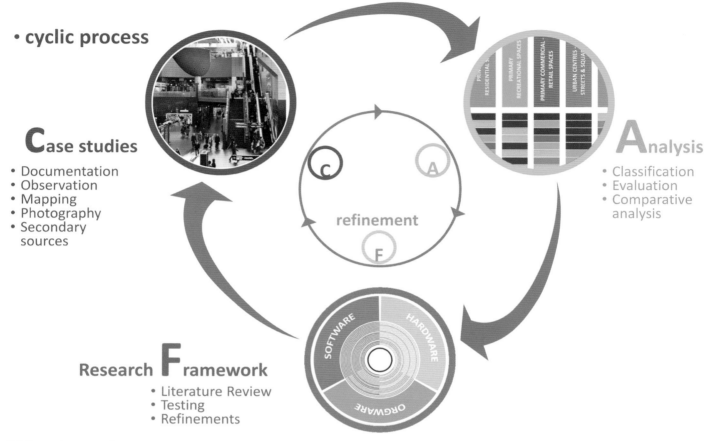

• **cyclic process**

Case studies
• Documentation
• Observation
• Mapping
• Photography
• Secondary
  sources

Analysis
• Classification
• Evaluation
• Comparative
  analysis

refinement

Research **F**ramework
• Literature Review
• Testing
• Refinements

3.1 Research process diagram.

new typologies and high level of complexity in terms of both hybrid spatial configurations and the high intensity of use.[2] Final documentation comprises a total of over 50 local (Singaporean) and international case studies, including cases from Beijing, Tokyo, New York, Melbourne, Berlin, Rotterdam and Copenhagen, among other cities.[3]

Figure 3.2 shows the distribution of all case studies in terms of their levels of density and intensity. All case studies are highlighted in one of five colors, representing the five initial urban space typologies identified based on primary uses that are predominant in space, namely: residential, recreational, mixed use, urban centers (streets, promenades, squares and plazas), and infrastructural transit-led spaces.

Density in this chart refers to "built density" and is measured by Gross Plot Ratio (GPR) or Floor Area Ratio (FAR), which is defined as the ratio of buildings' total floor area to the size of the parcel of land upon which they are built. For spaces without any built structures that are subject to GPR/FAR calculation, such as streets, plazas and squares, GPR for the surrounding context (400m in radius) is taken. For all other spaces the value in the chart reflects

either GPR/FAR per site/development or GPR/FAR per context (400m radius), whichever is larger. In the context of Singapore, GPR between 2.00 and 3.00 is considered high density, while GPR above 3.00 is considered very high density.

Intensity is, on the other hand, a much looser property and the available measures vary considerably. Figure 3.2 indicates the level of intensity through the relative number of programs within and along the urban space boundaries per 100 square meters of an urban space area. An average value of these measures is provided as a reference to the level of intensity.

Documentation Techniques
Documentation techniques employed in this research primarily involve structured first-person observations commonly used in Post-Occupancy Evaluation (POE),[4] including: on-site recording of qualitative (and some quantitative) data related to spatial typologies, features, activities and intensities of uses, using classification and evaluation checklists (prepared in advance), mapping, drawing, photography, textual description and occasional interviews.

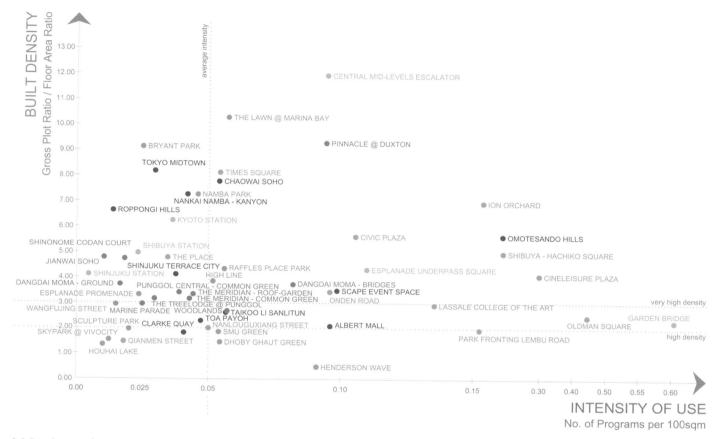

3.2 Distribution of case studies based on density and intensity levels—Gross Plot Ratio (GPR) and number of programs within and along urban space boundaries per 100 m² of urban space area.
Legend: RESIDENTIAL, RECREATIONAL, URBAN CENTERS, MIXED-USE, INFRASTRUCTURAL TRANSIT-LED

Focus Area of Observation

For each space investigated, a focus area of observation was established. Figure 3.3 shows an example of established urban space boundaries, that of the context, the development and the core urban space. In some cases development/site boundary overlaps with the boundary of the core urban space.

Initial Mapping and Photo-documentation

The initial mapping involved recording key spatial features available on site, namely: built structures (buildings), activities, softscape and hardscape areas, as well as water bodies or features (Figure 3.4). These initial maps serve as simple diagrams, comparable across all urban spaces to be analyzed.[5]

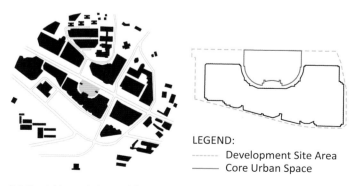

LEGEND:
----- Development Site Area
——— Core Urban Space

3.3 Spatial boundaries and focus area of observation. Example: Civic Plaza, Singapore.

BUILDINGS 55 %

Tokyo Midtown comprising of six buildings includes office, residential, commercial, hotel, museum and leisure space, as well as the tallest building in Tokyo and the new quarters of the Suntory Museum of Art. A main open space in the middle connects these five buildings, while the residential tower is slightly separated behind.

ACTIVITIES (Ground)

Pedestrian traffic is high and hectic in the public spaces at Midtown Tokyo, with people busily heading to and from offices, retails, shops, restaurants, homes, galleries and subway stations across the large main plaza. The main plaza is the primary urban entry into the project directly from the street and subway.

SOFTSCAPE 22.5 %

Midtown Tokyo design includes 4 hectares of open space, blending the rarity of large green lawns and parks intertwined with contemplative intervals that are more traditionally Japanese, in urban settings. One hundred and forty mature trees were preserved on site, including 25 transplanted cherry trees.

HARDSCAPE 19.7 %

The plaza hardscape is finished in cream granite paving with decorative black banding. The pattern, coloring and proportions of the hardscape are based on tatami mats, the traditional Japanese woven rice straw floor coverings, with 2:1 proportions of buff color and black borders.

WATER 2.8 %

A central feature of the park is the romanticized reinterpretation of a stream that once existed on site. Water jets, terraced pools and weirs simulate the mountain stream's descent to valley lowlands — a 30-meter grade change — to meandering pathways and the "Great Lawn."

3.4 Initial mapping and photo-documentation. Example: Tokyo Midtown, Tokyo, Japan.

Review of Secondary Sources

As a means of preparation for the site visit, as well as verification of data gathered on site, the documentation also involved a comprehensive review of secondary sources of the design parameters and planning policies, relevant for particular urban space (books, papers, reports, drawings, internet websites, map resources, such as Google Earth, etc.).

URBAN SPACE INSTRUMENT

The Urban Space Instrument represents direct application of the Urban Space Framework. It consists of classification and evaluation systems, which are descriptive mechanisms developed to identify key attributes of urban spaces, categorize them according to their hardware, software and orgware properties, and to assess their overall performances (Figure 3.5). They are accompanied by classification and evaluation checklists, and a scoring system.

HOW TO CLASSIFY URBAN SPACE

The classification system consists of a number of neutral descriptors and tags that are used to label urban spaces and classify them into primary, secondary and hybrid urban space typologies and conditions. While the majority of tags are qualitative (descriptive), some are measured or calculated, such as the scale, building coverage, Gross Plot Ratio (Floor Area Ratio) or percentage of softscape area. It sets the foundation for in-depth qualitative analysis, as well as for speculation on hybrid urban space typologies and conditions. A total of 27 descriptors with their associated tags are grouped according to hardware, software and orgware categories (Figure 3.6).

"S1: PRIMARY USE OF SPACE" within software components is considered the key descriptor, based on which five default urban space typologies can be created, namely: urban spaces in residential areas, recreational spaces, urban centers (streets and parks), mixed-use developments and infrastructural transit-led spaces. In addition, the default sub-typologies are further established based on "H1: URBAN FOOTPRINT," which refers to the predominant geometry and role of urban space in urban fabric, such as housing precincts, squares, parks, streets, promenades or bridges.

Establishing key urban space typologies, in reference to well-known land uses, is useful, as it provides a common language for the urban design practitioners. However, the analysis is not solely limited to the primary urban space typologies. By combining different tags, it is possible for each space to simultaneously belong to multiple typologies and hybrid conditions. As such, the classification system challenges static and conventional typologies by providing a means for multi-layered explorations of the emerging hybrid, dynamic and transformative configurations of urban spaces.

CLASSIFICATION		EVALUATION SYSTEM		
Descriptors:		Values:	Attributes:	Evaluators [Urban Space Qualities]:

Descriptors	Value group	Value	Attribute	Evaluators [Urban Space Qualities]
	HARDWARE	NODAL VALUE	A: ACCESSIBILITY	1: Pedestrian Access Points
				2: Universal Access
				3: Types and Distribution of Universal Access
				4: Prioritizing the Pedestrians
URBAN FOOTPRINT - H1			B: CONNECTIVITY	5: Movement Patterns
SCALE - H2				6: Node Connectivity
SHAPE - H3				7: Sightlines and Way-finding
ELEVATION - H4			C: MOBILITY MEANS	8: Bicycle-friendly Design
ENCLOSURE - H5				9: Public Transport
EDGE POROSITY - H6		SPATIAL VALUE		10: Vehicular Access
ECO-SYSTEM - H7				11: Drop-off and Taxi Stands
GPR/FAR per Site - H8			D: LEGIBILITY & EDGES	12: Spatial Layout
GPR/FAR per 400m radius - H9				13: Focal Points of Activity
URBAN SPACE [%] per Core- H10				14: Visual Landmarks
OPEN SPACE [%] per 400m radius- H11				15: Permeability
GFA (Gross Floor Area) per Site - H12			E: SPATIAL VARIETY	16: Spatial Variety
GFA per 400m radius - H13				17: Spatial Adaptability
		ENVIRONMENTAL VALUE	F: ENVIRONMENTALLY FRIENDLY DESIGN	18: Greenery and Water – Availability and Access
				19: Greenery – Form, Pattern and Diversity
				20: Biodiversity
				21: Environmentally Friendly Strategies
				22: Environmental Integration
			G: USER COMFORT	23: Protection from Weather Conditions
				24: Shade and Sunlight
				25: Air Control and Optimization
				26: Noise Control and Optimization
PRIMARY USES - S1	SOFTWARE	USE & SOCIO-PERCEPTUAL VALUE	H: DIVERSITY & INTENSITY OF USE	27: Diversity of Activities: Within Urban Space
SECONDARY USES - S2				28: Choice of Activities: Around Urban Space
GENDER - S3			I: SOCIAL ACTIVITIES	29: Seating Amenities
AGE - S4				30: Seating: Condition and Variety
SUB-CULTURES - S5				31: Interactivity
TIME SPECIFICITY - S6				32: Intimacy and Exposure
			J: IDENTITY (IMAGE & CHARACTER)	33: Imageability
				34: History and Symbolic Value
				35: Art, Culture and Alternative Culture
				36: Unique Nature
CLIMATE - O1	ORGWARE	OPERATIONAL VALUE	K: PROVISION OF AMENITIES & SERVICES	37: Hygiene Facilities
GEOGRAPHY - O2				38: Lighting
LOCATION - O3				39: Information Facilities
ROLE & BEHAVIOR - O4				40: Healthcare and Social Services
CATCHMENT/INFLUENCE - O5			L: SAFETY & SECURITY	41: Safety and Image
TIME REGULATION - O6				42: Security
CAPACITY - O7			M: MANAGEMENT & REGULATIONS	43: Rules and Regulations
GOVERNANCE - O8				44: Access Regulation and Management
				45: Time and Program Regulation and Management
				46: Permissions and Management
				47: Affordability and Equality

3.5 The Urban Space Instrument.

URBAN SPACE CLASSIFICATION SYSTEM
HARDWARE

descriptors:		tags:
H1	URBAN FOOTPRINT	housing precincts parks squares & plazas streets promenades hybrid developments bridges & tunnels
H2	SCALE (core area)	S (<2 500 sqm) M (2 500-5 000 sqm) L (5 000-10 000 sqm) XL (> 10 000 sqm)
H3	SHAPE	linear compact fluid
H4	ELEVATION	ground (<2.00 m) elevated (>2.00 m) underground
H5	ENCLOSURE	open – 100% exposed covered – having any shelter semi-enclosed - <75% fully enclosed - >75% fully enclosed
H6	EDGE - BOUNDARY	defined porous complex/undefined
H7	ECO-SYSTEM	built artificial built with greenery natural/landscaped
H8	GPR/FAR per Site/ Development	Not Applicable (0) low (< 1.20) medium 1.20-1.99) high (2.00-2.99) very high (> 3.00)
H9	GPR/FAR per 400m radius	low (< 1.20) medium (1.21-2.00) high (2.01-3.00) very high (> 3.00)
H10	URBAN SPACE per Core Area	S (<20%) M (20.01-50%) L (50.01-75%) XL (>75%)
H11	OPEN SPACE [%] per 400m radius	S (<20%) M (20.01-50%) L (50.01-75%) XL (>75%)
H12	GFA per Site/ Development	Not Applicable (0) S (0-1 000 sqm) M 1 001 - 10 000 sqm) L (10 001 - 100 000 sqm) XL (>100 000 sqm)
H13	GFA per 400m radius	S (> 600 000 sqm) M (600 001 - 1 000 000 sqm) L (1 000 001 - 1 500 000 sqm) XL (>1 500 000 sqm)

HARDWARE

URBAN SPACE CLASSIFICATION SYSTEM
SOFTWARE

descriptors:		tags:
S1	PRIMARY USES	residential recreational urban centers commercial - retail infrastructural
S2	SECONDARY USES	office events art & culture alternative culture education religion night-out areas tourist attractions
S3	GENDER	men women
S4	AGE	young children youth - teenagers elderly
S5	SUB-CULTURES	religious groups ethnic groups tourists artists & performers other
S6	TIME SPECIFICITY	morning night weekend occasional

SOFTWARE

URBAN SPACE CLASSIFICATION SYSTEM
ORGWARE

descriptors:		tags:
O1	CLIMATE	tropical continental
O2	GEOGRAPHY	local–Singapore rest of Asia Europe North America South America Australia and Oceania Africa
O3	LOCATION	downtown near suburbs far suburbs
O4	ROLE & BEHAVIOR	unit joint/connector network/system
O5	CATCHMENT/ INFLUENCE	urban block neighborhood town/district city/state
O6	TIME REGULATION	24-hour use restricted
O7	CAPACITY	restricted number no restrictions
O8	GOVERNANCE	public private

ORGWARE

3.6 Urban Space Instrument: classification system.

3.7 Examples of urban space footprints: bridge—Dangdai Moma, Beijing, China (left), street—Qianmen Street, Beijing, China (middle), hybrid development—Tokyo Midtown, Tokyo, Japan (right).

HARDWARE **Descriptors and Tags**

H1 **URBAN FOOTPRINT**: defines the geometry and role of urban space in urban fabric, namely housing precincts, parks, squares and plazas, streets, promenades, bridges and tunnels, and hybrid developments (Figure 3.7).

H2 **SCALE**: relates to area of core urban space; four scales are identified, namely S—smaller than 2,500m^2, M—2,500–5,000m^2, L—5,000–10,000m^2 and XL—larger than 10,000m^2.

H3 **SHAPE**: relates to the predominant shape/geometry of urban development, namely linear, compact and fluid.

H4 **ELEVATION**: defines the relationship of urban space with the main level of predominant pedestrian flow, namely ground level, elevated or underground.

H5 **ENCLOSURE**: defines the relationship between indoor and outdoor environments, namely open—100 percent exposed, covered, semi-enclosed and enclosed.

H6 **EDGE-BOUNDARY**: defines the level of visual and physical porosity of spatial boundaries. Figure 3.8 shows an analysis of the visual and physical porosity of Bryant Park, New York, using the length of the physically and visually accessible boundary as an indicator.

H7 **ECOSYSTEM**: defines the amount of softscape, greenery and water in space, differentiating built artificial, built with greenery and natural/landscaped urban spaces. Figure 3.9 shows an example of the natural element analysis.

H8 **GROSS PLOT RATIO (GPR) OR FLOOR AREA RATIO (FAR) per site/development**: refers to the ratio of buildings' total floor area to the size of parcel of land upon which they are built. GPR between 2.00 and 3.00 is considered high density, while GPR above 3.00 is considered very high density.

H9 **GROSS PLOT RATIO (GPR) OR FLOOR AREA RATIO (FAR) per 400m radius**: refers to the ratio of buildings' total floor area to the size of 400m radius area (the context, 502,400 m^2) that surrounds the urban space investigated (Figure 3.3). The values calculated are approximate and include roads.

H10 **URBAN SPACE per Core Area**: refers to the percentage of usable urban space allocated within the core area (Figure 3.3).

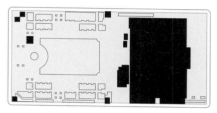

Physically accessible site boundary

Visually accessible site boundary

3.8 Example of a visual and physical porosity analysis: Bryant Park, New York, USA.

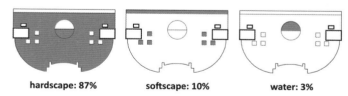

hardscape: 87%   softscape: 10%   water: 3%

3.9 Example of green and water feature analysis: Civic Plaza, Singapore.

H11 **OPEN SPACE per 400m radius**: refers to the percentage of all non-built areas (including roads) within the context of a 400m radius area.

H12 **GROSS FLOOR AREA (GFA) per site/development**: refers to the total floor area of all buildings on site/development.

H13 **GROSS FLOOR AREA (GFA) per 400m radius**: refers to the total floor area of all buildings within 400m radius area.

SOFTWARE Descriptors and Tags

S1 PRIMARY USES: refers to primary land use within and along the space boundaries, namely residential, recreational, urban centers (streets and squares), commercial and infrastructural (transit-led).

S2 SECONDARY USES: refers to other uses provided within and along the space boundaries, including office, event spaces, art and culture, educational and religious activities, among others.

S3 GENDER: recorded only if space obviously caters to particular users' gender.

S4 AGE: recorded only if space obviously caters to particular age group(s).

S5 SUBCULTURES: recorded only if space obviously caters to particular subculture(s).

S6 TIME SPECIFICITY: recorded only if activities occurring in space have obvious peak(s) at particular point(s) in time (day, week, month, season, year).

ORGWARE Descriptors and Tags

O1 CLIMATE: identifies general climate context: tropical or continental.

O2 GEOGRAPHY: refers to whether urban space belongs to a local (Singaporean) or international context.

O3 LOCATION: defines urban space location in relation to a city's downtown area.

O4 ROLE and BEHAVIOR: defines the role of space in the existing surrounding urban network, namely unit, joint/connector or network/system.

O5 CATCHMENT/INFLUENCE: identifies the area of influence of urban space, i.e., the user targets and catchment, such as local residents or the general public.

O6 TIME REGULATION: defines uses of space in a temporal dimension.

O7 CAPACITY: identifies regulations regarding the number of users that the space can (or is allowed to) accommodate.

O8 GOVERNANCE: identifies ownership and responsibility in governance and space management.

HOW TO QUALITATIVELY ASSESS URBAN SPACE

The evaluation system highlights the desired qualities of urban spaces, based on literature review, continuous site visits and the initial analyses. It consists of sets of evaluators and descriptive criteria that have an intrinsic positive value, with the aim of both describing and positively assessing urban spaces. The evaluation system is organized according to the three key components of the Urban Space Framework (as illustrated in Figure 3.5):

1 Each key **urban space component** (hardware, software and orgware) consists of urban values, namely nodal, spatial, environmental, use and socio-perceptual and operational value.

2 Each **urban value** consists of two or three attributes (13 in total).

3 **Urban space attributes** are further defined by two to five evaluators (47 in total).

4 Finally, each **evaluator** has two positive **criteria**, which makes it 94 in total.[6]

Scoring System

Urban spaces are scored using a structured evaluation checklist, which includes all criteria (design principles) proposed in the evaluation system. The rule is simple and straightforward: space scores 1 if it meets a criterion, and it scores 0 if it fails to meet the same criterion. The final score is an average sum of cumulative hardware, software and orgware scores, and forms the overall urban space value, which represents the overall performance of space shown in percentages. However, such an overall value is basic and serves for quick comparison only.

Evaluation Checklist

A full evaluation checklist (Figure 3.10) is provided in the following pages as a ready-made tool for urban space performance evaluation.[7] However, the list of proposed criteria (design principles) is not exhaustive. All urban spaces are assessed based on this checklist of evaluation criteria. Each criterion is of equal importance, i.e., criteria are not weighted. The sum of all the met criteria (as a percentage) within each component represents the space's HARDware, SOFTware and ORGware performance. An average of the component performances creates the overall urban space value (USV).

Circular Chart: Urban Space Value Diagrams

For the purposes of more comprehensive comparisons of urban space performances and the enhancement of visual communication, a set of urban space value diagrams has been crafted. The diagram is an integrated device that can serve both as an evaluation sheet and as a scoring chart, and has a form similar to a circular pie-chart.

The circular chart consists of three segments with respect to the identified three key urban space components: hardware, software and orgware. Each segment is divided into stripes, each representing one criterion. Colored stripes represent criteria (design principles) that are met by the investigated urban space, and the sum of all colored stripes creates the overall urban

URBAN SPACE EVALUATION CHECKLIST

HARDWARE

Attributes & Evaluators:	Criteria:	
A: ACCESSIBILITY		
1: Pedestrian Access Points	1A: At least 2 horizontal or 1 vertical access points are provided.	
	1B: More than 2 horizontal or 1 vertical access points are provided. Formal (main entrances) and informal access points are well distinguished.	
2: Universal Access	2A: There is at least 1 universal access point when level changes occur.	
	2B: More than 1 universal access points are available when level changes occur.	
3: Types and Distribution of Universal Access	3A: At least 2 types of universal access are available.	
	3B: Universal access points are fairly and logically dispersed over site.	
4: Prioritizing the Pedestrians	4A: At least 2 direct and safe pedestrian access points, well separated from vehicular traffic are provided.	
	4B: Urban space is completely pedestrianized.	
B: CONNECTIVITY		
5: Movement Patterns	5A: Space is well connected to dominant external pedestrian route(s).	
	5B: Space provides well-interconnected internal pathways, without dead-end situations.	
6: Node Connectivity	6A: Space connects 2 or more activity nodes in its immediate surroundings.	
	6B: Space is a destination with facilities for long-term activities.	
7: Sightlines and Way-finding	7A: Majority of horizontal and vertical directions are visible from every entry point.	
	7B: Main entry/exit points are visible from both within and out of space.	
C: MOBILITY MEANS		
8: Bicycle-friendly Design	8A: Bike stand facilities are available within space or in its vicinity (up to 200m).	
	8B: Designed cycling areas/lanes are provided, well separated from pedestrian walkways.	
9: Public Transport	9A: Access to public transportation means is available in the vicinity of urban space (up to 400m).	
	9B: At least 2 types of public transportation are available.	
10: Vehicular Access	10A: Parking facilities are provided in the vicinity (up to 400m).	
	10B: Parking facilities are integrated within space, without conflicting with pedestrian movement.	
11: Drop-off and Taxi Stands	11A: Pick-up/drop-off points are available on site.	
	11B: Taxi stands are provided within space or in its proximity (up to 400m).	
D: LEGIBILITY & EDGES		
12: Spatial Layout	12A: Pedestrian networks are clearly differentiated from other activities.	
	12B: The hierarchy of pedestrian network is provided. Major and minor pedestrian routes are clearly differentiated.	
13: Focal Points of Activity	13A: At least 2 legible nodes of different types of activities are provided within space.	
	13B: Nodes are visible from major access points.	
14: Visual Landmarks	14A: At least 1 visual landmark is provided.	
	14B: More than 1 visual landmark is provided.	
15: Permeability	15A: Space has good visual connection with surroundings - edges are porous or see-through.	
	15B: Edges are visually rich and active when permeability is reduced.	
E: SPATIAL VARIETY		
16: Spatial Variety	16A: Space is divided into sub-spaces.	
	16B: Sub-spaces have different visual, aesthetic and/or experiential qualities.	
17: Spatial Adaptability	17A: Space has capacity to adopt temporary programs.	
	17B: Space has flexible layout or adjustable structural elements to create different spatial arrangements and conditions.	

3.10 Evaluation checklist.

F: ENVIRONMENTALLY FRIENDLY DESIGN

Attribute	Criteria	
18: Greenery and Water – Availability and Access	18A: Greenery and/or water features are available in space.	
	18B: Space allows interaction with greenery and/or water elements provided.	
19: Greenery – Form, Pattern and Diversity	19A: Greenery has diverse forms and patterns.	
	19B: Greenery appears at different locations of the urban space (such as ground level, roof, or vertical greenery, for instance).	
20: Biodiversity	20A: Space emphasizes the usage of local flora species.	
	20B: Space is linked to a larger ecosystem enabling ecological continuity.	
21: Environmentally Friendly Strategies	21A: At least 1 environment-friendly strategy is employed in the design of urban space.	
	21B: More than 1 environment-friendly strategy is employed. Environmental awareness and environmentally friendly usage of space is clearly promoted.	
22: Environmental Integration	22A: Urban space respects and preserves (where applicable) existing natural environment.	
	22B: Space enhances natural experience through landscape design.	

G: USER COMFORT

Attribute	Criteria	
23: Protection from Weather Conditions	23A: Major pedestrian pathways are covered.	
	23B: Larger covered or enclosed areas are available in space.	
24: Shade and Sunlight	24A: Space provides a variety of shaded and sunlit areas.	
	24B: Flexible/adjustable shading means are provided in space.	
25: Air Control and Optimization	25A: Space is not exposed to substantial air pollution and has good ventilation.	
	25B: The design employs techniques to improve or enrich the air quality.	
26: Noise Control and Optimization	26A: Space is free from external and/or internal noises.	
	26B: Space employs techniques to improve or enrich the aural quality.	

URBAN SPACE EVALUATION CHECKLIST

SOFTWARE

Attributes & Evaluators:	Criteria:	

H: DIVERSITY & INTENSITY OF USE

Attribute	Criteria	
27: Diversity of Activities: Within Urban Space	27A: At least 1 public amenity for specific active use(s) is available within urban space.	
	27B: At least 2 well-integrated public amenities for specific passive and active uses of different types are provided within urban space.	
28: Choice of Activities: Around Urban Space	28A: At least 2 different activities are available in immediate surroundings of urban space.	
	28B: More than 2 different activities are available in immediate surroundings of urban space.	

I: SOCIAL ACTIVITIES

Attribute	Criteria	
29: Seating Amenities	29A: Sufficient formal seating amenities are provided in space.	
	29B: Secondary/informal seating is available in space.	
30: Seating: Condition and Variety	30A: Seating is available in both sun and shade.	
	30B: At least 2 different types of seating amenities are available in space.	
31: Interactivity	31A: Space provides flexible, movable and/or adjustable seating amenities (and/or tables).	
	31B: Interactive elements are available in urban space.	
32: Intimacy and Exposure	32A: Both exposed and inward-looking seating arrangements are provided.	
	32B: Space provides semi-permeable or adjustable barriers to reduce exposure.	

J: IDENTITY (IMAGE & CHARACTER)

Attribute	Criteria	
33: Imageability	33A: Space is memorable for its unique feature(s).	
	33B: Space and its features are well-known to larger public.	
34: History and Symbolic Value	34A: Tangible traces of historical/cultural heritage are available on site.	
	34B: Design has clear associations with local history and culture.	
35: Art, Culture and Alternative Culture	35A: Art and culture-oriented program(s) are provided.	
	35B: Space caters to alternative uses and/or user groups (subcultures).	
36: Unique Nature	36A: Space has unique natural features that substantially contribute to its visual identity.	
	36B: Natural elements have strong links to preservation, history or religion.	

URBAN SPACE EVALUATION CHECKLIST

ORGWARE

Attributes & Evaluators:	Criteria:	
K: PROVISION OF AMENITIES & SERVICES		
37: Hygiene Facilities	37A: Space is clean and kept in good physical condition.	
	37B: Sufficient number of at least 2 hygiene amenities are available in space.	
38: Lighting	38A: Adequate lighting along main pathways and activity nodes is provided.	
	38B: Space provides ambient and/or adjustable lighting.	
39: Information Facilities	39A: At least 1 public communicational facility is available in space.	
	39B: Good signage and way-finding facilities are available.	
40: Healthcare and Social Services	40A: Affordable general healthcare service for all age groups is available within urban space or in its vicinity (up to 400m).	
	40B: Services for 'vulnerable' user groups (elderly, children, the disabled, etc.) are available within urban space or in its vicinity (up to 400m).	
L: SAFETY & SECURITY		
41: Safety and Image	41A: Design prevents physical injuries.	
	41B: Space appears safe due to approachable and inviting design.	
42: Security	42A: Space employs security measures.	
	42B: Security measures are employed in non-intrusive manner.	
M: MANAGEMENT & REGULATIONS		
43: Rules and Regulations	43A: Space fosters inclusion and regulation rather than exclusion and restriction.	
	43B: Active users' participation in space management is encouraged.	
44: Access Regulation and Management	44A: Space is partially accessible 24 hours a day (passing through).	
	44B: Space is entirely accessible 24 hours a day.	
45: Time & Program Regulation & Management	45A: Space is a setting of occasional events and programs.	
	45B: Space provides means to facilitate regular events and programs.	
46: Permissions and Management	46A: Space allows, manages and facilitates non-designed activities with an adequate permission.	
	46B: Informal activities occur without any permission.	
47: Affordability and Equality	47A: At least 1 public program, service or facility available in space is free of charge.	
	47B: All public facilities/services are free of charge or largely affordable.	

3.10 Evaluation checklist (continued).

space value (Figure 3.11, top left). More specific comparisons are enhanced by another simplified chart, which consists of two circles. The outer circle shows the performance of space (in %) for each urban space value component—the sum of stripes of the same color. The inner circle (pie-chart) shows to what extent each of the components takes part in the creation of overall urban space value (Figure 3.11, bottom left).

Finally, for enhanced visual communication, this pie-chart is further simplified into a final urban space value circular diagram, as used in this book (Figure 3.12).

HOW TO ANALYZE URBAN SPACE PERFORMANCE

In addition to qualitative analysis, a descriptive statistical consistency analysis is undertaken for all urban spaces of the same type (tag) for each criterion in the evaluation framework in order to investigate the critical attributes that shape their performance. An average score deviation has been calculated for each criterion, based on which a hierarchy of criteria has been established (Figure 3.13).

Consistency analysis establishes a hierarchy of criteria, based on an average score deviation for each criterion (Figure 3.14). Essentially, it shows how frequently each criterion in the Urban Space Framework is met by a selected group of evaluated case studies. The hierarchy differentiates:

(a) **Basic/Necessary** criteria: most frequently met (fundamentally important for the urban space performance and the most feasible to meet; high priority).

(b) **Value Add** criteria: often met (feasible to meet; high priority).

(c) **High Value Add** criteria: most inconsistently met by all urban spaces of the same type (highest priority due to the highest

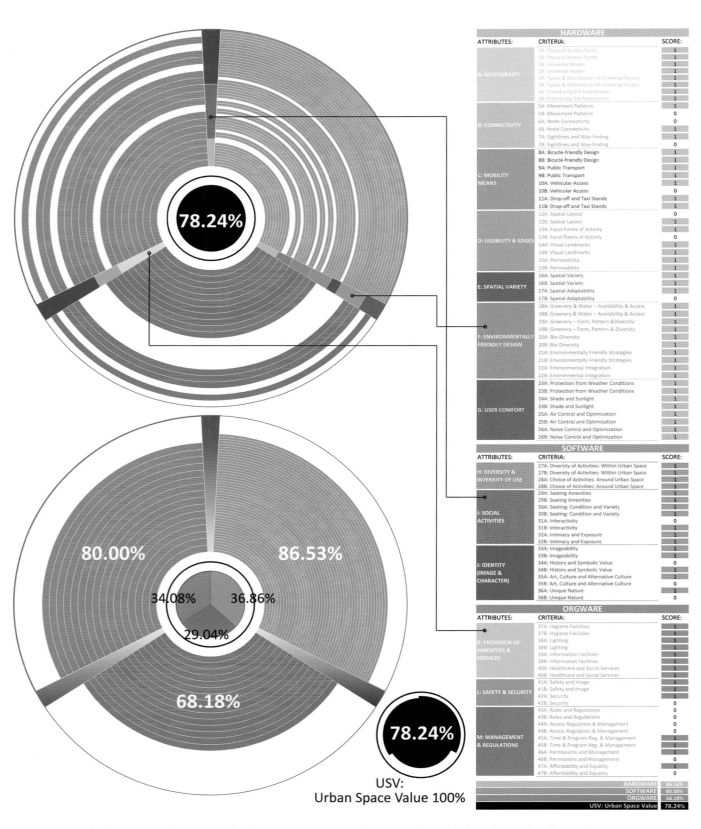

3.11 An example of evaluation and urban space value diagrams: initial circular chart [top] and simplified circular pie-chart [bottom].

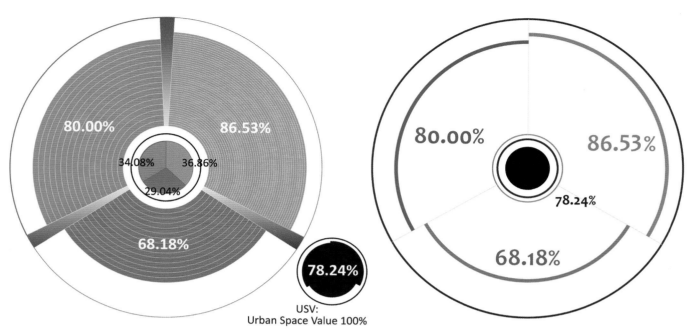

3.12 Final urban space value circular diagram.

Average score:	Hierarchy of criteria:
0.90-1.00	BASIC/NECESSARY
0.65-0.90	VALUE ADD
0.35-0.65	HIGH VALUE ADD
0.10-0.35	GOOD TO HAVE
0.00-0.10	DESIRED

3.13 Hierarchy of criteria.

corrective potentials for the improvement of overall urban space performance).

(d) **Good to Have** criteria: inconsistently met (low feasibility; low priority).

(e) **Desired** criteria: never or rarely met (lowest feasibility; lowest priority).

The key objectives of consistency analysis and hierarchy of criteria are:

1 To identify criteria that are most consistently (frequently) met.[8]
2 To identify criteria that are most inconsistently met.[9]

The main focus is on "basic" and "high value add" criteria, which are recognized as the most feasible to meet and as having the highest corrective potentials respectively to improve the overall urban space performance.

While it depends on the number of spaces selected for evaluation, the consistency analysis, with the hierarchy of criteria as the outcome, provides fruitful means to guide the initial process of designing urban spaces by highlighting urban space properties that are critical for the overall performance and by prioritizing the design actions for particular urban space typology or hybrid conditions. In other words, it prompts the designer to focus on "basic" and "high value add" criteria first, rather than on "desired" criteria.

URBAN SPACES IN PRIMARILY RESIDENTIAL AREAS	The Meridian: ROOF-GARDEN Singapore	The Treelodge @ Punggol Singapore	MARINE PARADE Singapore	WOODLANDS Singapore	LINKED HYBRID - GROUND Beijing, China	PINNACLE @ DUXTON Singapore	LINKED HYBRID - BRIDGES Beijing, China	The Meridian: COMMON GREEN Singapore	PUNGGOL CENTRAL Singapore	JIANWAI SOHO Beijing, China	SHINONOME CODAN COURT Tokyo, Japan	CONSISTENCY ANALYSIS: average scores	Hierarchy Of Criteria
27A: Diversity of Activities: Within Urban Space	1	1	1	1	1	1	1	1	1	1	1	1.00	
27B: Diversity of Activities: Within Urban Space	0	1	1	1	1	0	1	1	1	1	1	0.82	
28A: Choice of Activities: Around Urban Space	0	1	1	1	1	1	1	1	1	1	1	0.91	
28B: Choice of Activities: Around Urban Space	0	0	1	0	1	1	1	1	1	1	1	0.73	
29A: Seating Amenities	1	1	1	1	1	1	1	1	1	1	1	1.00	
29B: Seating Amenities	1	1	1	1	1	0	1	1	1	1	1	0.91	
30A: Seating: Condition & Variety	1	1	1	1	1	1	0	1	1	1	1	0.91	
30B: Seating: Condition & Variety	1	1	1	1	1	1	1	1	1	1	1	1.00	
31A: Interactivity	0	0	0	0	0	0	1	0	0	0	1	0.18	
31B: Interactivity	0	0	1	0	1	1	1	1	1	1	1	0.82	
32A: Intimacy and Exposure	1	1	1	1	1	1	1	1	1	1	1	1.00	
32B: Intimacy and Exposure	0	1	0	0	0	0	0	1	1	0	1	0.36	
33A: Imageability	1	1	0	0	1	1	1	0	0	1	1	0.64	
33B: Imageability	0	0	0	0	1	1	1	0	0	1	1	0.45	
34A: History and Symbolic Value	0	0	0	0	0	0	0	0	0	0	0	0.00	
34B: History and Symbolic Value	0	0	0	0	0	0	0	0	0	0	0	0.00	
35A: Art, Culture & Alternative Culture	0	0	1	0	1	0	1	0	0	1	1	0.45	
35B: Art, Culture & Alternative Culture	0	0	0	0	0	0	0	0	0	0	0	0.00	
36A: Unique Nature	1	1	0	0	1	1	0	1	1	1	1	0.73	
36B: Unique Nature	0	0	0	0	0	1	0	0	0	0	0	0.09	

Average score:	Hierarchy of criteria:
0.90-1.00	BASIC/NECESSARY
0.65-0.90	VALUE ADD
0.35-0.65	HIGH VALUE ADD
0.10-0.35	GOOD TO HAVE
0.00-0.10	DESIRED

3.14 Consistency analysis: an example of average scores for software criteria within the group of all urban spaces in primarily residential areas.[10]

The following tables and comparative insights provide two examples to illustrate how the hierarchy of criteria may be used for prioritizing design actions. The first set of hierarchy of criteria shows how it can be used for prioritizing design actions for primary use typologies. The second set of hierarchy of criteria is used to exemplify the prioritization of design actions for a hybrid typology or condition. Among numerous combinations of hybrid conditions, this example combines two tags, namely S1: Primary Use (software) and H2: Scale (hardware).

Hierarchy of Criteria: Design Actions for Default Urban Space Typologies (Primary Use)

Figure 3.15 summarizes the hierarchy of criteria for the default typologies, for three urban space components: hardware, software and orgware. Summary tables serve as a quick reference to hierarchy of criteria and priority of design actions for the default types of urban spaces. They also provide a comparative insight into properties that are critical for the overall performance of each default type of urban spaces.

HARDWARE

RESIDEN-TIAL	RECREAT-IONAL	MIXED USE	URBAN CENTERS	INFRA-STRUCTU-RAL	CRITERIA [DESIGN PRINCIPLES]:

CRITERIA [DESIGN PRINCIPLES]:

1A: Physical Access Points
1B: Physical Access Points
2A: Universal Access
2B: Universal Access
3A: Types and Distribution of Universal Access
3B: Types and Distribution of Universal Access
4A: Prioritizing the Pedestrians
4B: Prioritizing the Pedestrians
5A: Movement Patterns
5B: Movement Patterns
6A: Node Connectivity
6B: Node Connectivity
7A: Sightlines and Way-finding
7B: Sightlines and Way-finding
8A: Bicycle-friendly Design
8B: Bicycle-friendly Design
9A: Public Transport
9B: Public Transport
10A: Vehicular Access
10B: Vehicular Access
11A: Drop-off and Taxi Stands
11B: Drop-off and Taxi Stands
12A: Spatial Layout
12B: Spatial Layout
13A: Focal Points of Activity
13B: Focal Points of Activity
14A: Visual Landmarks
14B: Visual Landmarks
15A: Permeability
15B: Permeability
16A: Spatial Variety
16B: Spatial Variety
17A: Spatial Adaptability
17B: Spatial Adaptability
18A: Greenery and Water – Availability and Access
18B: Greenery and Water – Availability and Access
19A: Greenery – Form, Pattern and Diversity
19B: Greenery – Form, Pattern and Diversity
20A: Biodiversity
20B: Biodiversity
21A: Environmentally Friendly Strategies
21B: Environmentally Friendly Strategies
22A: Environmental Integration
22B: Environmental Integration
23A: Protection from Weather Conditions
23B: Protection from Weather Conditions
24A: Shade and Sunlight
24B: Shade and Sunlight
25A: Air Control and Optimization
25B: Air Control and Optimization
26A: Noise Control and Optimization
26B: Noise Control and Optimization

3.15 Hierarchies of criteria for default urban space typologies (residential, recreational, mixed use, urban centers, infrastructural transit-led).

SOFTWARE

	RESIDEN-TIAL	RECREAT-IONAL	MIXED USE	URBAN CENTERS	INFRA-STRUCTU-RAL	CRITERIA [DESIGN PRINCIPLES]:
						27A: Diversity of Activities: Within Urban Space
						27B: Diversity of Activities: Within Urban Space
						28A: Choice of Activities: Around Urban Space
						28B: Choice of Activities: Around Urban Space
						29A: Seating Amenities
						29B: Seating Amenities
						30A: Seating: Condition and Variety
						30B: Seating: Condition and Variety
						31A: Interactivity
						31B: Interactivity
						32A: Intimacy and Exposure
						32B: Intimacy and Exposure
						33A: Imageability
						33B: Imageability
						34A: History and Symbolic Value
						34B: History and Symbolic Value
						35A: Art, Culture and Alternative Culture
						35B: Art, Culture and Alternative Culture
						36A: Unique Nature
						36B: Unique Nature

ORGWARE

	RESIDEN-TIAL	RECREAT-IONAL	MIXED USE	URBAN CENTERS	INFRA-STRUCTU-RAL	CRITERIA [DESIGN PRINCIPLES]:
						37A: Hygiene Facilities
						37B: Hygiene Facilities
						38A: Lighting
						38B: Lighting
						39A: Information Facilities
						39B: Information Facilities
						40A: Healthcare and Social Services
						40B: Healthcare and Social Services
						41A: Safety and Image
						41B: Safety and Image
						42A: Security
						42B: Security
						43A: Rules and Regulations
						43B: Rules and Regulations
						44A: Access Regulation and Management
						44B: Access Regulation and Management
						45A: Time & Program Regulation and Management
						45B: Time & Program Regulation and Management
						46A: Permissions and Management
						46B: Permissions and Management
						47A: Affordability and Equality
						47B: Affordability and Equality

Average score:	Hierarchy of criteria:
0.90-1.00	BASIC/NECESSARY
0.65-0.90	VALUE ADD
0.35-0.65	HIGH VALUE ADD
0.10-0.35	GOOD TO HAVE
0.00-0.10	DESIRED

3.15 Hierarchies of criteria for default urban space typologies (residential, recreational, mixed use, urban centers, infrastructural transit-led) (continued).

Comparative Insights

The initial analysis of hardware, software and orgware performances shows that the majority of urban spaces score highest for hardware components. It may also be observed that the hierarchy of criteria differs according to each default typology. For example, establishing direct and safe connection to the dominant external movement route (5A), providing choice of public transportation (9B) and taxi stands (11B), providing unique and memorable spatial features (33A), retaining well-known characteristics (33B), employing passive and non-intrusive means of security (42B), and promoting inclusion and prevention through management, regulation and provision (43A) are found to be critical (High Value Add) for residential urban spaces only, while being basic for others, which makes them specific to this particular primary use.

Meanwhile, providing a sufficient number of pedestrian access points (1A), with universal design principles (2A), prioritizing the pedestrians (4A), parking facilities (10A), synergetic activities in the immediate surroundings of urban space (28A), providing adequate lighting (38A) and public communicational facilities (39A), safety (41A) and affordability (47A) are basic for all urban spaces regardless of their typology and may thus be considered as universal.

Hierarchy of Criteria: Design Actions for Hybrid Urban Space Typologies and Conditions

Hybrid Typology: Primary Use + Scale

Figure 3.16 summarizes the hierarchy of criteria for the hybrid typology defined by two classification tags: S1 Primary Use (software) and H2 Scale (hardware), for three urban space components—hardware, software and orgware. The specific hybrid typologies shown are extra-large residential urban spaces, extra-large recreational urban spaces and extra-large mixed-use urban spaces. They also provide comparative insights into properties that are critical for the overall performance and priority of design actions for each hybrid typology of urban spaces.

Comparative Insights

A number of criteria are of the same priority for all analyzed hybrids (as highlighted). Criteria that are critical (High Value Add) for all urban space hybrids are provision of designated cycling areas/lanes (8B), affordable general healthcare service for all age groups (40A) and facilitating regular events (45B). One criterion that is Good to Have for all urban space hybrids is related to preserving natural elements with strong links to preservation, history or religion (36B). Protection from weather conditions by providing covered walkways (23A) seems to be High Value Add for extra-large residential urban spaces only. Retaining or adding quality that is associated with history, historical events and/or people and culture (34B) seems to be High Value Add for extra-large recreational urban spaces only. Promoting environmental awareness and environmentally friendly use of urban space (21B), providing choice of types of seating amenities (30B) and free of charge for all public programs, services or facilities (47B) seem to be High Value Add for extra-large mixed-use urban spaces only.

* * *

The examples above show that the hierarchy of criteria, which is crucial for the relevant design actions to be taken for the improvement of urban space performance, is not a fixed set of rules. It is rather a flexible and adaptable guideline that may be applied according to the specific urban space conditions, whether it is a default or a hybrid typology. The hierarchies of criteria for default urban space typologies and for hybrid urban space typologies are different for each criterion (as shown above with the two examples). This affects the priority of design actions which highlights urban space properties that can substantially improve urban space performance for particular urban space typology or hybrid conditions. The hybrid urban space typology examples show that the qualitative analysis method suggested here is not limited to only one urban space typology, considering the assumption that with higher densities and intensified uses, urban spaces would become increasingly hybrid, less distinguishable and would have to provide more functions for a greater number of diverse user groups.

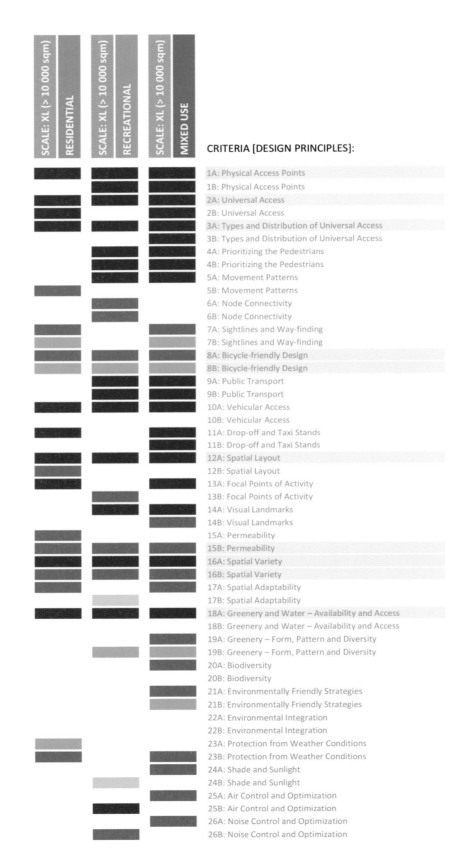

CRITERIA [DESIGN PRINCIPLES]:

1A: Physical Access Points
1B: Physical Access Points
2A: Universal Access
2B: Universal Access
3A: Types and Distribution of Universal Access
3B: Types and Distribution of Universal Access
4A: Prioritizing the Pedestrians
4B: Prioritizing the Pedestrians
5A: Movement Patterns
5B: Movement Patterns
6A: Node Connectivity
6B: Node Connectivity
7A: Sightlines and Way-finding
7B: Sightlines and Way-finding
8A: Bicycle-friendly Design
8B: Bicycle-friendly Design
9A: Public Transport
9B: Public Transport
10A: Vehicular Access
10B: Vehicular Access
11A: Drop-off and Taxi Stands
11B: Drop-off and Taxi Stands
12A: Spatial Layout
12B: Spatial Layout
13A: Focal Points of Activity
13B: Focal Points of Activity
14A: Visual Landmarks
14B: Visual Landmarks
15A: Permeability
15B: Permeability
16A: Spatial Variety
16B: Spatial Variety
17A: Spatial Adaptability
17B: Spatial Adaptability
18A: Greenery and Water – Availability and Access
18B: Greenery and Water – Availability and Access
19A: Greenery – Form, Pattern and Diversity
19B: Greenery – Form, Pattern and Diversity
20A: Biodiversity
20B: Biodiversity
21A: Environmentally Friendly Strategies
21B: Environmentally Friendly Strategies
22A: Environmental Integration
22B: Environmental Integration
23A: Protection from Weather Conditions
23B: Protection from Weather Conditions
24A: Shade and Sunlight
24B: Shade and Sunlight
25A: Air Control and Optimization
25B: Air Control and Optimization
26A: Noise Control and Optimization
26B: Noise Control and Optimization

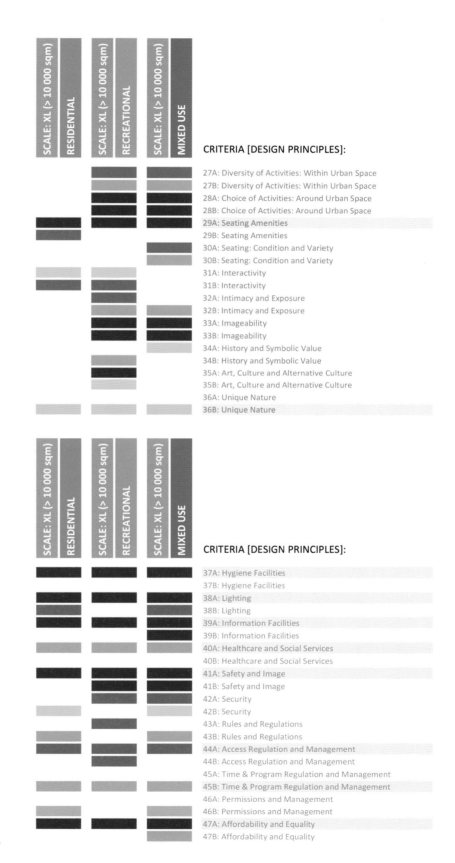

CRITERIA [DESIGN PRINCIPLES]:

27A: Diversity of Activities: Within Urban Space
27B: Diversity of Activities: Within Urban Space
28A: Choice of Activities: Around Urban Space
28B: Choice of Activities: Around Urban Space
29A: Seating Amenities
29B: Seating Amenities
30A: Seating: Condition and Variety
30B: Seating: Condition and Variety
31A: Interactivity
31B: Interactivity
32A: Intimacy and Exposure
32B: Intimacy and Exposure
33A: Imageability
33B: Imageability
34A: History and Symbolic Value
34B: History and Symbolic Value
35A: Art, Culture and Alternative Culture
35B: Art, Culture and Alternative Culture
36A: Unique Nature
36B: Unique Nature

CRITERIA [DESIGN PRINCIPLES]:

37A: Hygiene Facilities
37B: Hygiene Facilities
38A: Lighting
38B: Lighting
39A: Information Facilities
39B: Information Facilities
40A: Healthcare and Social Services
40B: Healthcare and Social Services
41A: Safety and Image
41B: Safety and Image
42A: Security
42B: Security
43A: Rules and Regulations
43B: Rules and Regulations
44A: Access Regulation and Management
44B: Access Regulation and Management
45A: Time & Program Regulation and Management
45B: Time & Program Regulation and Management
46A: Permissions and Management
46B: Permissions and Management
47A: Affordability and Equality
47B: Affordability and Equality

3.16 Hierarchies of criteria for hybrid urban space typologies and conditions S1 Primary Use + H2 Scale, namely extra-large scale residential, extra-large scale recreational and extra-large scale mixed-use urban spaces.

211

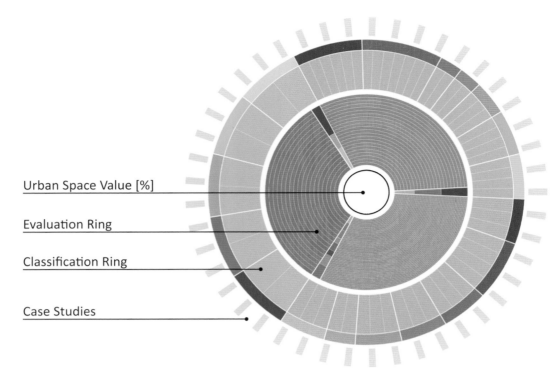

Urban Space Value [%]

Evaluation Ring

Classification Ring

Case Studies

3.17 TUSA conceptual design.

TUSA: TOOL FOR URBAN SPACE ANALYSIS

As a result of the synthesis of the initial comparative analysis, an interactive computational Tool for Urban Space Analysis (TUSA) has been conceptualized,[11] to automate and facilitate cataloging, classifying, evaluating, comparing and speculating on hybrid urban space typologies and their performances. Figures 3.18 to 3.24 provide snapshots of the TUSA interface and its main capacities.

TUSA integrates all elements of the Urban Space Instrument and Framework in a flexible manner and thus reflects the research process and analysis employed in this study of urban spaces. It is an integrative, intuitive, visually compelling and comprehensive communication platform for exploring the critical aspects of urban spaces, where any user can define his or her own way of search and analysis for a particular purpose. Unlike the majority of existing computational tools which operate with quantitative spatial parameters and involve modeling and simulation of urban forms and conditions, the TUSA is primarily based on the qualitative and descriptive assessment of urban spaces. It does not generate shapes or prescribe design solutions, but rather provides means to filter and analyze the key properties of urban spaces, speculate on their hybrid typologies, and finally inform on critical directions of the design process at its initial stage.

During research, TUSA has been primarily used as the key analytical tool to highlight the critical urban space performance

attributes as well as their relationships. The aim was to develop a dynamic application that would be adaptable to new conditions and design requirements, and fully embrace the concepts of hybridization, change and flexibility.

The TUSA Interface

The central design of the interactive TUSA interface visualizes the Urban Space Framework based on circular charts (Figure 3.17). It consists of four rings, namely:

- expandable case studies ring;
- classification ring;
- evaluation ring; and
- urban space value (%) circle.

The design fully reflects the color codes introduced in the Urban Space Framework, namely grey for HARDware, red for SOFTware and blue for ORGware, including the urban space attributes in the evaluation system.

Circular charts of an investigated space prompt the designer to seek out those case studies within the library that score well for its weakest components or specific criteria.

The main elements of the TUSA interface are shown in Figure 3.18.

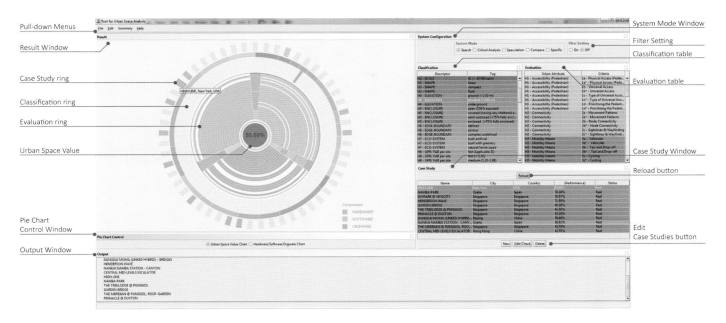

3.18 The TUSA interface.

TUSA Modes and Capacities

Dynamic System

The TUSA has been designed to readjust automatically once a new urban space is saved into the system, by allowing the easy and interactive addition of new case studies, using supplied classification and evaluation checklists. The hierarchy of criteria changes accordingly as it depends on the number of urban spaces within the database. The flexibility of the system is an essential aspect of the tool, as it preserves a certain level of intuitiveness which is an integral part of any design process, and gives the designer considerable freedom to search, evaluate, analyze and compare urban spaces choosing his or her own path. Moreover, such flexibility assures that the tool does not generate prescriptive design formulas, but rather suggests design actions in order to achieve good urban space performance.

Interactive Catalog: Search and Repository

The most basic capacity of TUSA is that it can serve as an interactive catalog which allows browsing through the existing database of case studies while narrowing the search using relevant descriptors in the classification ring, as well as desired design principles in the evaluation ring (Figures 3.19 and 3.20). More than one descriptor may be selected using both classification and evaluation rings, which enables the inclusion of hybrid typologies in the system. This multiple selection of desired descriptors narrows down the search to the most relevant cases in the database and helps the

designer/planner at the initial stage of decision-making (Figure 3.21).

Through descriptive classification and evaluation checklists embedded in "Search" mode, the TUSA enables the systematic categorization of urban spaces according to their hardware, software and orgware properties, as well as an assessment of their overall performances.

Tool for Critical Analysis

The research has primarily used the TUSA as an analytical tool, as it is its main and most elaborate capacity. It helps the user to highlight the most critical aspects of selected urban spaces while prioritizing design actions to improve performance. Once a new urban space is evaluated using the supplied evaluation sheet/checklist, the TUSA automatically generates the circular chart, which gives initial insights into the urban space's hardware, software and orgware performance components. The chart prompts the designer to seek out the best practices within the database that score higher compared to the weakest component of the investigated space (Figure 3.22). Through matching the consistency analysis and the established hierarchy of criteria embedded within the tool, the TUSA is able to highlight the most critical areas to focus on in order to improve the performance of each type of urban space. The hierarchy of criteria prompts the designer to focus primarily on "basic" criteria, since they are the most feasible to meet, and "high value add" criteria for having the highest corrective potentials to improve the overall urban

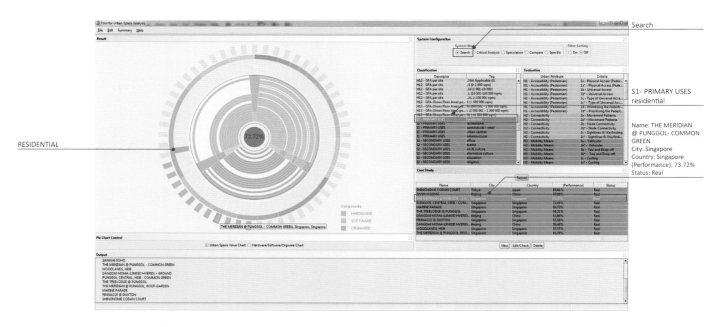

3.19 TUSA: "Search" mode, search by tag (Urban Space Value Chart).

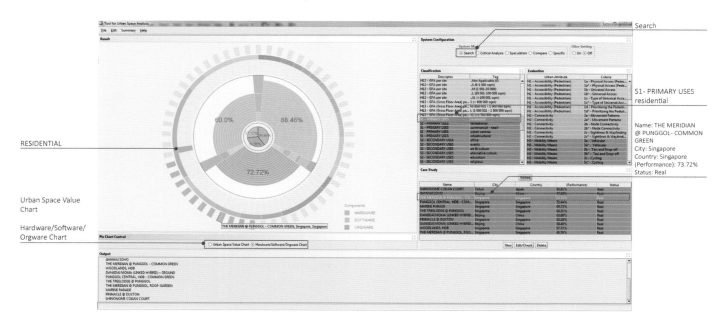

3.20 TUSA: "Search" mode, search by tag (Hardware/Software/Orgware Chart).

space performance, followed by "value add" and "good to have" criteria. Design recommendations to meet these criteria draw from the best examples in the database of case studies. Rather than dictating design solutions, the TUSA offers users the flexibility to determine which criteria and proposed design recommendations are most appropriate and practical in light of the specific project's goals, while prioritizing the design actions.

Speculative Tool

While the TUSA does not generate new hybrid typologies, it provides means to speculate on new spaces, by combining tags in the classification system. For example, for speculating on residential spaces in a very high-density local context (Figure 3.23), the tool highlights mutually basic, value add, high value add, good to have and desired criteria for such a hybrid typology.

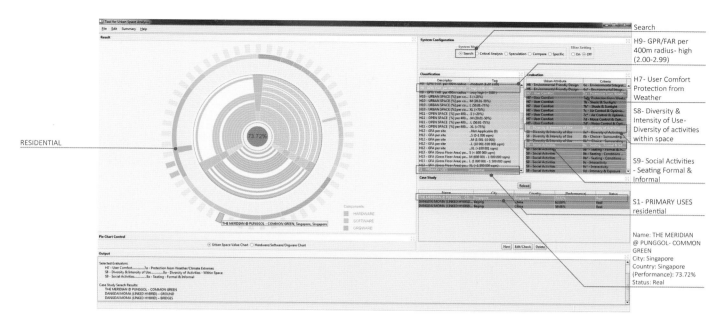

3.21 TUSA: "Search" mode, search by a combination of tags and descriptors.

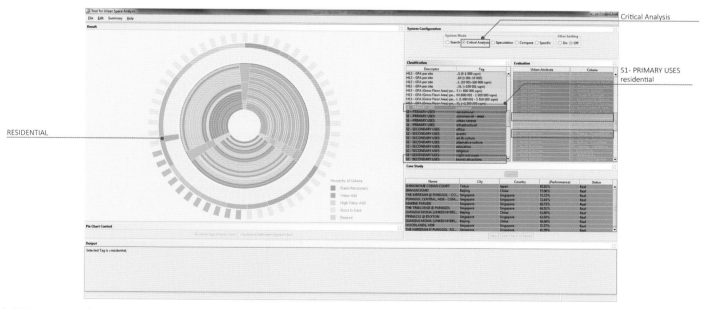

3.22 TUSA: "Critical Analysis" mode (selected tag: "Residential" within "S1 Primary Use" descriptor, an example).

Furthermore, this mode enables speculation on non-standard hybrid typologies by recombining attributes across different types of parameters. For example, one may speculate on underground parks, as shown in Figure 3.24. This becomes particularly interesting and relevant for high-density contexts where future urban development trajectories may in fact engender such hybrid spaces and conditions, rather than staying in the realm of hypothesis.

Discussions and Implications

With its various modes, capacities, innovative and intuitive ways of design communication, it is hoped that the TUSA can be a helpful new tool which contributes to better decision-making in the initial stages of the design process, as it fosters creativity and reinterpretations of design solutions rather than prescribing design formulas, and provides deeper insights into aspects which

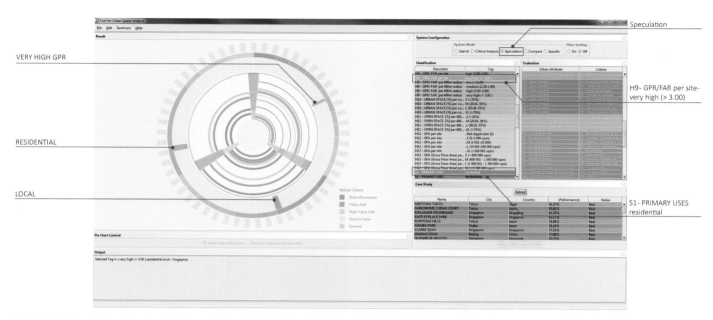

3.23 TUSA: "Speculation" mode, hybrid conditions (selected tags: "Residential" within "S1 Primary Use" descriptor; "very high (>3.01)" within "H8: GPR/FAR per Site" descriptor; and "local—Singapore" within "O2: Geography" descriptor, an example).

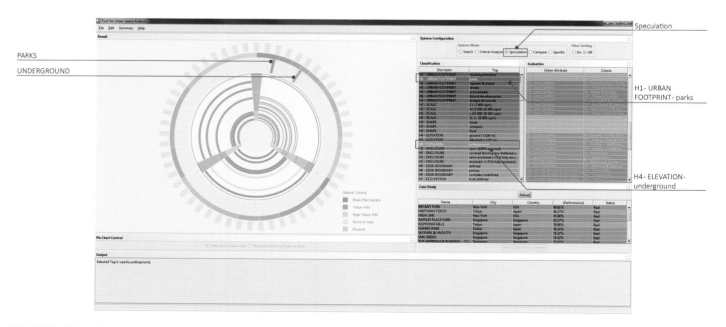

3.24 TUSA: "Speculation" mode, non-standard hybrid typologies (selected tags: "Parks" within "H1 URBAN FOOTPRINT descriptor" and "underground" within "H4: ELEVATION descriptor").

otherwise would be difficult to capture. However, the ways described are not exhaustive and users are encouraged to explore its capacities and find their own way of analysis.

The current TUSA database includes only 50 case studies, which makes consistency analysis somewhat limited, since not all tags and hybrid typologies provided by the TUSA are necessarily covered. With each new urban space added into the system, the hierarchy of criteria is automatically readjusted. The TUSA has been developed from the start to be flexible and to accommodate changes in the future. All TUSA modes are dynamic and changeable. Both classification tags and evaluation criteria can be edited (added or deleted) at any point in time, which makes the tool adaptable to new conditions and design requirements. This is an essential aspect of the TUSA, as it is a prerequisite for creating a dynamic and self-evaluative environment. By being self-critical, open and flexible, the tool reflects the demands of contemporary cities to be constantly reshaped and redesigned, and suggests a new way to investigate contemporary urban spaces.

Further adjustments would also make the TUSA applicable to other research projects, related to performance assessment, strategic planning and indexing of various types of urban environments. The flexibility of the tool and framework would allow the addition and adaptation of design attributes into the tool when needed (e.g., customization of the scoring system to give higher weighting to the presence of the informal activities in a space, over intentional programming), as well as to add new case studies into the tool.

Rather than directly generating "specific solutions" such as "forms," the TUSA is primarily developed as an analytical and speculative tool, providing fruitful means to systematically study, understand and guide urban space design in high-density contexts. With all its capacities, the TUSA also enables rethinking and re-conceptualizing the role and meaning of urban space in future development trajectories and becomes a guiding tool for projecting sustainable urban development and renewal.

URBAN SPACE CATALOG

For the purpose of systematic archival of documented data and initial findings, an Urban Space Catalog is proposed. The Catalog summarizes key information about each urban space in a comprehensive yet compact and visually compelling manner, including key space characteristics, namely classification (typology), quantitative measures (size, density measures, etc.), maps (spatial analysis), photographs, performance charts (evaluation) and textual information, consisting of on-site observations and a review of secondary sources, with a section commenting on lessons learned through investigation ("Strengths and Weaknesses" for local spaces and "How Does It Fit to Singapore?" for international spaces). The following pages provide two examples extracted from the Urban Space Catalog, namely Jianwai SOHO in Beijing, China (Figure 3.25) and ION Orchard in Singapore (3.26).

NETWORK PEDESTRIAN RECREATIONAL
INTENSE USE HYBRID OFFICE
PASSIVE ENVIRONMENTAL DESIGN HOUSING POROUS
PRIVATE EVENTS DOWNTOWN
RETAIL FLUID DOWNTOWN

0   25   75

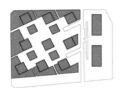

BUILDINGS 69%

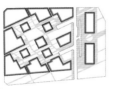

ACTIVITIES

SOFTSCAPE 28%

HARDSCAPE 52%

Layer Analysis

INTRODUCTION

Jianwai SOHO is a mega-complex in the central area of Beijing's CBD, 1.5 miles east of Tiananmen Square. The new complex of luxury residential, commercial and office buildings marketed to wealthy Chinese and foreigners replaced an old steel factory from the 1950s. The development includes 20 high-rise towers and four villas with 20 rooftop gardens and 16 pedestrian lanes.

INTENSITY OF USES

Although primarily residential, Jianwai SOHO also integrates offices, recreation facilities and retail outlets. There are about 200 shops ranging from 100 to 600 square metres in area. Two 28-story office towers, located next to the Third Ring Road, have total office area of 98,000 square metres. Jianwai SOHO offers both offices and residential apartments (more than 2,000 units), creating a convenient working and living environment. Moreover, each year Jianwai SOHO hosts over 40 events of various kinds.

EVENT SPACE

During the Summer Carnival, which runs for four months each year at the Jianwai SOHO, various concerts, poetry recitals, street displays and other events are taking place open for public.

DESIGN CONCEPT

The project was inspired by the maze of alleys in North African Islamic cities, namely Ceuta in Morocco, that are characterised by rich, diverse and vivid everyday life and ambiences. Narrow streets, covered passageways, play of light and shadow, smell and crowd are some of the elements that, with great spontaneity, create intriguing and exciting walking experiences. The intention of Jianwai SOHO was to recreate such an experience and generate urban space that can grow in every direction, being the main cell of the city.

High-rise high-density space (top)
Complex multi-layered public space network (bottom)

3.25 An excerpt from the Urban Space Catalog: Jianwai SOHO, Beijing, China.

LANDSCAPE AND PEDESTRIAN FRIENDLY DESIGN

Pedestrian and automobile flows are well-separated. The basement level is reserved for cars while the landscaped ground level is completely liberated for the pedestrians. The apartment towers and low-scale commercial buildings form a loose checkerboard plan at the ground level. Instead of organising the project around a large park or other urban-scaled focal point, the ground plane is riddled with sunken gardens that knit the two levels together and allow daylight to reach even the lowest levels. This multi-level space between the buildings is the most unique and striking element of the design. The roof of commercial buildings features green pedestrian walkways that connect all the buildings and allow free movement through the complex.

ENVIRONMENTAL DESIGN AND COMFORT

Rather than being grouped as close to each other as possible, Jianwai SOHO's residential towers are simple cubes (squares in basis) arranged in a checkerboard-like pattern so that the perimeter areas of each tower receive enough light and air. This is achieved by rotating the buildings slightly east (by 25°) from a direct southern exposure, coupled with variations in the height of the apartment towers which become progressively taller the farther they get from the water. In such a way, the passive environmental design is combined with the efficient use of the land. In terms of interior layout, the north corner of each floor is occupied by elevators and a communal room, while each of the other corners accommodates a spacious corner unit. There are only three units on each floor, which, apart from daylight, provides higher level of privacy.

HOW DOES IT FIT INTO SINGAPORE?

Due to its layout, Jianwai SOHO is characterized by the absence of a centre. Such an open layout with multiple levels may be well applicable to Singapore's highly dense residential areas. Integration of residential and commercial uses, as well as clever design of multi-level green public spaces, may become a good model for creating greater spatial diversity and intensification of space usage around local public housing areas.

Pedestrian-friendly multi-level green space network (top left and right)
Integrated fixed seating amenities (bottom)

Urban Space Diagram:
88.46% - 70.00% - 72.73%
Hardware-Software-Orgware

70.00%   88.46%

77.06%

72.73%

QUANTITATIVE DATA

Programming
# of Programme within and along Urban Space	5
# of Programme per 100sqm Area of Urban Space	0.010
% of Active Programme Space	0%
% of Flexible Space	0%
% of Internal Cirrculation	52%
% of F&B or Retail	40%

Landscape
% of Softscape Area	33%
% of Water or for Water Features	0%
# of Trees within Core Urban Space	240
# of Trees within Development Site	240
Ratio of Trees per 100 sqm of Usable Urban Space	0.50
Ratio of Trees per 100 sqm of Development Site	0.39

Accessibility
# of Entrances	10
# of Entrance per 100 sqm of Usable Urban Space	0.021
# of Formal/Main Entrances (from ground level)	8
# of Informal Entrances	1
% of Boundary that is Physically Accessible	26%
% of Boundary that is Visually Accessible	26%
Distance to Nearest Public Transport	30

Comfort
% Shaded Area at Noon	22%
% Shaded Area at Mid-afternoon	51%
% Shaded Area at Late-afternoon	69%
Total Covered/Enclosed Area	420
% of Covered Urban Space	1%

Seating
Units per 100 sqm of Usable Urban Space	N.A.
Capacity per 100 sqm of Usable Urban Space	N.A.
# of Seating Character	N.A.
# of Seating Types	N.A.
#of Seating Types per 100 sqm of Urban Space	N.A.

JIANWAI SOHO (PHASE 1)

BEIJING, CHINA
2004

PROJECT INFORMATION
Client: SOHO, China
Architects : Riken Ytamamoto & Field SHop
General Contractor: Parsons Brinckerhoff, Asia

PROJECT BRIEF
Primary Use: Residential
Adjacent Use: Office, Commercial/Retail, Event Space, Recreational

Urban Space
Site Area: 61,750 sq.m
Urban Space Area: 78%
Gross Plot Ratio(GPR): 4.78
Gross Floor Area(GFA): 295,000 sq.m

Building height: 73.5 m
Population Density: 1195.95

400m Radius Context
Open Space: 84%
Gross Plot Ratio (GPR): 3.10
Gross Floor Area (GFA): 1,558,220 sq.m

Context

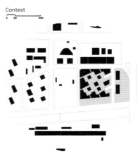

COMMERCIAL PLAZA
COVERED IDENTITY AMBIENT LIGHTING
DOWNTOWN NODE INFORMAL

0   25   50

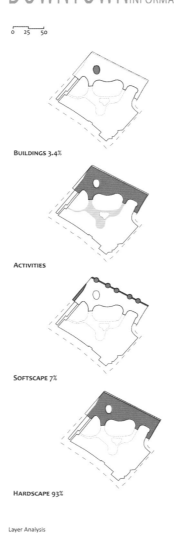

BUILDINGS 3.4%

ACTIVITIES

SOFTSCAPE 7%

HARDSCAPE 93%

Layer Analysis

INTRODUCTION

Located directly above Orchard MRT station, ION Orchard had rapidly established itself as a high speed, high volume retail heaven at the tip of Singapore's main retail strip. Due to its close proximity to the train station, ION orchard is elaborately integrated to the underground network system not only to serve its own commercial purpose, but to serve as part of a larger pedestrian infrastructure, which resulted in a complex yet successful hybrid urban space.

The ION Orchard complex consists of an open plaza, the podium block with 8 levels of retail program (4 above the ground and 4 underground) and a 48-storey residential tower.

INTEGRATED RETAIL EXPERIENCE

The retail outlets on the ground floor were clearly designed for the purpose of street level attraction, unlike many other malls along Orchard road. These street-facing retail outlets, in turn, became alternate entrances to the mall itself, providing an extended sense of permeability. However, like in many other consumption environments, the geometrical ambiguity of the interior space, and especially underground network, encourages human traffic to be channelled into the mall and lose the sense of direction. In contrast to the claustrophobic and maze-like environment within the mall, the public plaza provides a vast sense of space, making it highly appropriate as a meeting place for various user groups.

ACTIVITIES AND SURVEILLANCE

The activities carried out on the plaza are mostly static, suggesting that it is primarily used as a form of resting spot, in between other activities. Its spatial grandeur does make it intimidating for informal activities to happen. The informal activities, such as F&B or busking, still happen well beyond the boundary of the development. This sense of intimidation is further encouraged by the frequent flow of maintenance personnel on the public square. No other forms of surveillance were observed on site.

Meeting space (top)
Covered organic space (bottom)

3.26 An excerpt from the Urban Space Catalog: ION Orchard, Singapore.

PEDESTRIAN FRIENDLY AND INTENSITY OF USE

Due to its proximity to the public transport infrastructure, ION Orchard is relatively well connected to its adjacencies. However, such pedestrian connections are limited to underground network, which is often indirect and confusing. On the street level, due to the closure of pedestrian traffic across Orchard Road and Paterson Road, ION plaza seems to be somewhat disconnected. Yet, the plaza is well linked with other public plazas along the same side of Orchard Road, such as Ngee Ann City Civic Square (Civic Plaza), being part of the network of public event spaces.

MATERIALS, FORMAL AND INFORMAL SEATING

The floor materials used in ION Orchard's public plaza are largely monochrome and cool, aligning to the aesthetic of the overall development. This homogenous use of material is accented at various points by bright and loud urban furniture, such as colourful sculptures and seats. This creates certain sense of spatial interest, and activities tend to be observed around these amenities. Apart from the formal seating amenities, that is often rearranged and situated under the glass eaves which protects from the rain, informal seating is available in form of stairs, which connects the level of the street and slightly elevated level of the plaza itself. The unique organic shape of the glass façade is further accentuated by the digital display and attractive lights during the night, which makes the entire development one of the most prominent visual landmarks in Orchard Road.

STRENGTHS AND WEAKNESSES

Multiple factors, such as the general district use, public infrastructure, underground pedestrian infrastructure, sufficient and diverse seating amenities and protection from the rain, contribute to the vibrancy seen around the ION Orchard plaza. The entire development seems to be a positive example of integration of a new public and commercial space with an already established and effective urban structure and transportation infrastructure.

Seating arrangements: formal (top left) and informal (top right)
Visual landmark (bottom)

Urban Space Diagram:
80.77% - 70% - 68.18%
Hardware-Software-Orgware

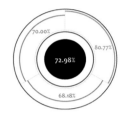

QUANTITATIVE DATA

Programming

# of Programme within and along Urban Space	7
# of Programme per 100sqm Area of Urban Space	0.155
% of Active Programme Space	0%
% of Flexible Space	50%
% of Internal Cirrculation	90%
% of F&B or Retail	0%

Landscape

% of Softscape Area	7%
% of Water or for Water Features	0%
# of Trees within Core Urban Space	20
# of Trees within Development Site	20
Ratio of Trees per 100 sqm of Usable Urban Space	0.44
Ratio of Trees per 100 sqm of Development Site	0.11

Accessibility

# of Entrances	9
# of Entrance per 100 sqm of Usable Urban Space	0.199
# of Formal/Main Entrances (from ground level)	2
# of Informal Entrances	7
% of Boundary that is Physically Accessible	6%
% of Boundary that is Visually Accessible	49%
Distance to Nearest Public Transport	0*

Comfort

% Shaded Area at Noon	25%
% Shaded Area at Mid-afternoon	30%
% Shaded Area at Late-afternoon	43%
Total Covered/Enclosed Area	2,000
% of Covered Urban Space	44%

Seating

Units per 100 sqm of Usable Urban Space	0.31
Capacity per 100 sqm of Usable Urban Space	2.48
# of Seating Character	5*
# of Seating Types	2
#of Seating Types per 100 sqm of Urban Space	0.04

ION ORCHARD

SINGAPORE
2006 - 2009

PROJECT INFORMATION
Client: Orchard Turn Developments Pte Ltd, a joint venture between Capital Land and Sun Hung Kai Properties
Architect: Benoy and RSP Architects
General Contractor: Wop Hup Holdings

PROJECT BRIEF
Primary Use: Urban Center
Adjacent Use: Commercial/Retail, Residential, Recreational, Infrastructural, Office, Event Space

Urban Space
Site Area: 18,000 sq.m
Urban Space Area: 97%
Gross Plot Ratio(GPR): 6.94
Gross Floor Area(GFA): 125,000 sq.m

400m Radius Context
Open Space: 68%
Gross Plot Ratio (GPR): 3.19
Gross Floor Area (GFA): 1,601,374 sq.m

Context

NOTES

1 A series of additional analytical explorations have also been conducted, including variations in space classification, morphology exercises, parametric modeling and simulation, with an aim to test and refine the framework, as well as to investigate various data visualization techniques.

2 Several cases do not fulfill high-density criteria, yet due to their innovative typology or high intensity that are highly relevant for densely built urban contexts, they were also included. These criteria do not necessarily refer to good practices in terms of quality, performance or success, but rather to good examples of the investigated conditions (built and population density, intensity of use, hybridity and spatial innovation). For example, observed high density of users (crowd) does not necessarily relate to high urban performance, although it may be an indicator of its popularity or intensity. Similarly, urban spaces that are less crowded, such as Henderson Waves in Singapore or Dangdai Moma in Beijing, for example, should not be a priori disregarded as potential good practices.

3 Some of the cases have been included after the research was completed, for the purpose of the book specifically. Figure 3.2 shows the list of initial case studies that were included in the original research project.

4 POE is commonly defined as "the process of evaluating buildings in a systematic and rigorous manner after they have been built and occupied for some time" (Preiser et al., 1988, p. 3). Numerous short-, medium- and long-term benefits of POE include: indications of problems in buildings and potential solutions, increased understanding of users' needs and building performance implications, increased understanding of the design intentions by users, better-informed and appropriate decision-making, reduction of costs, and improvements in future design quality, standards and measurements, etc. (Hassanain, 2007). This research adopted an indicative form of POE, which is defined as "a quick snapshot of the project." It is considered a broad-brush approach, where walk-through observations, interviews and sometimes short questionnaires are combined. The aim is to capture and highlight major strengths and weaknesses of spaces investigated. This method provides useful information quickly and forms the basis of a more in-depth study (HEFCE, 2006).

5 There are some limitations to on-site observation that need to be acknowledged. On-site visits were conducted under different weather conditions, and at different times of the day/week, which may have affected some observations. In addition, time spent on site was often not sufficient to accurately notify all activities, their intensity, peaks and patterns that may be important for space performance; to detect and collect such information, much longer observations, ethnographic research and a careful and consistent time schedule (including comparable specific weather conditions and days of the week) would be required.

6 The original terms used in the research have been changed to more intuitive and understandable terms for the book, as introduced in Chapter 2 (Urban Space Framework). Original research terms "urban value," "urban space attributes" and "criteria" have been changed to "urban space attributes," "urban space qualities" and "design principles" respectively, in the book.

7 The evaluation checklist should be used in reference to Chapter 2 of this book.

8 Criteria with high consistency are those that are very common among a selected group of case studies. They are very feasible to meet and may be considered as fundamental requirements for a particular type of urban space. Accordingly, they should be particularly considered in early stages of planning and design process, mainly in design brief development. This, however, does not mean that such criteria are necessarily more important than others. All criteria in the Urban Space Framework are considered equally important.

9 It is most likely that basic requirements (frequently met criteria) are fulfilled by the majority of urban spaces analyzed. Thus, in order to prioritize the design interventions to enhance the performance of an urban space more strategically, it is critical to look at those criteria that are most inconsistently met. Such criteria are read as having the highest value add factor and thus possess the highest priority in terms of the order of design interventions. Their impact on enhancing the overall urban space performance (value) is considered higher than that of basic requirements. Finally, they are feasible and the reference to good design measures is available.

10 Values toward 1.00 reflect high consistency in meeting a criterion. Values toward 0.00 express low consistency in meeting the criterion, i.e., high consistency in failing it.

11 The TUSA is designed using MySQL, which is an open source relational database management system (RDBMS) that runs as a server providing multi-user access to a number of databases. MySQL Workbench, a free integrated environment, is used to graphically administer MySQL databases and visually design database structures.

REFERENCES

Batty, M. (2005). *Cities and Complexity: Understanding Cities with Cellular Automata, Agent-based Models, and Fractals*. Cambridge, MA: MIT Press.

Ellin, N. (2006). *Integral Urbanism*. New York: Routledge.

Hassanain, M. A. (2007). Post-occupancy Indoor Environmental Quality Evaluation of Student Housing Facilities. *Architectural Engineering and Design Management*, 3, 249–256.

HEFCE. (2006). *Guide to Post Occupancy Evaluation* [Electronic Version], 1–62. Retrieved from http://www.smg.ac.uk/documents/POEBrochureFinal06.pdf.

Meredith, M., Lasch, A., & Sasaki, M. (2008). *From Control to Design: Parametric/Algorithmic Architecture*. Barcelona: Actar.

Preiser, W. F., Rabinowitz, H. Z., & White, E. T. (1988). *Post-occupancy Evaluation*. New York: Van Nostrand Reinhold.

Chapter 4

Guide to Design Actions

Through different design purposes and design actions, this chapter suggests practical means of Urban Space Framework application. Each design or decision-making action will be depicted in the form of visual diagrams to ease the communication and interpretation of findings. Several examples for each design purpose are shown, with sequential visual diagrams to explain the full processes of analysis and application.

Design Brief Development
Strategic Intervention—Evaluation and Enhancement
Comparison and Benchmarking

IMPROVING THE QUALITY OF URBAN SPACE BY STRATEGIC DESIGN GUIDANCE

While Chapter 3 provided ready-to-use instruments for the documentation, classification, evaluation and analysis of urban spaces, this chapter focuses on the operational aspects of the design process and decision-making, i.e., how to interpret and efficiently use the tools, procedures and findings. It will demonstrate, with exemplary cases that have been introduced in the previous chapters, how the Urban Space Instrument, which consists of classification and evaluation systems, which are descriptive mechanisms, enveloped by the HARDware, SOFTware and ORGware components of the Urban Space Framework, may be applied as a useful tool to guide various purposes of the design process involving various actors and to improve the overall design quality of urban space.

Design quality is a problematic term however, not least because it may mean different things to different actors and stakeholders (Carmona et al., 2010). Depending on the complexity of the project, reaching a consensus about what is high design quality can become a very challenging task to achieve. Often, during the implementation stage, poor or different understanding of quality of urban space among various actors, intuition and subjectivity in decision-making and design, and communication gaps or poor cooperation among multiple parties involved in the design process lead to lack of design integration and the results are often described as disappointing, with good examples scarce (Chapman, 2011; Sandercock & Dovey, 2002).

In response to such challenges, strategic design guidance that would shape better decisions at all levels, enable prompt communication among the various actors to facilitate more transparent decision-making process and ultimately deliver improved outcomes is of critical importance.

This is even more crucial for dense and hybrid urban conditions emerging globally, where the emerging types and conditions of urban spaces require the re-examination and re-conceptualization of conventional approaches. This includes investigating new, systematic yet flexible approaches, frameworks and instruments to understand, analyze, assess and guide the design and management of emerging urban spaces that would reflect their qualities and performances as holistic, relative, dynamic and pluralistic conceptions.

APPLICATION OF THE URBAN SPACE INSTRUMENT

Based on the research process and analysis, the application of the Urban Space Instrument proposes a holistic mechanism for more systematic and analytical investigations into those attributes of urban space that are critical to its performance that can lead to design actions to improve the performance of urban spaces of particular typologies or in specific high-density conditions. This should be used as a reference to a set of design recommendations, rather than as prescriptions, at the initial stage of new design processes or as an assessment tool for the existing urban space performances.

In applying the Urban Space Instrument, we are aware of "the danger of generally desirable design principles becoming inflexible dogma" (Carmona et al., 2010, p. 11). Rather, this is a tool established with an aim to facilitate:

> the active process of design that relates general principles to specific situations through the application of design intelligence: design principles should be used with the flexibility derived from a deeper understanding and

appreciation of their bases, justifications and interrelations. In any design process there are no wholly "right" or "wrong" answers—substantially because design involves relating general, and generally desirable, principles to specific sites, where the totality of the outcome is what matters.

(Carmona et al., 2010, p. 11)

In this regard, this chapter will elaborate on how the Urban Space Instrument may be used in an intuitive and flexible case-by-case manner to identify strengths and weaknesses in the design of specific urban spaces, with a view to informing possible design interventions to improve urban space performance, serving various planning and design purposes, as summarized in Table 4.1.

Design Brief Development

Design briefs are common means of providing site-specific design guidance by ensuring that important design issues are considered, offering a straightforward means of providing greater certainty and transparency in the design decision-making process. Because they set out design principles (preferably) in advance of development interest for particular sites, they can help unlock complex urban sites, by establishing core principles around which negotiations may occur (Carmona et al., 2010).

The hierarchy of criteria (design principles) established in the Urban Space Instrument provides useful assistance in developing the design briefs and facilitates the pre-design phase in the overall design process. Based on selected individual or multiple spatial characteristics (tags), the Urban Space Instrument generates checklists that identify and prioritize the essential and critical attributes the new designs should address. The design brief developer should focus on "Basic" criteria first, since they are fundamentally important for the urban space performance, being the most frequently met and thus the most feasible, followed by "Value Add" and "High Value Add" criteria (design principles) for their high priority with corrective potentials to improve the urban space performance.

Two scenarios will be discussed to illustrate how the Urban Space Instrument may be applied to facilitate design brief development (Figures 4.1 and 4.2).

"Design Brief Development" for Residential **Hybrid Typology**
(Case A: Residential + Medium Scale + High Density + Open Enclosure) (Figure 4.1)

1 Assistance in Developing the Design Brief
— Generate hierarchy of criteria:

First, the hierarchy of criteria is generated for residential typology (**S1 Primary Use**: Residential). Specific tags may be selected further depending on the desired hybrid typology. In this particular scenario, three more tags, i.e., **H2 Scale**: Medium; **H8 Gross Plot Ratio (GPR) per Site/Development**: High (GPR: 2.00–2.99, which is considered high density); **H5 Enclosure**: Open (100% exposed) are selected. The addition of tags enables one to narrow down the criteria that are mutually met across the HARDware, SOFTware and ORGware components by all selected tags.

2 Inform the Designer
— Generate checklists for design brief:

Based on the hierarchy of the criteria that are mutually met by all selected tags, a checklist is generated for the design brief. It is recommended that the design brief should focus on "Basic" criteria first (such as "Provide safe and direct pedestrian accesses that clearly prioritize the pedestrians over the vehicular traffic" and "Provide synergetic activities in the immediate surroundings of urban space" in this case) and then further incorporate "High Value Add" criteria (such as "Provide designated cycling areas/lanes") into the checklist. Furthermore, best practice case studies in the database may be examined to understand how other successful cases have implemented the recommended criteria (design principles).

"Design Brief Development" for Recreational **Hybrid Typology**
(Case B: Recreational + Large Scale + Very High Context Density + Elevated Elevation) (Figure 4.2)

1 Assistance in Developing the Design Brief
— Generate hierarchy of criteria:

In this scenario, the hierarchy of criteria is generated for recreational typology (**S1 Primary Use**: Recreational). Three more tags are selected, i.e., **H2 Scale**: Large; **H9 Gross Plot Ratio (GPR) per 400m radius (context)**: Very high (GPR: above 3.00, which is considered very high density); **H4 Elevation**: Elevated (above 2m) are selected. The addition of tags enables one to narrow down the criteria that are mutually met across the HARDware, SOFTware and ORGware components by all selected tags.

2 Inform the Designer
— Generate checklists for design brief:

The design brief should focus on "Basic" criteria first (such as "Divide space into sub-spaces," "Provide unique and memorable spatial features" and "Provide a variety of public programs, services or facilities that are free of charge"),

Table **4.1** Application of the Urban Space Instrument for specific design purposes

Design Purpose	Design Actions
Design Brief Development	**Assistance in Developing the Design Brief** Generate Hierarchy of Criteria **Inform the Designer** Generate Checklists for Design Brief
Strategic Intervention—Evaluation and Enhancement	**Evaluate** **Identify** Components and criteria to be enhanced **Analyze and Prioritize** Consult Hierarchy of Criteria Attend to Critical principles first (Basic and High Value Add)
Comparison and Benchmarking	**Evaluate Performance** **Compare** **Benchmark** A. Against the average performance B. Against the hierarchy of criteria (number of criteria met) C. Recommendation based on benchmarking

followed by "Value Add" and "High Value Add" criteria (such as "Activate impermeable edges" and "Provide adjustable filters to create physical or visual barriers") for enhanced urban space performance. Best examples in the library of case studies, which show strength in those particular criteria (design principles), may be referred to for more practical design guidance.

Strategic Intervention: Evaluation and Enhancement

Strategic intervention includes identifying a specific opportunity for improvement, selecting a set of improvement goals, designing the overall structure of a set of tools that can take them forward, and prioritizing the design actions that enhance the quality of urban space.

The Urban Space Instrument provides useful means to classify and evaluate both existing spaces and new design projects, and in such a way helps in strategic intervention for the planning and design process. Once the space is classified and evaluated, the Urban Space Instrument proposes areas (design principles) for enhancement, as well as prioritizing the enhancement actions, based on the hierarchy of design principles. Among the design principles that require improvements, the Urban Space Instrument prompts the designer to focus primarily on "Basic" criteria, since they are the most feasible to meet, and "High Value Add" criteria for having the highest corrective potentials to improve the overall urban space performance, followed by "Value Add" and "Good to Have" criteria. Design recommendations to meet these criteria draw from the best examples in the library of case studies. Rather

than dictating design solutions, the Urban Space Instrument offers users the flexibility to determine which criteria and proposed design recommendations are most appropriate and practical in light of the specific project's goals.

The scenarios below demonstrate how the Urban Space Instrument may be applied for strategic intervention (Figures 4.3 and 4.4).

"Strategic Intervention" for Residential Hybrid Typology (Case A: Dangdai Moma/Linked Hybrid, Beijing, China; and Case B: Treelodge@Punggol, Singapore) (Figures 4.3 and 4.4)

1 **Evaluate**

First, the cases are assessed using the structured evaluation checklist, which includes all criteria proposed in the evaluation system.

2 **Identify**

— Components and criteria to be enhanced:
A set of urban space value diagrams (initial circular chart [left] and simplified circular pie-chart [right]) are generated based on the result of the evaluation. Colored stripes in the initial circular chart [left] represent criteria that are met by the investigated urban space and the sum of all colored stripes creates the overall urban space value (in %). More specific comparisons are enhanced by another simplified circular pie-chart [right] which shows the performance of space (in %) for each urban space value component—the sum of stripes of the same color. In

DESIGN BRIEF DEVELOPMENT
1: Assistance in Developing the Design Brief
Generate Hierarchy of Criteria

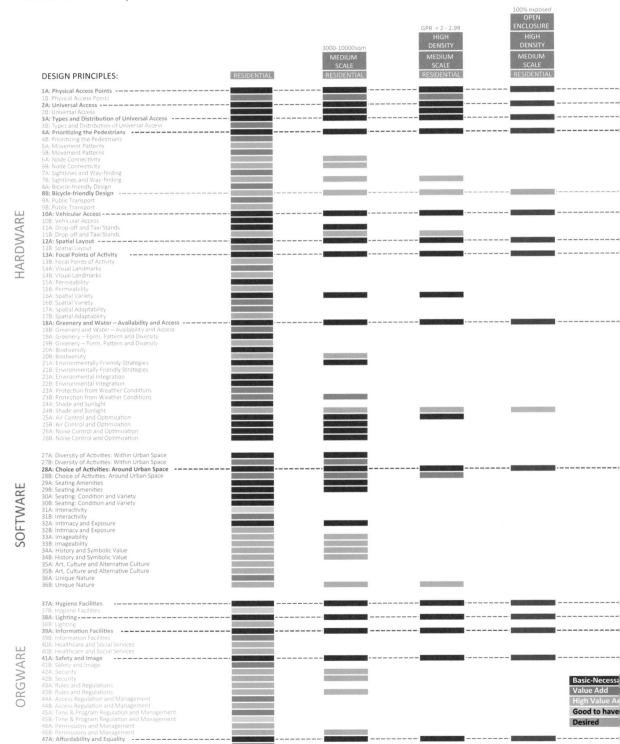

2: Inform the Designer
Generate Checklists for Design Brief

4.1 "Design brief development" for Residential hybrid typology (Case A: Residential + Medium Scale + High Density + Open Enclosure).

Basic/Necessary

High Value Add

Provide sufficient number of pedestrian access points

Provide means of universal access when level changes occur

Provide different types of universal access

Provide safe and direct pedestrian accesses that clearly prioritize the pedestrians over the vehicular traffic

Provide designated cycling areas/lanes

Provide parking facilities

Make pedestrian network visible and differentiated from other activities

Provide diversity of activity nodes

Provide sufficient green and water features

Provide synergetic activities in the immediate surroundings of urban space

Keep the space in clean and good physical condition

Provide adequate lighting along main pathways and activity nodes

Provide public communicational facilities

Employ adequate design measures to prevent physical injuries

Provide a variety of public programs, services or facilities that are free of charge

A. Safety fences clearly demarcates vehicular and pedestrian traffic. *Onden Road*, Tokyo, Japan.

B. Fully pedestrianized areas safeguard the pedestrian movement. *Albert Mall*, Singapore.

C. Multi-level fully pedestrian space that connects major infrastructural transit-led nodes. *Shinjuku Terrace City*, Tokyo, Japan.

D. Provision of adequate bike lanes, separated from pedestrian lanes. *Times Square*, New York.

E. Integration of adequate bike lanes within urban space. *Superkilen*, Denmark.

F. Space provides a range of different programs and activities. *Times Square*, New York.

G. The open space is surrounded by local shops, street vendors and temples. *Albert Mall*, Singapore.

H. Unique illuminated signs and directions grab users' attention. *Shibuya Station*, Tokyo, Japan.

I. Site maps and signage are well-integrated into urban furniture. *Shinonome Codan Court*, Tokyo, Japan.

DESIGN BRIEF DEVELOPMENT
1: Assistance in Developing the Design Brief
Generate Hierarchy of Criteria

2: Inform the Designer
Generate Checklists for Design Brief

4.2 "Design brief development" for **Recreational** hybrid typology (Case B: Recreational + Large Scale + Very High Context Density + Elevated Elevation).

Basic/Necessary

Value Add

High Value Add

Provide sufficient number of pedestrian access points

Provide means of universal access when level changes occur

Provide different types of universal access

Provide parking facilities

A. Slight level changes from the main circulation contribute to spatial subdivision. **High Line**, New York.

B. Different patterns and forms of greenery mark the spatial division. **Bryant Park**, New York.

C. The use of different textures and colors enhance spatial differentiation. **Superkilen**, Denmark.

Activate impermeable edges

Divide space into sub-spaces

Provide sufficient green and water features

Provide at least one public amenity for specific active use within urban space

Provide a variety of well-integrated public amenities for specific passive and active uses within urban space

Provide sufficient formal seating amenities

Provide flexible/movable seating and/or tables

Provide adjustable filters to create physical or visual barriers

Provide unique and memorable spatial features

D. Distinct architectural features, accompanied by the immediate vicinity of the Singapore River provide memorable quality to the space. **Esplanade Promenade**, Singapore.

Provide affordable general healthcare service for all age groups

Keep the space in clean and good physical condition

Provide adequate lighting along main pathways and activity nodes

Provide public communicational facilities

Employ adequate design measures to prevent physical injuries

Employ design strategies that make space appear approachable, inviting, and thus - safe

E. The space provides a number of game and sports amenities for users for free depending on weather conditions and on event calendar. **Bryant Park**, New York.

Provide a variety of public programs, services or facilities that are free of charge

STRATEGIC INTERVENTION - EVALUATION AND ENHANCEMENT

1: Evaluate

2: Identify
Components & Criteria to be Enhanced

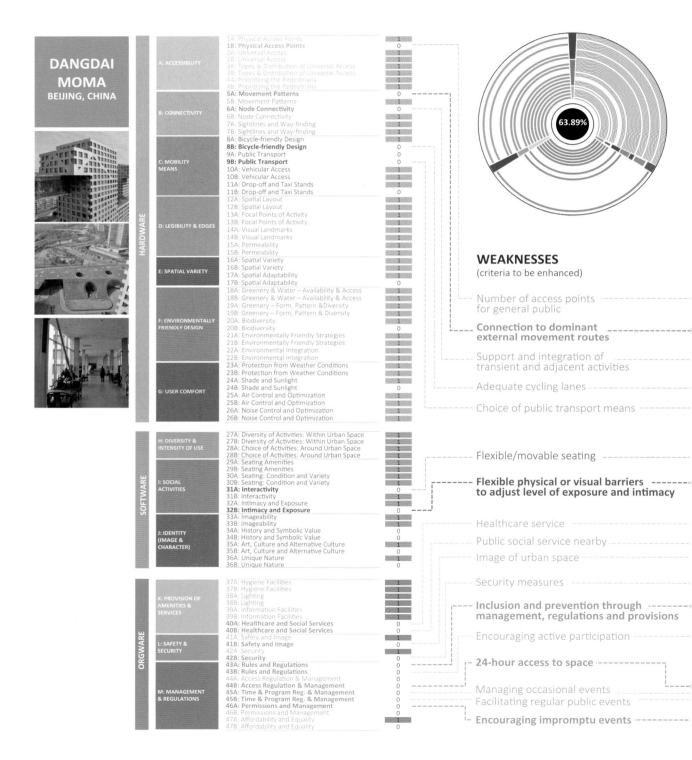

DANGDAI MOMA
BEIJING, CHINA

HARDWARE

A: ACCESSIBILITY
1A: Physical Access Points — 1
1B: Physical Access Points — 0
2A: Universal Access — 1
2B: Universal Access — 1
3A: Types & Distribution of Universal Access — 1
3B: Types & Distribution of Universal Access — 1
4A: Prioritizing the Pedestrians — 1
4B: Prioritizing the Pedestrians — 1

B: CONNECTIVITY
5A: Movement Patterns — 0
5B: Movement Patterns — 1
6A: Node Connectivity — 0
6B: Node Connectivity — 1
7A: Sightlines and Way-finding — 1
7B: Sightlines and Way-finding — 1

C: MOBILITY MEANS
8A: Bicycle-friendly Design — 1
8B: Bicycle-friendly Design — 0
9A: Public Transport — 0
9B: Public Transport — 0
10A: Vehicular Access — 1
10B: Vehicular Access — 1
11A: Drop-off and Taxi Stands — 1
11B: Drop-off and Taxi Stands — 0

D: LEGIBILITY & EDGES
12A: Spatial Layout — 1
12B: Spatial Layout — 1
13A: Focal Points of Activity — 1
13B: Focal Points of Activity — 1
14A: Visual Landmarks — 1
14B: Visual Landmarks — 1
15A: Permeability — 1
15B: Permeability — 1

E: SPATIAL VARIETY
16A: Spatial Variety — 1
16B: Spatial Variety — 1
17A: Spatial Adaptability — 1
17B: Spatial Adaptability — 0

F: ENVIRONMENTALLY FRIENDLY DESIGN
18A: Greenery & Water – Availability & Access — 1
18B: Greenery & Water – Availability & Access — 1
19A: Greenery – Form, Pattern &Diversity — 1
19B: Greenery – Form, Pattern & Diversity — 1
20A: Biodiversity — 1
20B: Biodiversity — 0
21A: Environmentally Friendly Strategies — 1
21B: Environmentally Friendly Strategies — 1
22A: Environmental Integration — 1
22B: Environmental Integration — 1

G: USER COMFORT
23A: Protection from Weather Conditions — 1
23B: Protection from Weather Conditions — 1
24A: Shade and Sunlight — 1
24B: Shade and Sunlight — 0
25A: Air Control and Optimization — 1
25B: Air Control and Optimization — 1
26A: Noise Control and Optimization — 1
26B: Noise Control and Optimization — 1

SOFTWARE

H: DIVERSITY & INTENSITY OF USE
27A: Diversity of Activities: Within Urban Space — 1
27B: Diversity of Activities: Within Urban Space — 1
28A: Choice of Activities: Around Urban Space — 1
28B: Choice of Activities: Around Urban Space — 1

I: SOCIAL ACTIVITIES
29A: Seating Amenities — 1
29B: Seating Amenities — 1
30A: Seating: Condition and Variety — 1
30B: Seating: Condition and Variety — 1
31A: Interactivity — 0
31B: Interactivity — 1
32A: Intimacy and Exposure — 1
32B: Intimacy and Exposure — 0

J: IDENTITY (IMAGE & CHARACTER)
33A: Imageability — 1
33B: Imageability — 1
34A: History and Symbolic Value — 0
34B: History and Symbolic Value — 0
35A: Art, Culture and Alternative Culture — 1
35B: Art, Culture and Alternative Culture — 0
36A: Unique Nature — 1
36B: Unique Nature — 0

ORGWARE

K: PROVISION OF AMENITIES & SERVICES
37A: Hygiene Facilities — 1
37B: Hygiene Facilities — 1
38A: Lighting — 1
38B: Lighting — 1
39A: Information Facilities — 1
39B: Information Facilities — 1
40A: Healthcare and Social Services — 0
40B: Healthcare and Social Services — 0

L: SAFETY & SECURITY
41A: Safety and Image — 1
41B: Safety and Image — 1
42A: Security — 1
42B: Security — 0

M: MANAGEMENT & REGULATIONS
43A: Rules and Regulations — 0
43B: Rules and Regulations — 0
44A: Access Regulation & Management — 0
44B: Access Regulation & Management — 0
45A: Time & Program Reg. & Management — 0
45B: Time & Program Reg. & Management — 0
46A: Permissions and Management — 0
46B: Permissions and Management — 0
47A: Affordability and Equality — 1
47B: Affordability and Equality — 0

63.89%

WEAKNESSES
(criteria to be enhanced)

Number of access points for general public

Connection to dominant external movement routes

Support and integration of transient and adjacent activities

Adequate cycling lanes

Choice of public transport means

Flexible/movable seating

Flexible physical or visual barriers to adjust level of exposure and intimacy

Healthcare service

Public social service nearby

Image of urban space

Security measures

Inclusion and prevention through management, regulations and provisions

Encouraging active participation

24-hour access to space

Managing occasional events

Facilitating regular public events

Encouraging impromptu events

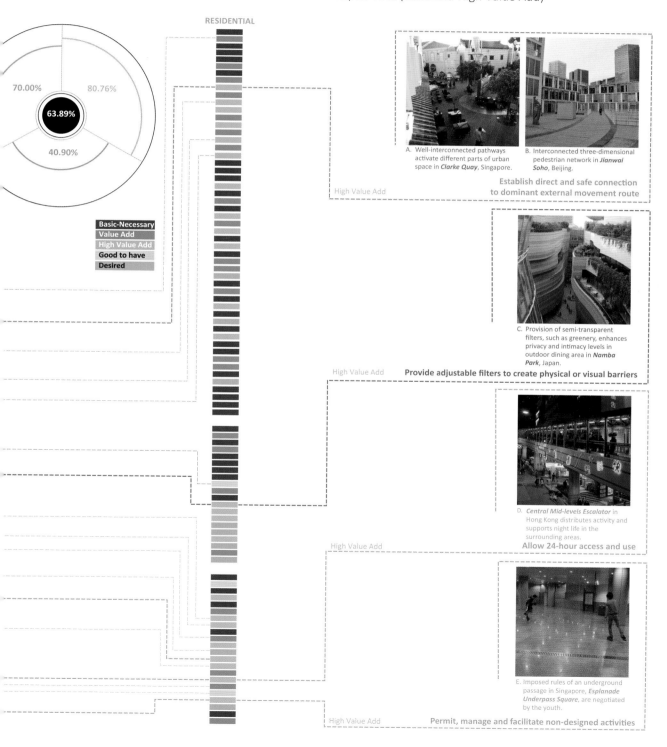

4.3 "Strategic intervention" for Residential hybrid typology (Case A: Dangdai Moma/ Linked Hybrid, Beijing, China).

3: Analyze and Prioritize
- Consult Hierarchy of Criteria
- Attend to Critical Principles First (Basic and High Value Add)

RESIDENTIAL

70.00%   80.76%

63.89%

40.90%

Basic-Necessary
Value Add
High Value Add
Good to have
Desired

A. Well-interconnected pathways activate different parts of urban space in *Clarke Quay*, Singapore.

B. Interconnected three-dimensional pedestrian network in *Jianwai Soho*, Beijing.

High Value Add

Establish direct and safe connection to dominant external movement route

C. Provision of semi-transparent filters, such as greenery, enhances privacy and intimacy levels in outdoor dining area in *Namba Park*, Japan.

High Value Add   **Provide adjustable filters to create physical or visual barriers**

D. *Central Mid-levels Escalator* in Hong Kong distributes activity and supports night life in the surrounding areas.

High Value Add   **Allow 24-hour access and use**

E. Imposed rules of an underground passage in Singapore, *Esplanade Underpass Square*, are negotiated by the youth.

High Value Add   **Permit, manage and facilitate non-designed activities**

STRATEGIC INTERVENTION - EVALUATION AND ENHANCEMENT

1: Evaluate

2: Identify
Components & Criteria to be Enhanced

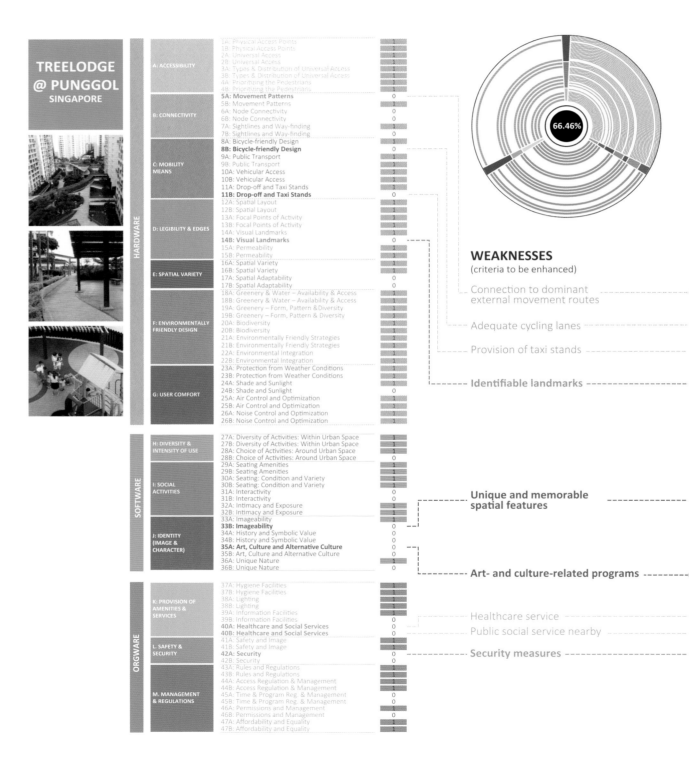

TREELODGE @ PUNGGOL SINGAPORE

HARDWARE

A: ACCESSIBILITY
- 1A: Physical Access Points — 1
- 1B: Physical Access Points — 1
- 2A: Universal Access — 1
- 2B: Universal Access — 1
- 3A: Types & Distribution of Universal Access — 1
- 3B: Types & Distribution of Universal Access — 1
- 4A: Prioritizing the Pedestrians — 1
- 4B: Prioritizing the Pedestrians — 1

B: CONNECTIVITY
- **5A: Movement Patterns** — 0
- 5B: Movement Patterns — 1
- 6A: Node Connectivity — 0
- 6B: Node Connectivity — 0
- 7A: Sightlines and Way-finding — 1
- 7B: Sightlines and Way-finding — 0

C: MOBILITY MEANS
- 8A: Bicycle-friendly Design — 1
- **8B: Bicycle-friendly Design** — 0
- 9A: Public Transport — 1
- 9B: Public Transport — 1
- 10A: Vehicular Access — 1
- 10B: Vehicular Access — 1
- 11A: Drop-off and Taxi Stands — 1
- **11B: Drop-off and Taxi Stands** — 0

D: LEGIBILITY & EDGES
- 12A: Spatial Layout — 1
- 12B: Spatial Layout — 1
- 13A: Focal Points of Activity — 1
- 13B: Focal Points of Activity — 1
- 14A: Visual Landmarks — 1
- **14B: Visual Landmarks** — 0

E: SPATIAL VARIETY
- 15A: Permeability — 1
- 15B: Permeability — 1
- 16A: Spatial Variety — 1
- 16B: Spatial Variety — 1
- 17A: Spatial Adaptability — 0
- 17B: Spatial Adaptability — 0

F: ENVIRONMENTALLY FRIENDLY DESIGN
- 18A: Greenery & Water – Availability & Access — 1
- 18B: Greenery & Water – Availability & Access — 1
- 19A: Greenery – Form, Pattern &Diversity — 1
- 19B: Greenery – Form, Pattern & Diversity — 1
- 20A: Biodiversity — 1
- 20B: Biodiversity — 1
- 21A: Environmentally Friendly Strategies — 1
- 21B: Environmentally Friendly Strategies — 1
- 22A: Environmental Integration — 1
- 22B: Environmental Integration — 1

G: USER COMFORT
- 23A: Protection from Weather Conditions — 1
- 23B: Protection from Weather Conditions — 1
- 24A: Shade and Sunlight — 1
- 24B: Shade and Sunlight — 0
- 25A: Air Control and Optimization — 1
- 25B: Air Control and Optimization — 1
- 26A: Noise Control and Optimization — 1
- 26B: Noise Control and Optimization — 1

SOFTWARE

H: DIVERSITY & INTENSITY OF USE
- 27A: Diversity of Activities: Within Urban Space — 1
- 27B: Diversity of Activities: Within Urban Space — 1
- 28A: Choice of Activities: Around Urban Space — 1
- 28B: Choice of Activities: Around Urban Space — 0

I: SOCIAL ACTIVITIES
- 29A: Seating Amenities — 1
- 29B: Seating Amenities — 1
- 30A: Seating: Condition and Variety — 1
- 30B: Seating: Condition and Variety — 1
- 31A: Interactivity — 0
- 31B: Interactivity — 0
- 32A: Intimacy and Exposure — 1
- 32B: Intimacy and Exposure — 1

J: IDENTITY (IMAGE & CHARACTER)
- 33A: Imageability — 1
- **33B: Imageability** — 0
- 34A: History and Symbolic Value — 0
- 34B: History and Symbolic Value — 0
- **35A: Art, Culture and Alternative Culture** — 0
- 35B: Art, Culture and Alternative Culture — 0
- 36A: Unique Nature — 1
- 36B: Unique Nature — 0

ORGWARE

K: PROVISION OF AMENITIES & SERVICES
- 37A: Hygiene Facilities — 1
- 37B: Hygiene Facilities — 1
- 38A: Lighting — 1
- 38B: Lighting — 1
- 39A: Information Facilities — 1
- 39B: Information Facilities — 0
- **40A: Healthcare and Social Services** — 0
- **40B: Healthcare and Social Services** — 0

L: SAFETY & SECURITY
- 41A: Safety and Image — 1
- 41B: Safety and Image — 1
- **42A: Security** — 0
- 42B: Security — 1

M: MANAGEMENT & REGULATIONS
- 43A: Rules and Regulations — 1
- 43B: Rules and Regulations — 1
- 44A: Access Regulation & Management — 1
- 44B: Access Regulation & Management — 1
- 45A: Time & Program Reg. & Management — 0
- 45B: Time & Program Reg. & Management — 0
- 46A: Permissions and Management — 1
- 46B: Permissions and Management — 0
- 47A: Affordability and Equality — 1
- 47B: Affordability and Equality — 1

66.46%

WEAKNESSES
(criteria to be enhanced)

Connection to dominant external movement routes

Adequate cycling lanes

Provision of taxi stands

Identifiable landmarks

Unique and memorable spatial features

Art- and culture-related programs

Healthcare service

Public social service nearby

Security measures

234

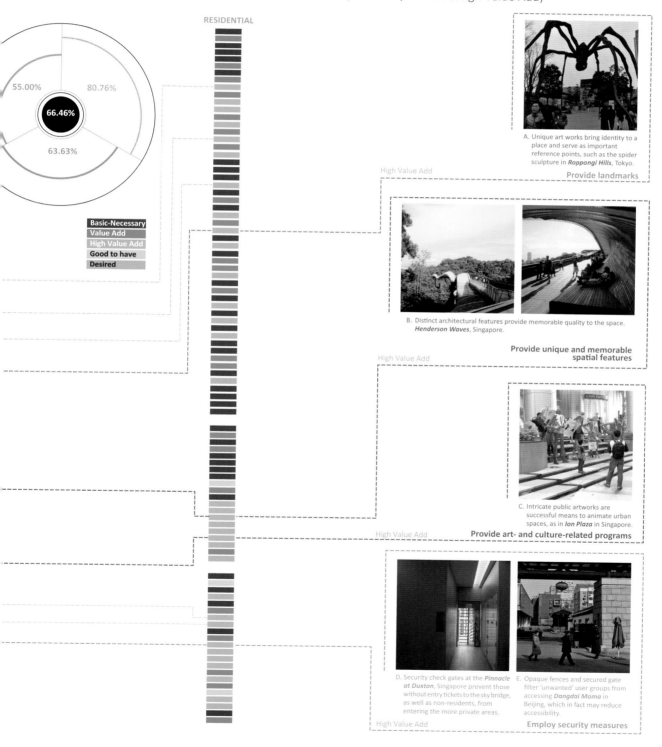

4.4 "Strategic intervention" for
Residential hybrid typology (Case
B: Treelodge@Punggol, Singapore).

3: Analyze and Prioritize
- Consult Hierarchy of Criteria
- Attend to Critical Principles First (Basic and High Value Add)

RESIDENTIAL

55.00%   80.76%

66.46%

63.63%

Basic-Necessary
Value Add
High Value Add
Good to have
Desired

A. Unique art works bring identity to a
place and serve as important
reference points, such as the spider
sculpture in *Roppongi Hills*, Tokyo.

High Value Add   **Provide landmarks**

B. Distinct architectural features provide memorable quality to the space.
Henderson Waves, Singapore.

**Provide unique and memorable
spatial features**

High Value Add

C. Intricate public artworks are
successful means to animate urban
spaces, as in *Ion Plaza* in Singapore.

High Value Add   **Provide art- and culture-related programs**

D. Security check gates at the *Pinnacle
at Duxton*, Singapore prevent those
without entry tickets to the sky bridge,
as well as non-residents, from
entering the more private areas.

E. Opaque fences and secured gate
filter 'unwanted' user groups from
accessing *Dangdai Moma* in
Beijing, which in fact may reduce
accessibility.

High Value Add   **Employ security measures**

this manner, the strengths and weaknesses of a particular case are easily identified and this informs which criteria should be enhanced for overall urban space improvement.

3 Analyze and Prioritize

—Consult hierarchy of criteria:

In order to prioritize the enhancement actions, the hierarchy of criteria is generated for residential typology (**S1 Primary Use**: Residential) against which the criteria identified as weakness are compared.

—Attend to critical principles first (Basic and High Value Add): This guides the design action to attend to the critical criteria (design principles) first, prompting the designer to focus primarily on "Basic" criteria and "High Value Add" criteria, followed by "Value Add" and "Good to Have" criteria. Design recommendations to enhance these design qualities derive from the best practice case studies in the database library, which serve as references that successfully implemented such design principles (although different contextual differences should be taken into account).

Comparison and Benchmarking

After the evaluation is completed and the design recommendations are given on how to meet the criteria for improvement, the Urban Space Instrument may be used for benchmarking best practices with the following specific stages:

1 Benchmarking against the average performance of the overall urban space value, and HARDware, SOFTware and ORGware values.
2 More refined benchmarking against the hierarchy of criteria (which shows the number of criteria met).

In this research, the baseline for good performance is suggested as the average value among all spaces of the same type. Spaces that perform higher than average are considered to be performing well. While, ideally, the maximum value would be 100 percent for urban space value and for each component— HARDware, SOFTware and ORGware—the tool highlights the highest available performance among all spaces of the same type in order to provide more meaningful and feasible reference for urban space improvement.

The following scenarios illustrate how the Urban Space Instrument may be applied for comparison and benchmarking purposes (Figures 4.5 and 4.6).

"Comparison and Benchmarking" for Residential **Hybrid Typologies** (*Case A: Dangdai Moma, Beijing, China; Treelodge@ Punggol, Singapore; Shinonome Codan Court, Tokyo, Japan*) (*Figure 4.5) and* Recreational *Hybrid Typologies* (*Case B: Skypark@VivoCity, Singapore; Namba Park, Osaka, Japan; the High Line Park, New York, USA) (Figure 4.6)*

1 Evaluate Performance

All cases are assessed using the structured evaluation checklist.

2 Compare

Simplified circular pie-charts are generated based on the result of the evaluation for quick comparison among the case studies and for easy identification of the strengths and weaknesses.

3 Benchmark

A Against the average performance

The benchmark value which is the average value (performance) among all spaces of the same type (residential for case A and recreational for case B) is shown as a dotted line in the circular charts, which may be compared with the actual case study value (urban space performance). The tool also highlights the highest available performance among all spaces of the same residential type (Shinonome Codan Court for case A, which scores the highest in all components of HARDware, SOFTware and ORGware) and recreational type (the High Line Park for case B), which becomes the benchmark reference for urban space improvement.

B Against the hierarchy of criteria (number of criteria met)

The tool also provides means of more complex and qualitative comparison between two or more cases and in such a way benchmarks them against one another. More precisely, a summary table may be generated which sums up the criteria met by each selected case across the hierarchy of criteria. In other words, it sums the number of basic/necessary, value add, high value add, good to have and desired criteria met by each selected space, while highlighting the highest numbers for easier comparison. More detailed information of specific criteria (for case A, a desired criterion—"Link greenery to a larger ecosystem"—which is met by Treelodge, but is very rarely met by the same residential type and hence may indicate a highly unique design feature of Treelodge compared to other cases, and for case B, a good to have criterion—"Provide flexible/movable seating and/or tables"—which is met by VivoCity, but is inconsistently met by the same recreational type and hence can indicate a unique design feature of VivoCity compared to other cases) may be further provided by the database library.

C Recommendation based on benchmarking

Based on the benchmarking results and the weaknesses identified compared to the benchmarking reference (Shinonome Codan Court for case A and the High Line Park for case B), more informed recommendations may be derived to address the specific criteria to be enhanced (for case A, ORGware criteria in Dangdai Moma and SOFTware criteria in Treelodge; and for case B, ORGware criteria in VivoCity and Namba Park) by referring to the successful implementation of such criteria in the benchmarking reference (Shinonome Codan Court for case A and the High Line Park for case B).

DISCUSSIONS AND IMPLICATIONS

The examples discussed above exemplify how the Urban Space Instrument may be used for different design purposes and facilitate optimum design actions to enhance the urban space design quality. These examples are certainly not exhaustive. The Urban Space Instrument may further be used for other design purposes such as pre-evaluation of a design proposal, speculation of a new hybrid typology, and many more which are demonstrated in Chapter 3. This may be done using the TUSA (Tool for Urban Space Analysis), an integrated computational tool serving as an automated means of analyzing urban spaces, which integrates all the research findings and operations in the system with capacities to automatically generate design recommendations according to the specific design purpose (refer to Chapter 3, section on the TUSA: Tool for Urban Space Analysis). Furthermore, the TUSA allows greater flexibility in the research analysis and for the accommodation of future changes, as well as a means of updating the existing database and adding new spaces. With such capacities it is a useful guiding tool in practice, policy-making, decision-making, design brief development and urban space pre- and post-evaluation; ultimately, it is a tool for predicting and testing future urban space scenarios.

The intention here is not to propose a regulatory instrument based on rigid, static, ready-made and inflexible sets of design principles. The framework and research instrument outlined in this book rather aim to respond to change, hybridity, complexity and dynamism, which are the essential and unavoidable elements of contemporary high-density urban environments. It establishes a temporary integrated mechanism that can facilitate initial decision-making for timely, flexible, intuitive and context-sensitive urban space interventions on a case-by-case basis. This allows a shift to more decentralized bottom-up approaches, more strategic and spontaneous planning, and dynamic and pluralistic design processes (Ellin, 2006; Meredith et al., 2008), which is in line with the recent tendencies in urban design and urban planning.

The Urban Space Framework and Instrument proposed in this volume is only a starting point for further in-depth investigation into the complexities and qualities of contemporary urban spaces in high-density contexts. Implications for further research include enriching the Urban Space Framework further, with a stronger focus on the social, behavioral and operational facets of urban space design and performance, and exploring methods for capturing and/or measuring intangible and dynamic elements that substantially shape the experiential quality of an urban environment.

REFERENCES

Carmona, M., Tiesdell, S., Heath, T., & Oc, T. (2010). *Public Places Urban Spaces: The Dimensions of Urban Design* (2nd edn). London: Architectural Press.

Chapman, D. (2011). Engaging Places: Localizing Urban Design and Development Planning. *Journal of Urban Design, 16*(4), 511–530. doi: 10.1080/13574809.2011.585840.

Ellin, N. (2006). *Integral Urbanism*. New York: Routledge.

Meredith, M, Lasch, A., & Sasaki, M. (2008). *From Control to Design: Parametric/Algorithmic Architecture*. Barcelona: Actar.

Sandercock, L., & Dovey, K. G. (2002). Pleasure, Politics and the "Public Interest": Melbourne's Riverscape Revitalization. *Journal of the American Planning Association, 68*(2), 151–164. doi:10.1080/01944360208976262.

COMPARISON AND BENCHMARKING

1: Evaluate Performance

2: Compare

3: Benchmark

A. Against the average performance

——— case study values

- - - - benchmark values

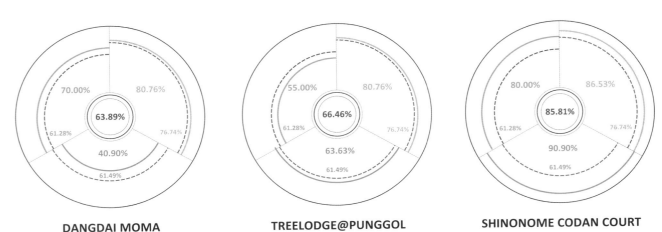

DANGDAI MOMA **TREELODGE@PUNGGOL** **SHINONOME CODAN COURT**

	DANGDAI MOMA	TREELODGE	SHINONOME	benchmark values for residential spaces
HARDWARE	80.76%	80.76%	86.53%	76.74%
SOFTWARE	70.00%	55.00%	80.00%	61.28%
ORGWARE	40.90%	63.63%	90.90%	61.49%
USV - URBAN SPACE VALUE	63.89%	66.46%	85.81%	66.65%

WEAKNESSES
(criteria to be enhanced)
Variation of well-integrated public amenities for passive and active uses within urban space
Flexible/movable seating
Art- and culture-related programs

WEAKNESSES
(criteria to be enhanced)
Public social service nearby
Image of urban space
24-hour access to space
Support and manage informal activities

4.5 "Comparison and benchmarking" for Residential hybrid typologies (Case A: Dangdai Moma, Beijing, China; Treelodge@Punggol, Singapore; Shinonome Codan Court, Tokyo, Japan).

B. Against the hierarchy of criteria (number of criteria met)

COMPONENT	HIERARCHY	DANGDAI MOMA	TREELODGE	SHINONOME
HARDWARE	Basic/Necessary	23	23	23
	Value Add	12	13	13
	High Value Add	7	5	9
	Good to have	0	0	0
	Desired	0	1	0
SOFTWARE	Basic/Necessary	7	7	7
	Value Add	4	2	4
	High Value Add	3	2	4
	Good to have	0	0	1
	Desired	0	0	0
ORGWARE	Basic/Necessary	5	5	5
	Value Add	1	3	5
	High Value Add	2	5	7
	Good to have	1	1	2
	Desired	0	0	1
OVERALL	Basic/Necessary	35	35	35
	Value Add	17	18	22
	High Value Add	12	12	20
	Good to have	1	1	3
	Desired	0	1	1

A. Link greenery to a larger ecosystem

B. Provide sufficient amount and diversity of hygiene amenities

C. Recommendation based on benchmarking

C. Provide diversity of activities in the immediate surroundings of urban space

D. Provide flexible/movable seating and/or tables

E. Provide art- and culture-related programs

F. Provide affordable social services specifically catering to 'vulnerable' user groups

G. Employ design strategies that make space appear approachable, inviting, and thus - safe

H. Allow partial 24-hour access to space (passing through)

I. Permit, manage and facilitate non-designed activities

COMPARISON AND BENCHMARKING

1: Evaluate Performance

2: Compare

3: Benchmark

A. Against the average performance

—————— case study values

- - - - - benchmark values

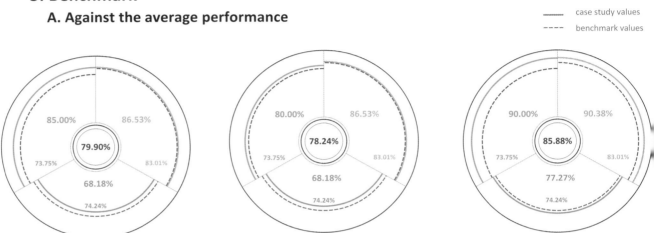

VIVOCITY   NAMBA PARK   HIGH LINE

	VIVOCITY	NAMBA PARK	HIGH LINE	benchmark values for recreational spaces
HARDWARE	86.53%	86.53%	90.38%	83.01%
SOFTWARE	85.00%	80.00%	90.00%	73.75%
ORGWARE	68.18%	68.18%	77.27%	74.24%
USV - URBAN SPACE VALUE	79.90%	78.24%	85.88%	77.00%

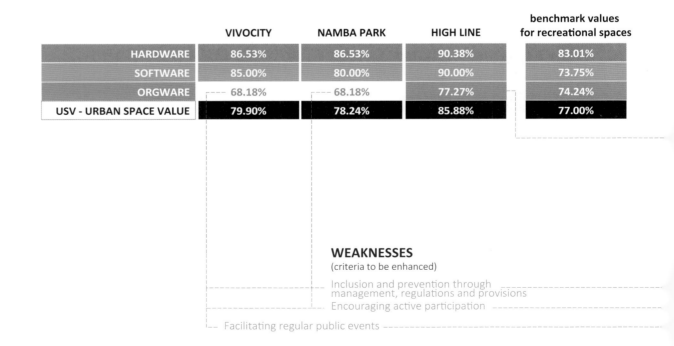

WEAKNESSES
(criteria to be enhanced)

Inclusion and prevention through management, regulations and provisions

Encouraging active participation

Facilitating regular public events

4.6 "Comparison and benchmarking" for **Recreational** hybrid typologies (Case B: Skypark@VivoCity, Singapore; Namba Park, Osaka, Japan; the High Line Park, New York, USA).

B. Against the hierarchy of criteria (number of criteria met)

COMPONENT	HIERARCHY	VIVOCITY	NAMBA PARK	HIGH LINE
HARDWARE	Basic/Necessary	29	28	**30**
	Value Add	11	10	**13**
	High Value Add	2	4	2
	Good to have	2	3	2
	Desired	0	0	0
SOFTWARE	Basic/Necessary	9	9	9
	Value Add	4	4	4
	High Value Add	2	3	4
	Good to have	**2**	0	1
	Desired	0	0	0
ORGWARE	Basic/Necessary	9	9	9
	Value Add	5	2	3
	High Value Add	1	4	4
	Good to have	0	0	1
	Desired	0	0	0
OVERALL	Basic/Necessary	**47**	**46**	**48**
	Value Add	**20**	16	**20**
	High Value Add	5	**11**	10
	Good to have	**4**	3	**4**
	Desired	0	0	0

A. Provide covered walkways

B. Provide flexible/movable seating and/or tables

C. Recommendation based on benchmarking

C. Promote inclusion and prevention through management, regulations and provision

D. Facilitate regular events

E. Employ ways to encourage users' participation in space management

5

It is expected that cities will transform over time. However, with globalization and technological advancements, cities are perhaps transforming at a faster rate today than in any other period in human history. The urban conditions underpinning such cities in transition are also evolving in more complex ways, thus renewing interest in urban design and public space as potential mechanisms for achieving environmental, social and economic sustainability.

Many examples of urban societies and spaces undergoing rapid transformation may be found in the Singapore and East Asian case studies included in this volume; high density in these cities is not a choice but a preordained condition given the large influx of populations from the surrounding hinterland. It is not the intention of this book to search for or define Asian-ness, itself a problematic term when the geographical extent encompasses cultures that are vastly different from one another. Rather, the conditions of hybridity, space limitations and high density are prevalent in many of the cities from which we draw our case studies. Where these conditions exist—in Europe, Asia, Latin America or Africa—we are seeing new typologies of public space emerging; some more successful than others.

Many of these new urban spaces provide for a variety of uses across time and/or space. The ability to accommodate very different programs and the intensity of use lend richness and vibrancy to the spaces concerned. This capacity of urban space is especially important in emerging and evolving high-density hybrid conditions where land shortage is coupled with complex, varied and changing user profiles. In some instances such spaces are stacked above one another and change over time to accommodate different uses—a testimony to the lack of space and the importance of location in the context of congestion and density. In the best cases these spaces are inclusive, welcoming and where people of all socio-economic classes are able to feel at ease.

Increasingly, however, such spaces are anomalies in today's era of globalization and neo-liberalism where mega-structures tend to adopt a more inward-looking nature. Not only are these developments commonly armored and cladded in reticent glass and steel but, more often than not, they also offer little in the way of fostering tolerance and social cohesion. In these privatized realms, concessions for public space, if any are made at all, are designed, programmed and managed in ways that marginalize the lower strata of society. Flexible and open forms of public spaces are disappearing, particularly in urban areas with fervent land speculation, at an alarming rate.

In the most extreme cases, for example, disadvantaged communities, without other possibilities, eke out a living by making use of the open space on and along railway tracks and in its surroundings for their makeshift stands and stalls, risking life and limb to remove the goods and wares several times a day to enable the passage of trains. Safe, accessible and nurturing public spaces should never be compromised. Unfortunately, the reality of this situation illuminates the inequities of spatial proportions that are dividing cities between the haves and have-nots. Moreover, the complexity of such urban conditions highlights the urgent need to understand the many roles of public space for different users. On an encouraging note, we are beginning to see more examples of private residential and even commercial developments that are planned and designed to accommodate the larger public within their boundaries. Even if this may be only a gesture, it is a good beginning.

One of the difficulties in the planning, programming and management of public space is the lack of an objective set of indicators or criteria, if nothing else, to remind urban managers and designers of the importance of these different dimensions and aspects that ensure a better outcome. As we have seen in the examples in this volume, not all urban space types perform well across the different dimensions. In many instances, the programming of the space determines to a large extent its success. On the other hand, poor programming and management may compromise the best design efforts. It is not uncommon to think that returning existing plans back to the design table can redeem existing spaces that have been devastated by insufficiencies in programming and management. Urban design, however, is but one means to an end and not an end in itself, as our human agency enables us to shape and be shaped by urban spaces. Thus, knowledge of the interconnectedness between the physical and human dimensions of urban space needs always to be factored into both the processes and criteria for design.

Developing this knowledge is becoming more and more critical in contemporary cities where conditions of hybridization and densification prevail. Here, the sheer range of users and agencies together with the necessity to "make do" with space limitations have created opportunities for the emergence of new typologies of urban space. This combination of diversity and congestion, in turn, will cause conditions to evolve that lead to the invention of further new typologies. How city managers and designers respond to the continual change of urban conditions resulting in greater hybridity of public space typologies will depend on the planning instruments and tools available to them.

In this volume, an integrated Urban Space Framework and Instrument, including the interactive computational tool—the Tool for Urban Space Analysis (TUSA)—is applied in the research to catalog, evaluate, analyze, hypothesize and guide decision-making in the planning and design of complex urban space configurations in high-density conditions. The Urban Space Instrument and the TUSA's capacity to demonstrate flexibility, incorporate new criteria and speculate on unprecedented hybrid conditions is an innovative step toward a systematic framework with an influential impact on the planning and design process. An instrument like the TUSA possesses both quantitative and qualitative utilities, but can the characteristics of quality public spaces indeed be measured objectively and their success replicated? This is the conundrum of dealing with the notion of public space, since the experience (both good and bad) is often a subjective one. Nevertheless, it is often possible within our own communities to arrive at a consensus of the key characteristics contributing to quality public space; but, then, are these principles and standards of design shared universally and therefore replicable elsewhere and everywhere?

Re-Framing Urban Space is premised on cities where hybridity, space limitations and high density converge to produce a fruitful environment for new typologies of public space. Under these urban conditions, the question of measurability and replicability is turned into one of ideology; that is, the merit of immortalizing "timeless" principles and standards of design in urban contexts that are perpetually evolving. How far do we tread in either safeguarding or compromising the beloved urban spaces of our cities when confronted with complex conditions of densification, intensification, hybridity and sustainability? The core of the issue does not lie solely within the realm of planning and design but also within the larger spheres of policy-making, culture and economy. In this sense, *Re-Framing Urban Space* presents research insights to inform urban space design, planning, policy- and decision-making, while *re-framing urban space* (the action) is very much a collaborative effort involving people and organizations, both private and public, with long-term interests in the quality and character of their cities for today, tomorrow, and for generations to come.

Index

Page numbers in *italic* indicate figures and in **bold** indicate tables.